Building Resilience in Students Impacted by Adverse Childhood Experiences

For all of my colleagues, who are driving school busses,
taking care of school grounds, feeding, teaching, leading,
and caring for youth in the NEW NORMAL.

—Victoria E. Romero, M.Ed.

This book is dedicated to my mom
and to all children and survivors who transform bitterness
to sweetness, pain to compassion.

—Ricky Robertson, M.Ed.

To every individual that allowed me to be a part of your life through
sharing your experience with me, especially my Edison Elementary
students and Danville Freedom School Babies, what a privilege
and honor to serve you.

—Amber Warner, LCSW

Building Resilience in Students Impacted by Adverse Childhood Experiences

A Whole-Staff Approach

Victoria E. Romero, Ricky Robertson,
and Amber Warner

Foreword by Gary R. Howard

CORWIN
A SAGE Publishing Company

FOR INFORMATION:

Corwin
A SAGE Company
2455 Teller Road
Thousand Oaks, California 91320
(800) 233-9936
www.corwin.com

SAGE Publications Ltd.
1 Oliver's Yard
55 City Road
London EC1Y 1SP
United Kingdom

SAGE Publications India Pvt. Ltd.
B 1/I 1 Mohan Cooperative Industrial Area
Mathura Road, New Delhi 110 044
India

SAGE Publications Asia-Pacific Pte. Ltd.
3 Church Street
#10-04 Samsung Hub
Singapore 049483

Program Director: Jessica Allan
Associate Editor: Lucas Schleicher
Editorial Assistant: Mia Rodriguez
Production Editor: Tori Mirsadjadi
Copy Editor: Diane DiMura
Typesetter: C&M Digitals (P) Ltd.
Proofreader: Sally Jaskold
Indexer: Joan Shapiro
Cover Designer: Candice Harman
Marketing Manager: Charline Maher

Library of Congress Cataloging-in-Publication Data

Names: Romero, Victoria E., author. | Robertson, Ricky, author. | Warner, Amber, author.

Title: Building resilience in students impacted by adverse childhood experiences : a whole-staff approach / Victoria E. Romero, Ricky Robertson, and Amber Warner ; foreword by Gary R. Howard.

Description: First edition. | Thousand Oaks, California : Corwin, [2018] | Includes bibliographical references and index.

Identifiers: LCCN 2018003288 | ISBN 9781544319414 (pbk. : acid-free paper)

Subjects: LCSH: Abused children—Education. | Children with social disabilities—Education. | Psychic trauma in children. | Post-traumatic stress disorder in children.

Classification: LCC LC4601 .R58 2018 | DDC 371.9—dc23
LC record available at https://lccn.loc.gov/2018003288

This book is printed on acid-free paper.

SFI label applies to text stock

19 20 21 22 10 9 8 7 6 5

Contents

Foreword

By Gary R. Howard

Victoria Romero and I met over thirty-five years ago when we were both young social justice educators collaborating in the creation of the REACH Center for Multicultural Education. We were part of a multiracial team of teachers and activists driven by a vision of possibility and a hope that schooling in the United States could be made more just, more inclusive, and more effective in serving marginalized students.

I have deep respect for the way Victoria has continued in this work over many decades. As a teacher, a trainer, a principal, and a systemic school change consultant, she has consistently carried forth our early vision of hope and possibility. As the struggle for social justice and educational **equity** has continued, deepened, and become even more complex over the years, she has stayed in the trenches of committed activism and grown ever stronger in her commitment. Now, in this new book, she has joined with two deeply talented and richly experienced colleagues, Ricky Robertson and Amber Warner, to forge some very important new ground—expanding the equity and social justice lens to include students and adults dealing with trauma-related adverse childhood experiences (ACEs).

The **trauma-informed** perspective presented in this book affirms both our diversity and our unity. As the authors clearly demonstrate, trauma-related experiences occur across all racial, economic, and cultural groups, yet the way these experiences show up in school, and the way educators and other service providers respond to students, often vary greatly based on demographic differences. Because of this potential for disparate treatment, a deep understanding of ACEs phenomenon is crucial for any educator or any school system that is serious about equity issues today. In this sense, equity, ACEs, and the whole arena of socioemotional learning are part of the same larger work. If we are to realize our vision of a socially just society that is truly committed to the education and well-being of all of our children, we will have to continue to grow and support the kind of trauma-informed transformationist educators whose attributes and actions are described in this book. In the pages that follow, Romero, Robertson, and Warner set forth an evidence-based, classroom-tested, and actionable pathway to that possible future.

Preface

I am loath to tell people to mortgage their houses and lease their children to acquire tickets to a hit Broadway show. But Hamilton, *directed by Thomas Kail and starring Mr. Miranda, might just about be worth it—at least to anyone who wants proof that the American musical is not only surviving but also evolving in ways that should allow it to thrive and transmogrify in years to come.*

—Ben Brantley
New York Times Review
August 6, 2015

What is it about this musical that captivates its audiences? Is it because American history is told in hip-hop or because the Founding Fathers are portrayed by men of color? Or, could the reason be this hit musical illustrates the complexities and contradictions thirteen colonies struggled with in making a new nation? Our Founding Fathers formed a more perfect union that was imperfect from the very beginning. In a rap battle in the musical, we see the Founding Fathers spitting rhymes debating the advantages of freedom from British rule while allowing slavery to exist in all the colonies. While the Founding Fathers are discussing ideals that are inclusive—liberty, the pursuit of happiness, and inalienable rights—women, European indentured servants, Native Americans, and free Africans were left out. The Constitution was so full of contradictions, amendments were added almost immediately. The Thirteenth Amendment was a compromise between the northern and southern states to count enslaved Africans as three-fifths of a human being. This allowed slave-holding states to count their human property and gain seats in the House of Representatives. These contradicting dualities are expressed brilliantly in the musical's lyrics and the audience, looking at actors who are men of color rap hip-hop, is reminded that elitism, racism, and sexism still plague us in contemporary times. Our Founding Fathers set us up.

Perhaps even more compelling, the musical gives us a peek into the Founding Fathers' personalities and their lives. We learn things left out of our history books. Some of them were advocates for slavery while others were staunch abolitionists. Some wanted more central government control and others wanted the newly formed states to act on their own. Their personalities were as complex and contradictory as the debates and documents they were writing. But it was the life of Alexander Hamilton, the Founding Father on the ten-dollar bill, who established the first national bank, the U.S. Mint, and the U.S. Coast Guard that was most extraordinary. Of all the Founding Fathers, he was perhaps the most conservative and contradictory. He wanted to establish a monarchy and at times, when it suited his political and career ambitions, was an abolitionist and an advocate for slavery. A political survivor, Alexander Hamilton pushed Alexander Hamilton's agenda. Hamilton was an immigrant and an adult survivor of adverse childhood experiences. He was a poster child for ACEs.

Hamilton was born on the West Indian island of Nevis. His mother was married to a man who was so abusive she left him, which for the time was a courageous social action for a woman to take. They did have a son, Peter. Rachel Lavien describes her first husband as "crude and insufferable" (Chernow, 2004, p. 10). Using a Danish law, her husband had her arrested for adultery and she was imprisoned. This would infer that Johann Lavien was able to prove that his wife had had extramarital affairs after she left him. In that era, it was hard for a woman to divorce a man. At some point, she met and settled into a common-law relationship with James Alexander and had two more sons, James Jr. and Alexander. Her first husband had legal custody over her first born.

Since she and James Alexander never married, their sons' births were considered illegitimate, a status that carried heavy negative legal, moral, and social repercussions. For example, children born out of wedlock could not inherit property and were socially ostracized. Subsequently any claim to property that the Hamilton sons might have had because of her legitimate marriage would be a mute issue. Only their half-brother Peter could inherit property.

Compounding the stigma the illegitimacy caused, the Hamiltons were an impoverished family. James Hamilton was never able to provide for his family on a consistent basis and abandoned them when Alexander was ten years old. Three years later, Alexander and his mother became violently ill. Alexander survived; his mother did not. Because his father had deserted the family and his mother died, both Hamilton boys were now considered orphans and were sent to live with his mother's first cousin. A year later, the first cousin committed suicide. At sixteen and fourteen years old, respectively, James Jr. and Alexander were without parents or guardians.

In their short lifetimes, James Jr. and Alexander suffered the deprivations of poverty, abandonment by their father, the death of their mother, scandals about their illegitimacy, and the suicide of a caregiver. As a result, the brothers would be separated for the rest of their lives. James Jr. was apprenticed to a carpenter and Alexander was a clerk for a mercantile company where his intelligence and ambition were noted. By his sixteenth birthday, Alexander basically ran the operations when one of the owners returned to the states because of health issues.

In 1772, a hurricane devastated St. Croix, Nevis, and St. Kitts. Alexander, now seventeen, penned an essay about the devastation that was published in the local newspaper and caused such a positive reaction that islanders, including the governor, wanted to know who was this Alexander Hamilton. Funds were raised to send this youth, gifted with words, to the United States to be educated. On his way to America, the ship caught fire but sailed into Boston Harbor three weeks after leaving the West Indies.

Alexander Hamilton arrived to start his new beginning just as the political climate in the American colonies was agitating for the same—a new beginning. His intelligence, drive to be successful, and the political climate in the northern colonies coalesced at a perfect time. He saw this developing nation through the eyes of the immigrant that he was—an opportunity to move ahead. Hamilton became a lawyer and was George Washington's right-hand man, handling correspondence and later heading a battalion during the Revolutionary War. President George Washington appointed Hamilton to be America's first Secretary of the Treasury, building on the business skills he had learned as a sixteen-year-old in Nevis.

As Hamilton was helping to build this new nation, his personal and professional life was rife with political conflicts, sexual scandals, and personality clashes. Being an immigrant, from a country that was not European, his detractors would sometimes refer to him as being creole, a mixed-race person. Compounding this intentional racial slight, Hamilton was the only Founding Father who was not from a wealthy family. He married into one.

Alexander Hamilton was an insecure man driven by his ambitions and aspirations to make something of himself. He was quick to anger, hypersensitive to any slight, real or imagined. Living among the gentry, he was ashamed of his childhood experiences. He would go to extreme lengths to protect his political, professional, and intellectual reputation, once at the expense of his wife's and children's standing in the community. He published an account about a three-year sexual affair to clear his name of accusation of misuse of federal spending while Secretary of the Treasury. We know that his life was cut short in a duel with the third vice-president of the United States, Aaron Burr.

If Alexander Hamilton had grown up in New York during contemporary times, an immigrant, poor, orphaned, a ward of the state after his cousin's suicide, hypersensitive at the lease provocation, and belligerent, what would have been the chances of his academic and social success? As he moved up in the school system, would his K–12 teachers, school counselors, and principals have seen him as a potential CEO or brilliant innovator?

If he attended public school in our times, and were to be a successful, emotionally mature adult, he would need educators who were not only trauma informed and equipped with strategies to help him grow his innate resiliency but educators who knew themselves well enough to teach the socioemotional work.

Founding Father, war hero, and statesman, Alexander Hamilton is a textbook example of how multiple adverse childhood experiences, or ACEs, have lingering dysfunctional effects on a functioning adult. Although Hamilton survived his childhood, his adult life was a train wreck. Even his untimely death at an early age fits the ACEs mortality data point (Anda et al., 2009; Felitti et al., 1998). Hamilton, the architect of the U.S. Treasury, which helped the thirteen newly united states to become the United States, sabotaged his own career and life because of his abrasive confrontational personality and sexual proclivities, two more behaviors that impact adult survivors of adverse childhood experiences.

Building Resilience in Students Impacted by Adverse Childhood Experiences: A Whole-Staff Approach is a workbook for school district employees who work with the youngest and most vulnerable members of our society, our children. If the institution of education has earned the brand **school-to-prison pipeline**, something is symptomatically wrong. People do not elect to become educators or work with children to be complicit with the penal system. The information and activities in this workbook will help them get back in touch with their ideals, understand that behavior is a language, and know that many students enter our schools speaking a behavior language that prevents them from being optimal learners. Other students manage school culture well, behave accordingly, but suppress their inner turmoil and act out in other ways. Students living with adverse childhood experiences are attending our suburban, rural, and urban schools.

This workbook connects the dots between research from the 1970s to the latest studies:

- o   Felitti and Anda's Adverse Childhood Experiences (ACEs) research,

- o   the effects of trauma on learning and socioemotional development,

- o   compassion fatigue and burnout in school employees,

- o   Howard's Achievement Triangle,

- o   Transformationist Teaching and Learning,

- o   Socioemotional Competencies,

- o   Benard's Resiliency Framework,

- o   Dweck's Growth Mindset,

- o   Response to intervention (RTI) Framework, and

- o   Edmonds's and Sizemore's characteristics of high-poverty, high-performing schools and districts,

to propose ways schools or school systems can reframe how instructional services are delivered to all students attending public and private schools in suburban, rural, and urban America.

Why do we need to adapt our current practices? In a national survey of 95,677 children, eighteen years old and younger, from all economic levels and ethnic backgrounds, 46 percent experienced at least one adverse childhood experience and the prevalence of exposure to ACEs increased with age (Sacks, Murphey, & Moore, 2014). According to an article by Valerie Strauss (2018) published in the *Washington Post*, campus shootings have occurred at 170 American elementary and secondary schools since the Columbine massacre in 1999. Mass shootings have become an event with the predictable consequence of traumatizing the entire school community: staff, students, and families.

At the same time, schools and school districts need to attend to the adults working with or for young people. According to a survey conducted by New Teacher Center, one million teachers change schools each year and 40–50 percent quit within their first five years (Neason, 2017). They want to be good teachers but today's students, as evidence by the data, have needs that are more complex than just providing academic content.

Another consideration to think about, Felitti and Anda's ACEs research was conducted on 17,000 adults. There are adult survivors of ACEs working with young people who are living with adverse childhood experiences—adults who may not be in touch with why certain student or adult behaviors trigger emotional reactions that influence how they respond or react. All staff members need to understand themselves at a deeper level to better serve our young people and to sustain collaborative and professionally trusting relationships with colleagues.

Since 1997, social service providers (Larkin, Felitti, & Anda, 2011), mental and physical health care givers (Chapman et al., 2004), and public health agencies (Centers for Disease Control and Prevention, 2010) have used the findings of Felitti and Anda's research to create trauma-informed approaches to promote emotional health outcomes from infancy to adulthood. Washington state was the first state to pass an ACEs reduction law (SHB 1965) in 2011 (Kagi, Jinkins, & Frockt, 2011–12). SHB 1965 changed public policy to address the relationship between ACEs scores, health-related problems, and criminal involvement. Other states have followed to advance awareness in primary prevention, community engagement, and policy (e.g., Alaska, California, Missouri, and Vermont). The criminal justice system has also conducted studies and made recommendations to change its policies.

In 2014, the *Journal of Juvenile Justice* published a study examining the prevalence of ACEs in 64,329 juvenile offenders in Florida. Researchers learned adverse childhood experiences not only increased the likelihood of young people being involved in the juvenile system, they were more likely to reoffend. They recommended school and health professionals consider overeating, substance abuse, smoking, disruptive behavior, and bullying as plausible ACEs behaviors and to create ways to screen students before they offend. In summarizing their findings, Michael T. Baglivio and team saw suspending or expelling students from school as removing these students from a safe environment and described it as deprivation. They believe school staff are in the best position to help students learn behaviors that build resiliency and strengthen self-regulatory skills (Baglivio et al., 2014).

In the thirteen or fourteen years America's children are in public or private educational systems, educators most certainly have ample time to reteach behaviors while keeping students academically engaged. But first, we must make sure school *is* their safe space.

Building Resilience in Students Impacted by Adverse Childhood Experiences: A Whole-Staff Approach is a workbook designed to help school staff

o become more knowledgeable about how ACEs impacts teaching and learning;

o incorporate instructional strategies and reconstruct systems to make sure school remains accessible and proactive for all students; and

o bring in professionals in physical and mental health, child welfare agencies, community resources to support school staff in meeting the needs of students and families in more therapeutic and compassionate ways.

Bottom line, the premise of the work in this book is about **equity**. Knowing each student and adult employee by name and need is a requisite for school systems in the 21st century. When we reframe our thinking about why some students are disruptive, or withdrawn, or bully others by thinking of behaviors as a form of communication, the child is no longer a bad kid or from a bad family. Informed, we understand the behavior is caused by things beyond the child's control. When we learn there are strategies that will help teach new forms of behavior communication and that it may take years for a student to learn and apply a new behavior language, we can prepare. We can change the trajectory of a child's life toward a positive direction.

Just like academic learning, socioemotional learning is cumulative. By the time students are in their thirteenth or fourteenth year of our educational systems, they can be college, career, and socioemotionally ready to live the rest of their lives well. As student satisfaction increases, so will our graduation rates, community college, vocational schools, and university enrollments. Our jobs will become easier because we will not only learn from each other, we will take care of each other. We will earn back the respect from our community that we deserve.

Educators already know what we do is one of the most complex professions. When we understand the need for school systems to attend to the socioemotional needs of the adults, we will be able to retain new teachers and have others aspire to become school administrators. Coming to work becomes a good deal and not an ordeal. When school staff explore the thin line between personal and professional to lessen the possibilities of negative biases coloring their professional choices, our professional judgments are objective.

Educators are our society's first responders. The nuclear physicist, poet, FedEx worker, teacher, medical assistant, soldier, all have their start in a PreK to 12th-grade system. As America's first responders, is it not our patriotic duty to prepare each student to live their best lives?

Each chapter in *Building Resilience in Students Impacted by Adverse Childhood Experiences: A Whole-Staff Approach* opens with ANTICIPATED OUTCOMES or goals the authors aspire readers will achieve. After READing evidence-based information, guiding questions help readers REFLECT on what they have read and then RESPOND to process and think about how they can apply the information, trauma-informed concepts, and strategies in their daily responsibilities. Read, Reflect, and Respond are the contemporary version of the 3 Rs—Reading, 'Riting and 'Rithmetic—which described the basic foundations of student education during the 18th century (Olah, 2017). Our 3 Rs are the basic foundations for readers who are teaching in the 21st century. Some of the guiding questions and portions of the narratives are specifically related to classroom or school employees. The majority of the guiding questions, however, are for all staff members regardless of their responsibilities.

At the end of each chapter are TOOLKIT TAKEAWAYS or summarizing thoughts. Toolkit Takeaways are the big ideas to be considered as readers think about their current practice. It's about moving from good teaching to transformationist teaching.

A GLOSSARY OF TERMS defines words or phrases not provided in the narrative.

ADDITIONAL RESOURCES provides related URL links, book and article titles, and sample templates (for restorative conversations, Tier I schoolwide behavior management).

Chapter 1, ACEs and the New Normal, introduces the reader to Drs. Vincent Felitti and Robert Anda's groundbreaking research about adverse childhood experiences (ACEs). There is a definition of *ACEs* and lists of examples. Chapter 1 also describes what most veteran educators already know—the students sitting in today's classrooms have different needs than the students they taught even fifteen years ago. Society has changed. What these young people are exposed to is unlike young people in previous generations were. News of mass shootings in schools, cyberbullying, access to prescription opioids, video games that glorify killing, and increasing poverty rates are new-age challenges that influence classroom behaviors. The authors have labeled these influences in today's classroom as the *new normal*.

Chapter 2, Put on Your Own Oxygen Mask Before Helping Others, focuses heavily on the socioemotional needs of school staff. If we are asking educators to know and support their students on a deeper socioemotional level, they must first know themselves on a deeper socioemotional level, understand the effects of secondary trauma, and recognize the symptoms of compassion fatigue and burnout. The authors aren't advocating good teaching; they are advocating transformationist teaching. Transformationist teaching gives school staff permission to first care for themselves and their colleagues in ways that are professional and emotionally supportive. When the adults practice self-care, they can share with their students their coping mechanisms for dealing with stress. School staff need to model for their students how to behave in professional settings for students to accept the notion that school is a sacred space for teaching, learning, and well-being.

Chapter 3, It's Easy to Have High Expectations—Hard to Grow a New Mindset, begins with sharing the characteristics of high-poverty, high-performing schools, a body of research that began in the late 1970s. Who are the people working in these schools and what is it that they know and are able to do to achieve such results? Chapter 3 lays the foundation for understanding transformationist teaching and trauma-informed strategies by tying together

- o Dweck's research on how mindset influences one's belief and capability,

- o Howard's Achievement Triangle that delineates the dynamics of transformationist teaching, and

- o Benard's Resiliency Framework, which identifies the characteristics of every human's inborn capacity for transformation and change.

School staff in high-poverty, high-performing schools probably have mindsets that are growth oriented. They work collaboratively and take ownership of their students' achievement and they create school cultures that build upon and strengthen each student's innate resiliency.

Chapter 4, The Effects of Trauma on the Brain, explains how areas of the brain are impacted by emotional states. Continuing the focus on adult self-care, the chapter starts with helping school staff deepen their understanding of how their emotions affect teaching and their reactions to the stresses of teaching. It is another dimension of the KNOW MYSELF in Howard's Achievement Triangle.

Chapter 4 then describes how emotions impair a student's ability to learn or regulate his or her behaviors and what school staff can do to mitigate these stressors in the time they have with young people.

Chapter 5, Teaching Behaviors, Differentiating Interventions, Changing Pedagogy, shares the elements of a student-centered approach to trauma-informed teaching: TALK, TRUST, FEEL, and REPAIR. Several case studies illustrate these restorative approaches to behavior management enabling school and the classroom to become a safe space for the adults and students.

An adapted version of the Response to Intervention tiered triangle illustrates how a school can differentiate behavior interventions once everyone is practicing trauma-informed strategies. The roles of school counselors, special education staff, and behavior specialists change to work with students needing targeted interventions in classes structured like English language learners (ELL) or for remedial academic groupings. At Tier I, 95 percent of the students spend the majority of their time in general education courses. At the highest level, Tier III, are the students whose behaviors are caused by organic issues. School counselors, special education staff, and school nurses coordinate services with community resources.

Chapter 6, Plan With the End in Mind: Visioning a Compassionate School, describes the process an imaginary school district undertook to increase its graduation rates and align its daily practice and policies, beginning at PreK, with its mission statement to prepare each student to be intellectually and socially equipped by graduation. This chapter may be wishful thinking for some but for others a standard to aim for. Readers can easily align information in previous chapters like the characteristics of high-poverty, high-performing schools, Howard's Achievement Triangle, Benard's Resiliency Framework, and Dweck's Growth Mindset as they read about the Innovative School District.

Chapter 7, From Theory to Practice: Transformationist Actions Convert ACEs to Aces, helps the readers process what they have read in the previous six chapters. At the heart of the chapter are partial lists that outline trauma-informed

o   schools and school districts,

o   school staff,

o   school counselors and school-based social workers,

o   school psychologists and nurses, and

o   school support staff (office, lunchroom, custodial, bus drivers, security, etc.).

There is also an activity where readers apply socioemotional competencies and concepts from Benard's Resiliency Framework and SEL Competencies to their self-care plans and when working with students. There are links to videos that illustrate how support staff (lunchroom, school-based police officer, bus driver, custodian, etc.) build trusting relationships with students in the brief moments they have with them.

Chapter 8, The Process, the Plan, the Transformation, shares the process, implementation guide, and plan for transforming a school or school district into a compassionate organization. It also argues the need to adjust the roles of the only staff members who have the therapeutic skillset to support the transition—professional school counselors, school nurses, special education staff and behavior specialists, school-based social workers, and educational psychologists.

Chapter 9, In Their Own Words, the final chapter, which you may actually want to read first, shares the testimonies of individuals one or more of the authors knows personally. Each contributor was impacted by multiple ACEs and shares his or her memories of their PreK to 12th-grade experience. All of them make a compelling case for why we need to have a healthy sense of urgency to establish a systemic approach for meeting the challenges of our students at every grade level. Changing behavior takes time—that we have as educators. Our students are in our professional care—six to seven hours per day, 182 days per year for thirteen or fourteen years.

THE AUTHORS

There are three distinct voices in this workbook. Collectively, the three authors represent multiple perspectives. Victoria Romero is an educational consultant, former principal, and classroom teacher. Ricky Robertson is a behavior specialist and former classroom teacher. Amber Warner is a licensed clinical social worker and former social worker assigned to public schools. They share their expertise and actual experiences in separate sections within most of the chapters to illustrate how theory flows into practice. Their names have been added at the beginning of their sections to help the reader shift to that author's contribution.

> *There are strong minds in every walk of life that will rise superior to the disadvantages of situation and will command the tribute due to their merit.*
>
> —Founding Father
> Alexander Hamilton
> Federalist No. 36

You are reading *Building Resilience in Students Impacted by Adverse Childhood Experiences: A Whole-Staff Approach* because you believe there's no such thing as a bad child, but there are children in bad systems.

Ideally, you are in a district that has decided to provide professional development for all employees. Or perhaps your principal has decided to do the same for his or her staff. But if you happened to find this book on your own to improve your practice, try to form a professional learning team with members of your grade level or department. Collaborative learning is much richer and more meaningful when you have partners to share with. This is especially important because you have now created your critical friend team. Never underestimate the power of teacher-leaders.

Victoria E. Romero, M. Ed.
Ricky Robertson, M. Ed.
Amber Warner, LCSW

Acknowledgments

ACKNOWLEDGMENTS FROM VICTORIA E. ROMERO, M. ED.

Special thanks to colleagues who read through the roughest rough drafts, school counselor Rachel Powers, reading specialist Jennifer Siegrist, and literacy specialist Jennifer Haynes. Thank you to Drs. Quentin Graham and Diana Stephens for the use of your matrices that will help educators self-assess and develop their socioemotional strengths. Susy Smothers, you are that school counselor who supports not only your students and their families, but you helped staff learn how to communicate more professionally. Thank you for your guide on restorative conversations. Ashley Pugh, my sorority sister, thank you for the graphics.

To my first editor, my husband, Colin "Tony" Romero, M.D. You are such a good reader and so glad the lessons in sentence diagramming you learned in Catholic school stuck. The greatest gift was the day that you told me you learned some new things in those early drafts and thought of questions family practice physicians and pediatricians could begin to ask their young patients about emotional well-being. I am grateful to my granddaughters, Kyra and Kyla, for helping me understand and appreciate what life is like for students in today's high schools and universities. Kristin Anderson, had you not asked me "So when will your book be ready?" at the first Deep Equity Corwin Press consultants training meeting, this book would not be in the hands of educators today. Thank you for seeing something in me that prompted you to ask that question. A few months later, cleaning out files, I came across one I had started while earning my masters in school counseling titled, "The Therapeutic Classroom." At that time, I decided to get my M.Ed. in counseling in hopes of being a better classroom teacher. I knew at the time the needs of my students were changing and that I needed to add socioemotional teaching skills to my toolkit—although, at the time, those words and curriculum were not part of our pedagogy. All of the papers I had written and articles I collected in the mid-1990s were the start of this work.

Kristin led me to editor Dan Alpert, and Dan, you steered me to Jessica Allan, our editor. Jessica, you were excited from the first e-mail introduction, encouraging and supportive from the start. After getting the first round of feedback from professionals in the field, you called a special session for Corwin's acquisition team. You felt a sense of urgency to get the information into the hands of practitioners. To our reviewers, your enthusiasm for our work and constructive critiques—well, you will read them in its published edition. We paid attention.

Lucas Schleicher, I imagine you and your team going through those permission logs with a magnifying glass. Your tips and suggestions were spot on.

To my coauthors, Ricky Robertson and Amber Warner, who added their professional expertise and in the process, also gave the work depth—something I know would not have been possible just from the limited point of view of my classroom teacher and principal lens.

Lastly, Antwone, Cleressa, Conor, Maria, and the Salomon family, you are the heart of this work. May your testimonies give educators the encouragement they need in order to change lives like the educators who changed yours.

ACKNOWLEDGMENTS FROM RICKY ROBERTSON, M.ED.

My dear friends, especially Liz, Gabriel, Beth, Khalya, Eric, Faith, and Poni, who bless me with love and refuge. Ruben Rangel, Michelle Barton, Miriam Wallace, and Mrs. Broadway, whether you taught me in first grade or in college, you shaped who I am today. My ancestors (Queer, familial, artistic, spiritual, and chosen), I am thankful for the ways you guide and strengthen me. My gratitude also to this beautiful earth, mother of us all, and the source of my resilience. Truly, this book would not be possible if it were not for the educators who give their time, money, mind, and heart to supporting their students; it has been an honor to be "in the trenches" with you. Finally, this work is inspired by those young people who bear the pain of this world yet still they rise.

ACKNOWLEDGMENTS FROM AMBER WARNER, LCSW

A very special thank you to my coauthors for allowing me the opportunity to collaborate with you on this effort. Victoria Romero, my mother, DST sorority sister, first teacher, closest mentor, and my most admired, words cannot express my gratitude that you thought enough of me to include me in this effort. Thank you, Victoria. Ricky Robertson, how I admire that you can put into words actions that make sense to others and gives them tangible steps to teach and support themselves and the most vulnerable. Colin Romero, my father, thank you for your example of being a supportive husband to mom during this effort. To the family of Mr. Mark Neil, Principal of Edison Elementary (2002–2007), he was my "best boss." Before he became a principal, he was a school counselor. He supported continuing education, respected my craft, fostered my leadership skills, led by example, and believed every child could succeed. He is very much missed. To ALL the students of Edison Elementary School, Danville, Illinois, from 2000 to 2008, thank you for being great teachers and making me a better social worker and most of all, a better human being. Vernessa Gipson, former Director of Freedom School at Champaign Ford Regional Office of Education, thank you for inviting me to be a part of the Freedom School Family; it was life changing, and this book aims to support professionals in finding the potential in ALL students, just like we did in Freedom School. Dr. Bryan Sexton of Duke University's Office of Patient Safety, thank you for your resiliency work and teaching me not only how to bounce back, but bounce forward. May other professions learn how to prevent and heal from burnout.

ACKNOWLEGMENTS FROM THE PUBLISHER

Corwin gratefully acknowledges the contributions of the following reviewers:

Lydia Adegbola
New Rochelle High School
New Rochelle, New York

Dustin Johnson, Ed.D.
High Point University
High Point, North Carolina

Delsia Malone
Alabama Department of Early Childhood Education
Montgomery, Alabama

Lynn Lisy-Macan
University at Albany—SUNY
Albany, New York

Rebecca Rupert
Monroe County Community School Corporation
Bloomington, Indiana

About the Authors

Victoria E. Romero taught elementary students in one suburban and two urban school districts; significantly improved the academic standing of two schools as a principal; and coached administrators, directors, and school leadership teams for sustainable school improvement in five school districts. She facilitated professional development for K–12 teachers on classroom strategies promoting student academic success, infusing multiple perspectives into regular curriculum, and establishing classroom management systems that promote autonomy, positive well-being, and resiliency.

Victoria co-authored the Reflection Guide for the third edition of Gary R. Howard's book, *We Can't Teach What We Don't Know*. She also coordinated two teams of science teachers, one in America and the other in the country of Namibia, to write a textbook for fifth graders in Namibia.

She is currently a consultant for Corwin, working once again with her colleague, Gary R. Howard, bringing his Deep Equity process to school districts around the country.

Ricky Robertson has had the privilege to work with students from Pre-K to 12th grade who have persevered in the face of adverse experiences and trauma. Drawing from experience as a teacher and behavior intervention specialist, Ricky coaches educators in developing a relationship-based approach to teaching and learning that inspires transformation through compassion, humor, deep listening, and "real talk."

Amber Warner is a licensed clinical social worker, with over twenty years of experience. She has had the privilege of serving as a community outreach case manager (four years), school social worker (eight years), medical social worker (five years), and behavioral health therapist (three years). As a school social worker, in addition to her work with children and their families, she was part of the schoolwide Modern Red School House Leadership Team and the Positive Behavior Interventions and Systems Team. She facilitated K–6 monthly classroom discussions utilizing Second Step and Character Counts curriculums.

In 2011, Amber worked in health care and as part of the organization's leadership team, she was introduced to the work of Dr. Bryan Sexton on health care providers' staggering burnout rates and the healing proponents of Positive Psychology. A new passion and interest developed for her. She became a Certified Duke Patient Safety Officer in 2013 at Duke University's Patient Safety Center. Amber has also studied under the direction of Dr. David Burns, leading psychiatrist and adjunct professor at Stanford University where TEAM—a new form of cognitive behavioral therapy for the treatment of depression and anxiety—was developed. She has achieved Level 2 TEAM certification from the Feeling Good Institute. She has a certification from the National Clearinghouse on Families and Youth in Trauma-Informed Care. Most of all, Amber has a passion for people, their wellness, and quality of life. She currently resides in California. She enjoys spending time with family and friends, hiking, Inferno Pilates, learning new things, traveling, community service, attending church, and an occasional new pair of shoes.

ACEs and the New Normal

We saw that things like intractable smoking, things like promiscuity, use of street drugs, heavy alcohol consumption, etc., these were fairly common in the backgrounds of many of the patients . . . These were merely techniques they were using, these were merely coping mechanisms that had gone into place.

—Vincent Felitti, M.D.,
Co-principal researcher of ACEs

Anticipated Outcomes

Readers will

o have a definition and examples of the three categories of adverse childhood experiences (ACEs)—Abuse, Family/Household Challenges, and Neglect;

o understand that ACEs affect adults and students in all ethnic groups and at all economic levels;

o make the connection that behavior is a language and another form of communication;

o understand interventions can mitigate the effects of ACEs and students can learn new behaviors over time;

o understand that we cannot continue to handle disruptive behaviors punitively or assume that students who are compliant are not experiencing traumatic events. The *new normal* describes the complexities of today's rural, suburban, and urban classroom.

The term *adverse childhood experiences* (ACEs) has its origins in a body of research conducted by the Centers for Disease Control and Prevention

(CDC) and Kaiser Permanente–San Diego, California. The principal investigators, Vincent Felitti, M.D. (Kaiser Permanente) and Robert Anda, M.D. (CDC) surveyed over 17,000 adults between 1995 and 1997 as part of their regular physical examinations. The respondents, members of Kaiser Permanente's health plan, were mostly White, middle class, and well educated. The survey asked questions about childhood incidences of abuse; dysfunctional home life; neglect; and current adult behaviors like smoking, alcohol, and food consumption.

The results demonstrated the strong correlation cumulative incidences of traumatic stress during childhood had with poor physical, mental and emotional behaviors and early mortality rates. The findings concluded that traumatic experiences occurring during childhood are common with two-thirds of adult participants reporting one or more adverse childhood experiences and 1 in 5 reporting three or more ACEs (Felitti et al., 1998).

Adverse childhood experiences (ACEs) describe traumatic events that occur before the age of eighteen and are categorized into three groups: abuse, family/household challenges, and neglect.

- o Abuse
    - o Emotional: humiliation, intimidation, badgering, withholding love, verbal put-downs, or any action which demeans the sense of identity, dignity, and self-worth
    - o Physical: punching, beating, kicking, slapping, burning, or any action done with malicious or cruel intent
    - o Sexual: stroking genitals, intercourse, rape, sodomy, or exposing naked body parts

- o Family/Household Challenges
    - o Domestic violence: pushing, slapping, kicking, hitting adult–adult; adult–child; and/or child–child
    - o Substance abuse: a family member is an alcoholic or addicted to drugs
    - o Mental illness: a family member has chronic depression, is bipolar, schizophrenic, or paranoid
    - o Acrimonious divorce: bitter and usually prolonged feuding between parents
    - o Incarceration: a family member is in prison

- o Neglect
    - o Emotional: failing to show affection or attention
    - o Physical: failing to provide the basics; withholding food; not providing proper hygiene, necessary medical care, supervision, protection from dangers; or exposing children to harmful situations (Centers for Disease Control and Prevention, 2016a)

In 2007, researchers David Finkelhor, Heather Turner, Richard Ormrod, Sherry Hamby, and Kristen Kracke, from the Crimes Against Children Research Center at the University of New Hampshire, conducted a study involving youth, 17 years old and under. Funded by the Office of Juvenile Justice and Delinquency Prevention, the results were republished in the October 2009 bulletin of the U.S. Department of Justice. One of the major findings corroborated Felitti and Anda's original ACEs research on adults—exposure to traumatic incidences and/or the impact of adverse childhood experiences on today's youth is a common occurrence. Of the 4,549 youth 17 years old and younger, more than 60 percent were exposed, directly or indirectly, to some form of trauma at the time of the survey (Finkelhor, Turner, Ormrod, Hamby, & Kracke, 2009).

The interview sample consisted of two groups: a national representation of 3,053 White youth and an oversample of Black, Latino, and low-income families to ensure a measurable number to analyze. The survey questions were divided into eight categories: conventional crime, child maltreatment, victimization by peers and siblings, sexual victimization, witnessing and indirect victimization, exposure to community violence and family violence, school violence and threats, and Internet victimization.

ACEs ARE AN EQUAL OPPORTUNITY OCCURRENCE

If you are an educator in a rural, suburban, or urban school, public or private, there are young people sitting before you who are impacted by one or more of the following adverse childhood experiences. Some of your colleagues are survivors of ACEs. Adverse childhood experiences are an equal opportunity occurrence, impacting all ethnic groups regardless of socioeconomic status or geographic location.

Finkelhor and associates also found that trauma exposure varies with chronological age. The most common from infancy to middle childhood were assaults by a sibling and physical and emotional bullying. Assaults increase in harshness as children enter their preteen to teen years. At these ages, they are more likely to be victims of a wider range of assaults like the following:

- Online sexual solicitation
- Dating: physical or emotional violence
- Assault with a weapon (pencil, bat, knife, martial arts weapons)
- Exposure to domestic and community violence
- Exposure to mass shooting, credible school threat of bombs, mass shooting, or attack
- Internet bullying
- Sexual assault
- Sexual harassment

This groundbreaking study is the first to interview youth and their caregivers who are living with ACEs. Since its publication, researchers at the University of New Hampshire added to this growing body of research by compiling a list of the most prevalent ACEs by state.

In 2014, Vanessa Sacks, David Murphey, and Kristin Moore, using data from the 2011–2012 National Survey of Children's Health, isolated eight specific ACEs impacting children and youth living in the United States and contrasted those ACEs in terms of prevalence in all fifty states.

The eight most prevalent ACEs impacting children in our country are as follows:

1. Poverty

2. Divorce, especially an acrimonious one

3. The death of a parent, caregiver, or close family member (sibling)

4. Having a parent or guardian who is or has been incarcerated

5. Living with anyone who was mentally ill, suicidal, or severely depressed for more than a couple of weeks

6. Living with anyone who has a problem with alcohol or drugs

7. Exposure to domestic violence (e.g., slapping, hitting, kicking, punching, or beating each other up)

8. Exposure to community violence

In terms of the prevalence of ACEs in our country, poverty is the most common adverse childhood experience and affects families in almost all fifty states. Only in Iowa, Michigan, and Vermont is divorce more common than economic hardship. Abuse of drugs and alcohol, the exposure to neighborhood violence, and living with anyone who is mentally ill, severely depressed, or suicidal for more than a few weeks are also the most commonly reported ACEs in our country. The rising opioid epidemic is sure to swell the numbers of White families impacted by drug addictions.

Children living in Connecticut and New Jersey have some of the lowest prevalence rates and Oklahoma has some of the highest. The most unsettling statistic is that 46 percent of America's children experienced at least one adverse childhood experience.

In the meantime, for today's educators, these are not mere statistics but children coming to school every day somewhere in America's rural, suburban, or urban regions.

Read, Reflect, Respond

1. Study the results of Drs. Sacks, Murphey, and Moore's analysis for your state on pages 3 or 4 of the PDF using this link: http://www.childtrends.org/wp-content/uploads/2014/07/Brief-adverse-childhood-experiences_FINAL.pdf.

2. After reviewing the data for your state, what are some implications for your practice?

3. Make a list of student behaviors that are the most challenging to manage in your classroom, school, school counseling sessions, or infirmary. We will refer to this list in later chapters.

Ricky Robertson, Behavior Specialist

LOST IN TRANSLATION

Imagine that you have a student in your class who only speaks Swedish. Her family speaks Swedish at home and has spoken it for generations. And, for the sake of this scenario, let's say that you don't know a word of Swedish. Yet, somehow, you must find a way to teach this student, even though the two of you do not share a common language.

Before your teacher's brain begins devising strategies that you would use to educate this student, I invite you to consider the following questions:

When this student is speaking, even though you don't understand her, is she still trying to communicate?

Could it be challenging, even frustrating, at times for the two of you to understand one another?

Whose fault is it that the two of you speak different languages?

Do you think this student is capable of learning a new language quickly and easily or will it take time and effort?

Now I'd like you to imagine a second student in your class. Most days, she is engaged and an active participant but sometimes she gets upset and you see a different side of her. She becomes argumentative and quickly escalates to yelling and throwing things. At times her anger is so volatile, it becomes scary and you feel a sense of relief when she storms out of your classroom and slams the door.

Sometimes it is easy for you to identify what has made her so upset and other times it seems like anything could trigger this reaction. You learn from other staff and the school counselor that her home life is chaotic. In her home, the family speaks a language called "Fist through the Wall." Whenever anyone in her household is upset, has an unmet need, or feels ignored, it is communicated by throwing things, screaming, or punching a hole in the wall, for example. Your student has been around this form of communication since she was born. You learn from senior colleagues who taught other members of her family that they have a history of similar behaviors. The adults in her life may have learned this from the adults in their lives. In fact, "Fist through the Wall" is the behavioral language this family has spoken for generations.

A behavioral language is a phrase I use to refer to a set of behaviors routinely used to express needs, desires, and emotions. To have her needs met, develop a sense of belonging, and survive in her family, this student has had to learn to speak her family's *behavioral language*. Due to repeated exposure to stressful life events, many of her behaviors have become so ingrained that they are like reflexes. This student is a classic example of a young person impacted by adverse childhood experiences, or ACEs.

Read, Reflect, Respond

1. When this student is expressing herself using her behavioral language, even though you don't understand her, is she still trying to communicate? Explain.

2. Could it be challenging, even frustrating, at times for the two of you to understand one another? Explain.

3. Whose fault is it that the two of you speak different behavioral languages?

4. Do you think this student is capable of learning a new behavioral language quickly and easily or will it take time and effort?

When a Student Impacted by ACEs Is Acting Out, She Is Trying to Communicate.

In the English lexicon, there is an expression, "Actions speak louder than words." This adage suggests behavior is a form of communication. Having worked with preschoolers all the way to high school seniors who have been impacted by adverse childhood experiences, I can say that their behavior speaks louder than words and can also be harder to understand and remediate.

In general, human behavior is a complex, ambiguous, and difficult to interpret form of communication. If we are to be successful when working with students who have behavioral issues because of exposure to the trauma of adverse childhood experiences, we must develop an understanding of the purpose of their behavior. The purpose, intent, or underlying need that is met by a behavior is commonly referred to as the behavior's *function*. In later chapters, we will explore the functions of behavior that are common to many ACEs students, namely, achieving a sense of safety, belonging, and feeling valued. By understanding a behavior's function, you can help the student translate a behavior into a more school-appropriate form of communication.

In my practice, I work with teachers everyday who are exhausted and frustrated—and understandably so. They come to work each day hoping it will be a good one only to leave work feeling as though they have failed because they were unable to manage a student's behavior. Many times, I have observed students behave so severely in class that it becomes impossible for the teacher to teach. I'll be frank; it's a miserable day not only for the teacher—but believe it—it is also a miserable day for the student.

I work with these students on a one-on-one basis and hear the ways they recognize their teacher's frustration and internalize it. They will often say things like, "I know she hates me. I hate her too," or "Why should I try? He doesn't want me in his class." These students are typically not emotionally mature enough to recognize the impact of their behavior and take responsibility for it. The result is that they and their teacher become trapped in a cycle of blame, frustration, and alienation. But this cycle is not fixed or inflexible. As you read this workbook, we will look at ways to interrupt this cycle and shift communication toward responsibility, in the interest of repairing relationships and building resiliency in our students.

It is also important to acknowledge the impact on the teacher who must respond to a myriad of behavioral, cognitive, and emotional needs while attempting to teach. Most of us choose this profession because we want to make a difference in the world through education. What many of us discover is that our work bears greater resemblance to that of being a social worker or having to reparent someone else's child. That isn't what most educators signed up for, yet it is the *new normal* for many in this field. The stresses of this work can have significant impact on the emotional, mental, and physical health of educators. I would argue that this chronic stress contributes to teacher burnout and retention. Therefore, in Chapter 2 we will discuss the impact of this challenging and vital work and ways to care for ourselves.

No One Is at Fault Because the Two of You Speak Different Behavioral Languages.

In times of challenge and conflict, it is natural to feel as though someone is to blame. We often blame the other person, or we blame ourselves. However, I would argue that it is neither you nor the student's fault that you speak different behavioral languages. Each of you has developed ways to communicate to navigate the environments you live in.

For the student impacted by ACEs, the repeated exposure to stressors and trauma in the home has shaped her neurological functioning. In future chapters, we will further explore the impact of ACEs on the brain as well as strategies that can be used to deescalate students and reengage the parts of their brains that help them to learn and make appropriate decisions.

This Student Can Learn a New Behavioral Language.

Think back to any time that you attempted to change your behavior; this could include going on a diet, starting an exercise routine, or changing your spending habits, for example. Think about what you discovered about yourself and your habits. I am willing to bet that there is one thing you quickly learned about your own behavior—that is, that it wasn't so easy to change.

I'll use a personal example; I used to smoke two packs of cigarettes a day. Looking back, I am not even sure how I had the time to smoke that much in a 24-hour period. Despite the best intentions, the support of my family, the encouragement of my doctor, it still took me three years of quitting and relapsing and quitting again, until I could finally say that I had broken the habit. As I write this, it has been almost ten years since I have smoked a cigarette. Quitting smoking taught me that changing behavior takes time, commitment, energy, and support. I also learned that to not give up, I had to believe that changing my behavior was in my best interest and that one day I would be successful in accomplishing it.

I think this awareness is helpful when working with our students who have been impacted by adverse childhood experiences. We are often asking them to change the behaviors that have been necessary to their survival at home in order to be successful in our classrooms.

It may take a student five to seven years to become proficient in academic English. Schools are more successful meeting the needs of ELL students because we have special programs at every grade level to support them and give them the time to learn a second language. The same is true for students impacted by trauma; interventions are needed at every grade level to help them learn a new behavioral language. Schools like Lincoln Alternative High School in a rural community and featured in the documentary *Paper Tigers* prove my point. Educators will continue to make a difference when they become trauma-informed and when we begin to provide support the moment these students enter our system.

THE NEW NORMAL

If you are a veteran teacher, one who has been teaching for a decade or more, you already know it's a new day. I often hear a common refrain, "It didn't used to be like this." For our novice educators just entering our profession, this is all they know and without adequate support and professional development, many do not last.

In 2015, for the first time in over fifty years, the number of public school students living in poverty exceeded 50 percent. In some states, the percentage of students living in poverty surpassed 70 percent. Consider for a moment the high correlation between poverty and adverse childhood experiences and traumas, such as domestic violence, homelessness, abuse, or neglect. Those who live in poverty are more likely to suffer chronic stress and repeated traumatization, while having less access to support and resources. In effect, most of our public school students now live in poverty with a higher likelihood of experiencing trauma than previous generations.

Consider that, alongside these higher poverty rates, we have also seen unparalleled advances in technology. No doubt many of these technological developments have greatly improved our capacity to access and share information, thereby helping us to educate our students. However, technology, especially smartphone technology and the growing popularity of social media, has shifted the ways in which we interact with one another. Research is now being done to look at the impact of smartphone use on parenting. Initial findings show a decrease in the duration and frequency of parental interaction. Parental interaction is essential for mirroring and modeling appropriate emotional responses and behaviors. It is also vital to forming the key attachments that allow us to have healthy relationships. Studies suggest that children are more likely to behave inappropriately, as means to get attention, when their parents are using mobile technology. The health of our society's children is in competition with our cell phones.

I invite you to consider just these two factors: poverty and technology. They alone suggest that we have a generation of children who have been exposed to higher rates of trauma while receiving less parental support. We have students with greater emotional needs who have less of an ability to express, regulate, and manage those needs. In the classroom, this looks like having more students that require near constant attention and novelty, while displaying greater emotional volatility and lacking many healthy relationship-building skills. Whether we like it or not, this is the new normal. We must accept this reality if we are to change it. It is our intention that in the pages that follow, you will find resources and perspectives that spark dialogue, collaboration, and intervention on behalf of children who deserve to be heard and to heal.

Read, Reflect, Respond

1. What are the interventions, at each grade level, that your school or school district currently provides to support students learning English as a second language?

2. What are the interventions, at each grade level, that your school or school district currently provides to support the student speaking a different behavior language?

3. What is your initial reaction or response to the information in Chapter 1? Any "aha" moments or validating moments? Explain.

Toolkit Takeaways

o   Adverse childhood experiences (ACEs) describe traumatic events that occur before the age of eighteen and are categorized into three groups: abuse, family/household challenges, and neglect.

o   Exposure to and impact of ACEs is a common occurrence in America. The numbers of adult survivors and students living with adverse childhood experiences are statistically significant. Although poverty is the most common adverse childhood experience, ACEs impact Americans regardless of ethnicity and economic level.

o   Behavior is a language. School staff can teach and provide opportunity for students to apply new ways to shift disrupting communication toward responsibility, repairing relationships, and supporting resiliency in our students.

o   Technology has reduced the time adults and youth spend in person-to-person interactions.

o   Like English language learners (ELLs), it may take years for some students to learn a new behavior language. Program models like ELL or remedial programs are needed at every grade level to provide targeted interventions to help students learn and apply a new behavior language.

2

Put on Your Own Oxygen Mask Before Helping Others

Self-care (is) an ethical imperative.

—John C. Norcross, Ph.D.
—Jefferey E. Barnett, Psy.D.

Anticipated Outcomes

Readers will

o   understand that the need to create or maintain working environments that support the socio-emotional well-being of school staff is a priority;

o   distinguish the difference between burnout, compassion fatigue, and vicarious traumatization;

o   understand that professional wellness is self-awareness of one's physical, emotional, and mental health;

o   learn strategies for self-care and use a template to start a self-care plan;

o   review the professional standards for school administrators that relate to creating and maintaining positive cultures and climates for staff, students, and families.

There's a reason why flight attendants tell passengers to put on their oxygen masks before trying to help others. If you become hypoxic because your

> *We routinely put the less experienced teachers with the neediest students. No other profession does this.*
>
> —Zaretta Hammond
> Author of *Culturally Responsive Teaching & The Brain*

brain is deprived of oxygen, you are of no benefit to anyone, especially yourself. The research findings of adverse childhood experiences and the studies conducted on a national sampling of youth may be part of explaining why turnover and retention rates for new teachers are a problem (Philips, 2015). In some areas around the country, there is a shortage of teachers (U.S. Department of Education, 2017). If universities and teacher colleges are not preparing incoming educators with knowledge about the new normal and trauma-informed strategies and new educators are not getting on-the-job professional development, we are doing them a disservice.

By not providing professional development opportunities about ACEs and trauma-informed strategies and district-level therapeutic supports, we are asking teachers to try and perform their jobs in environments that are not healthy and, in some schools, even toxic for their intellectual or emotional well-being. Subsequently, we cannot wonder why a kindergarten teacher may want a defiant five-year old student suspended from school. When educators do not know poverty is an adverse childhood experience, we cannot ask them to simply stop referring so many students from low-income families to be tested for self-contained behavior disorder classrooms. When we don't share the list of traumatizing ACEs behaviors, teachers will continue to misinterpret **compliant behaviors** as students being well emotionally. The dysfunctions these students deal with may be invisible because they know how to function in a school culture. The impact of adverse childhood experiences may not be obvious until they develop a drug addiction, bully others, become the victims of bullies, commit suicide, or, worse, commit mass murders at school.

Now that we have the ACEs research findings, the concept of *teaching in the new normal* will make sense to educators. Ricky says teachers actually sigh with relief when he explains *the new normal* to them. They are relieved when they realize the difficulty they are having with a student is not personal. Once they have a new understanding, Ricky says teachers become receptive and eager to work with him and the student to restore the relationship and make improvements that support socioemotional development.

Professional development for teaching in the new normal must include strategies for self-care and ways to mitigate compassion fatigue or burnout. Educators begin their careers with compassionate ideals; they want to make a difference in the lives of their students. Helping them keep breathing life-sustaining oxygen throughout their careers is aiding them to build and maintain a healthy stasis. Mother Teresa, founder of the Missionaries of Charity serving the poor in Calcutta, India, understood compassion fatigue and included in her plans a mandatory yearlong leave after four to five years of mission work so nuns could heal from the effects of daily exposure to distress and trauma (Halford, 2016).

The authors were intentional about focusing on self-care in this second chapter. Compassion fatigue is the physical and mental exhaustion and emotional withdrawal professionals experience when working with distressed children, adults, or families over extended periods of time. Educators like emergency room physicians and nurses, social workers, police officers, firefighters, and psychotherapists are prone to developing compassion fatigue. To date, the research about compassion fatigue as it relates to educators is not keeping pace with the increasing stresses of our professional responsibilities.

One of the reasons for this lag is that professional development for educators tends to focus on what to do for students. Even when a school or school district adopts a socioemotional curriculum, the training does not start with examining the needs of the employee first. Providing professional development about adverse childhood experiences should begin with staff first. The original study was done with adults. The inference here is that there are adult survivors of ACEs working and making decisions that impact the lives of young people. They need to first *know themselves well, be able to identify coping strategies they use, and identify triggers that cause them to react in irrational ways.* Teaching is more than technique and academic skills. Teaching is about relating to the learner. Parker Palmer (1997), author of *Courage to Teach,* says the premise of his book is good "*teaching cannot be reduced to technique; good teaching comes from the identity and integrity of the teacher. . . . Technique is used until the real teacher arrives*" (pp. 2, 13). Perhaps helping future educators delve deeper into self should be a prerequisite course at the university level.

Chapter 2 is about helping teachers put on their own oxygen mask first to regain their sense of professional identity and integrity and stop saying, "*Just tell me what to do.*" Unfortunately, there is no silver bullet or quick fix to help us navigate the new normal.

BURNOUT OR COMPASSION FATIGUE?

Much of the research and strategies to mitigate compassion fatigue reside in the fields of social work, psychology, psychiatry, law enforcement, and the military. As a matter of fact, much of the research regarding stress related to educators focuses on a symptom—burnout—of working in stressful conditions. Much has been written about teacher burnout, but very little about compassion fatigue. We prefer to use the term *compassion fatigue* to describe what happens to educators. Those who are called to teach decide to do so, not because they want a job, but because they want to make a difference. Educators tend to be a compassionate lot.

Mental health specialists see burnout and compassion fatigue as two different reactions to stress. They describe occupational burnout as general exhaustion and lack of motivation to do the necessary job-related tasks well. Individuals suffering from burnout are prone to physical and emotional breakdown. There are stages leading up to burnout, starting with a strong ambition at the beginning of the job, followed by overworking oneself, followed by an isolation from friends and family, followed by adverse negative effects on the personality, and culminating in depression, emptiness, and physical or emotional collapse (TheyDiffer.com, 2015).

Compassion fatigue, also known as secondary or vicarious trauma, is an individual's gradual decline in feelings of compassion. Individuals that work directly with victims of physical, psychological, or sexual trauma are prone. A number of symptoms characterize compassion fatigue: hopelessness, depression, and high levels of stress and anxiety (TheyDiffer.com, 2015). Catherine Nyhan, a licensed professional counselor in Portland, Oregon, states when educators are suffering from compassion fatigue, they avoid student contact and become cynical toward colleagues, parents, and students. They say things about their students' and parents' problems that lack empathy and use sarcasm as a form of humor. They begin to distance themselves emotionally from coworkers and friends. This may be especially true for educators who have a personal history of adverse childhood experiences (Nyhan, 2016). Compassion fatigue is the most appropriate description of what happens to staff working in school systems. Professionals who work with traumatized people are prone to develop vicarious trauma or secondary trauma and when they struggle trying to be responsive, other areas in their life suffer (Babbel, 2014).

Read, Reflect, Respond

We encourage you to self-assess and establish a baseline to determine if you are prone to or have compassion fatigue. There are several assessments available on the Internet. At the end of this chapter, you will be asked to write a self-care plan. Knowing where you are on the continuum will help you design a plan to meet your needs.

The following URL is a link to a self-test:

http://www.compassionfatigue.org/pages/selftest.html

You can also contact your health care provider to get started on your self-care plan.

Ricky Robertson, Behavior Specialist

THE NEW NORMAL: A CASE STUDY INTERVENTION

Chris was in the ninth grade. He was from an upper-middle-class, two-parent household. He was academically strong. His teachers described him as easygoing, insightful, and attentive. Chris was especially gifted in writing and had bonded with his freshman English teacher.

However, in December of his freshman year, something changed. It started with Chris forgetting to complete a couple of assignments on time, handing them in late. By February, he was skipping classes and in jeopardy of failing a number of his classes. His teachers had also noticed a dramatic shift in Chris's mood. The previously easy-going young man was now irritable and standoffish. Things had gotten particularly bad in his English class. Chris and his English teacher got into an argument that escalated to a yelling match and ended with Chris storming out of the classroom and leaving school grounds.

I scheduled an intervention team meeting with Chris's family and his teachers. Chris was invited to attend the meeting as well, but he declined. We started the meeting off discussing Chris's many strengths and then spoke about the sudden shift we had seen in his behavior and academic performance. Chris's parents listened to our concerns. They neither validated nor denied them. They said that they couldn't think of any reason for Chris to be acting this way at school. The only suggestion they offered was that perhaps Chris wasn't being academically challenged. The meeting ended with an intervention plan that included more challenging classwork and weekly check-ins with Chris's parents.

In the weeks following our meeting, Chris was offered more challenging classwork. He was also given the opportunity to choose among assignments in his English class, with the hopes that one would reignite his interest. None of this made any difference. If anything, Chris was becoming more despondent. Each Friday, Chris's English teacher called home to update his mother on her son's performance that week.

A month after our initial meeting, Chris's mother showed up at school unexpectedly and asked to meet with me and Chris's English teacher. What we learned at that meeting was eye-opening to say the least. Chris's mother explained that Chris had struggled with depression and anxiety since he was a child. She attributed his struggle to turmoil in her marriage that resulted in her and her husband separating when Chris was in second grade. The separation was bitter, lasted nearly a year, and left Chris emotionally devastated. Although she and her husband eventually got back together, Chris never seemed to bounce back.

During sixth grade, Chris started to experiment with drugs and alcohol. By the summer of his eighth-grade year, Chris was sent to a residential drug treatment program for teenagers. The treatment program was expensive and, even though the couple could afford it, Chris's mother believed that her husband resented their son for the cost the family incurred because of his addiction. She said that her husband didn't understand why Chris couldn't "just get over it and move on." The "it" was Chris's depression and anxiety.

She said that she knew that Chris wasn't currently using drugs. He was still meeting with his counselor weekly and being regularly drug tested. What she feared most was the change in Chris's mood. His bouts of depression always precipitated Chris acting out. In the past, it had been through substance abuse, but she feared this time it could be much worse. She and Chris had gotten into an argument the night before she came to see us. The yelling stopped after Chris said he wanted to kill himself. Hearing her son talk about suicide broke her heart. She didn't know what to do so she came to see us, a mother desperate and afraid of losing her son.

There was one other thing that happened the day of the meeting that is important to discuss. After the meeting, Chris's English teacher stayed in my office. She said that something had dawned on her while she was listening to Chris's mother speak. She now understood why the argument she and Chris had gotten into which resulted in him leaving her classroom had gotten so out of hand. Her own son struggled with severe depression when he was in high school. She went on to say that growing up, her parents were alcoholics and she later married a man with substance abuse issues. And although she and her husband eventually divorced, she blamed that relationship and, ultimately herself, for their son's depression.

Talking to Chris's mother had her realize why she was so reactive with Chris. When Chris had become withdrawn and despondent in her class, it triggered a fear inside of her similar to what she felt witnessing her son struggle with his depression. She said that she wondered why she had gotten so upset about Chris not turning in his assignments. She didn't get that upset when other students failed to turn in work. And her communication with him had been too emotionally charged. She saw now that she needed to look for ways to support Chris but also to detach and manage her own emotions.

As for Chris's intervention plan, we first obtained a Release of Information to be able to speak with Chris's counselor. We also started Chris on a daily Check-In/Check-Out program. The daily check-ins were an opportunity for Chris to establish a positive relationship with an adult in the building who wasn't one of his teachers. We let Chris choose any adult in the building as his check-in mentor. It just so happened that he chose the school counselor. Their daily check-ins were a chance for Chris to discuss interests, challenges, fears, hopes—anything he wanted to share in a space free of judgment. With time, Chris's morale improved, and we sought out a volunteer opportunity for him at a local animal shelter. Chris loved animals and benefited tremendously from having a few hours every Saturday to volunteer at the shelter.

Chris's story illustrates a number of important factors when working with ACEs students. One is that a student's socioeconomic status, or the outward appearance of a functional home life, does not determine the number of ACEs a student has endured nor the extent of their impact. Chris's story also illustrates the value of forming trusting partnerships with families of ACEs students. Chris's mother wasn't willing to divulge any information about Chris's addiction and mental health issues until she trusted us. We built that trust by including her feedback in Chris's intervention plan and implementing the plan with fidelity. The bond was strengthened by the consistent communication between Chris's English teacher and his mother.

Most importantly, Chris's story helps us to reflect, as educators, on how our personal histories impact our work with ACEs students. Chris's English teacher's personal life, including her own ACEs, caused her to both connect and struggle with Chris. Her story invites us to be aware of our triggers and mindful of the impact of our life experiences on our work as educators. To be effective in working with ACEs students, especially when their behaviors are escalated, we have to remain calm, assertive, and nonreactive.

Remaining calm in tense situations takes practice. It requires us to be aware of our own emotional and physiological state during the interaction and to use strategies to keep ourselves calm. In order to do this, it is essential to be aware of our triggers. Triggers can be any behavior, style of communication, or situation that evokes an intense emotional response in you. Sometimes these triggers are directly connected to our own experience of ACEs. I had a teacher tell me once that a student's tantrums reminded her so much of her abusive father that she froze in fear the first time that one happened. Triggers are not always connected with ACEs. Sometimes they are just little annoyances that, for whatever reason, elicit a disproportionate emotional response from us. For example, I was working with a teacher who said he would rather a student outwardly defy him than lie to him. Any time a student lied to him, he became unreasonably angry and the frustration impacted his ability to focus and teach.

If you can be aware of your triggers, then you will be more successful in navigating the emotional minefield of working with ACEs students. For me, as a behavior specialist, I am often in situations where I have to deescalate a student in the midst of a tantrum. One of my triggers is being intentionally spit on by a student. Anytime a student spits on me, I take a few deep breaths, scale back my level of engagement with the student, and silently say a prayer in my head. These little strategies work a lot better than losing my cool and making the situation worse.

Read, Reflect, Respond

1. ACEs tests are available online. What is your ACEs score? Regardless of whether your ACEs score is high or low, how do you think your ACEs history has impacted your teaching style?

2. Identify your triggers. What behaviors, styles of communication, topics, for instance, do you find personally triggering as a teacher? You could refer to the list of challenging behaviors that you made in Chapter 1. Make a list of three triggers. How do you typically respond to each one?

3. What are three "in the moment" strategies that you could use to remain calm when triggered by an interaction or event? Which one will you try this week?

Chris's story also teaches us when to let go and seek help. We needed to recognize that our school-based interventions were not enough to help Chris. We needed to speak with Chris's counselor and look for additional sources of support, both within and outside of our school. Fortunately, Chris's family had already placed Chris in counseling and they were able to afford ongoing care. For other students, seeking outside support may look like a referral to a social service agency or, in cases of suspected abuse or neglect, a call to Child Protective Services.

I encourage schools to think beyond crisis intervention and look for positive supports within the community as well. Chris's intervention plan included volunteering at an animal shelter because Chris loved animals. Transformative work can take place when a student is connected to a mentor, community organization, recreational program, or a volunteer, internship, or employment opportunity. Students thrive when we connect them with opportunities that tap into their interests and strengths and give them an opportunity to give back and feel valued and appreciated.

Read, Reflect, Respond

1. Know when to seek help. Describe your school's or school district's process for identifying students who struggle behaviorally or emotionally? When working with an ACEs student, at what point do you seek help from another professional in your building? What factors determine if you should seek help from an outside agency?

2. What community organizations, local businesses, or recreational programs are available in your community to support young people?

3. Describe your school's or school district's process and resources for supporting the socioemotional needs of the adults.

4. At what point would you seek support? Name the colleagues you know can support you. Explain.

It is common for the teachers who I work with to experience stress and difficult emotions when working with ACEs students. Teachers who care deeply for their ACEs students are vulnerable to vicarious trauma. I say from personal experience, it can be heartbreaking to learn about the abuse, trauma, or neglect that a young person has had to endure. And teachers are in a particularly challenging position because whether or not they have access to that knowledge, they are responsible for teaching and managing the behaviors of students impacted by ACEs. As we have mentioned, some of these behaviors can be severe and incredibly disruptive or aggressive. I have had teachers refer to classroom management with ACEs students as "navigating an emotional minefield" or "walking on eggshells." They do anything that they can to maintain a positive relationship with students and prevent them acting out or shutting down. All of this requires a great deal of the teacher's emotional, mental, and physical energy.

If we are to effectively teach ACEs students, then we must first take care of ourselves. As it stands, educators already face overwhelming workloads, high expectations, and challenging, often underresourced work environments. Add to that the demands of the unique socioemotional, learning, and behavioral needs of our students, especially those impacted by ACEs, and it becomes clear that something has to give. Unfortunately, the first thing that often gets sacrificed is our own health and well-being. The more we neglect ourselves, the quicker we will find ourselves in burnout.

It is vital that we step back and look at the impact of our work on our hearts, minds, and bodies. To avoid compassion fatigue, which can impact our health, finances, and effectiveness as teachers, I recommend adopting strategies for self-care. An easy way to start is by looking at the various areas of your life (e.g., health, relationships, finances) and choosing a small action you can take to benefit the area that feels most neglected. I also strongly suggest developing a daily habit to decompress and ease the burden of each work day. Otherwise, we risk carrying our stress and emotional baggage home to our loved ones. Whether it is such things as exercising, going for a walk, journaling, or meditating, I recommend choosing a healthy, sustainable habit that you can do at the end of each school day to relax and let go.

Read, Reflect, Respond

1. List three things that motivate you or lift your mood. Get out your calendar. Schedule a time over the next month to do each one of them, at least once.

2. Create a daily habit to decompress. Identify one activity that you can do after work to decompress and let go. Try it for one week.

Amber Warner, LCSW

SELF-CARE IS AN ETHICAL IMPERATIVE

Self-care is often easier talked or thought about than putting into practice. Professionals know they need to care for themselves but many don't. At times, we can even underestimate the necessity for self-care. Some may think self-care sounds selfish or something to only be mindful of during our private time, away from our professional setting. For others, self-care only comes into play after experiencing burnout or responding to a traumatic event. Self-care is more than just pampering oneself on special occasions, eating healthy meals, or exercising regularly. For certain professions, self-care is about emotional and professional survival. Self-care is attending to our physical, emotional, and mental health needs.

In an article written for clinical psychologists, "Self-Care as Ethical Imperative," authors John Norcross and Jeffrey Barnett tell clinical psychologists "without our own ongoing self-care, we become increasingly more limited in our ability to effectively assist others. It is vital to strike a balance between ongoing self-care and caring for others" (2008). In this light, self-care must be a proactive commitment and the number one intervention necessary to build professional resiliency. Research about the pressures today's educators face has already been established (Overman, n.d.; University of Houston, 2011). Therefore, educators can look to the mental health community for support, direction, and practices for self-care.

Educators, like doctors, nurses, social workers, and chaplains, are at risk for increased exposure to other people's trauma simply due to the nature of the work and the needed intimacy in which they serve. When we teach, we teach the whole person, whether we have been informed of any trauma they have experienced or not. Teaching and learning is relational. Teachers and principals respond daily to the effects of trauma when their students' behaviors disrupt the learning environment. When educators have exhausted all their management strategies and the behavior is unchanged, they are prone to feeling incompetent and ineffective. The compassion that they had at the start of the school year or the start of their career begins to wane into compassion fatigue.

When informed of the traumatic details in a student's life, the professional can also be adversely impacted. For the listener, these effects can be like experiencing

Vicarious tramatization

the traumatic event themselves. This is called *vicarious traumatization*. Vicarious trauma is the opposite of withdrawing into compassion fatigue. When educators overidentify with a student's disclosure, they might begin to exhibit similar symptoms.

According to psychologist Jeffrey Barnett, they may have intrusive thoughts and images about the student's disclosure, experience insomnia, physiologic arousal, and distressing emotions. Without realizing, a teacher will distance himself or herself to avoid his or her feelings or try to minimize what the student is sharing. Avoidance undermines the close relationship needed between an educator and his or her student. Dr. Barnett warns that failure to recognize the symptoms of vicarious trauma impairs professional decisions that clinicians and educators make. Arriving to school late or leaving early, resisting innovation, avoiding colleagues, wishing the student would stay home, and excessive requests to remove the student from class are just a few signs a teacher may be experiencing vicarious trauma and developing compassion fatigue.

Mass shootings or the credible threat of a mass shooting traumatizes the entire school community, its staff, students, and parents. The time has come for all schools and school districts to add to their response plans steps for dealing with posttraumatic stress syndrome. Planning must include the voices of the available district counseling personnel, community mental and physical health professionals, first responders, rotaries, and members of the clergy. Engaging community mental and physical health care givers and first responders are obvious choices. Rotaries and the clergy may not be. Rotaries raise funds for schools. After a mass shooting, survivors have to return to the same place within weeks. Perhaps rotaries can fund security surveillance measures for the building that a school or school district may not be able to immediately afford. Members of the clergy can provide spiritual support for the members of their respective religious communities.

Educating ourselves about the signs, symptoms, effects, and possibilities of exposure to vicarious traumatization and compassion fatigue helps us to be intentional and accepting of self-care as direct service providers. Understanding that violent acts, whether they happen in the community or at school, can induce posttraumatic reactions is also part of the *new normal*.

Individual Self-Care Plans at the start of the school year

Individual self-care plans should become part of each educator's goal setting at the start of the school year. Plans should have, at a minimum, one measurable objective for physical, emotional, and health wellness. Administrators and leadership teams should add measurable strategies for team care to their school climate strategic plans.

Connection & Community amongst Staff

A simple first step intervention for school teams to consider would be to check in with each other briefly, routinely, and formally, as part of a team or staff meeting. Allowing each participant to take a couple of minutes to share one thing about herself or himself personally, share a funny student-related story or one professional aha moment is a good emotional check-in. When we share our experiences, it tends to bring the human factor into the work we are doing and allows for us to empathize with each other and be coresponsible for taking care of one another.

When we work and give from a place of optimal wellness, we can achieve the best results in our areas of influence. My hope is that from this section not only will you as an individual enhance your self-care plan, but you and your team, with leadership support, will also integrate wellness activities throughout your work day and week. Group walks around the block after lunch, potlucks in the staff lounge, and regular staff just-because celebrations can be done during the work day. Self-care morphs into staff care.

You are unique and have your own likes, dislikes, and interests, which are important to embrace. You must find what outlets, support systems, and structures work best for you and make you feel your best.

Physical Health Wellness

Most physicians give patients a list of to-dos for a healthy heart. These heart healthy habits are self-care at its basic best—no smoking, low-sodium diet, healthy nutrition, and regular exercise. These same lifestyle habits along with staying hydrated, practicing restorative sleep hygiene, having daily movement and exercise, and decent grooming and hygiene are foundations of optimal physical wellness.

A proactive and consistent approach will help educators build a strong inner core. Then when we find ourselves faced with a crisis or trying to manage disruptive behaviors in the classroom, we can be more responsive and creative problem solvers. For example, what foods do you eat that help you feel good, satisfied, and sustained throughout the day? Certain foods, like spinach, nuts, and quinoa, keep blood sugars level and help us have more energy throughout the work day, be more alert, and feel fuller longer. This helps with concentration and creativity and can reduce mood swings.

Read, Reflect, Respond

Restorative sleep hygiene refers to the practices and habits necessary to have good nighttime sleep quality and full daytime alertness.

1. How much sleep do you require to feel your best, be alert, kind, and attentive throughout the day?

2. How do you handle restless or wakeful periods during the night?

3. How do you naturally relax and unwind after a work day or a stressful encounter? Do you have a regular routine or ritual to prepare for restorative sleep?

Emotional Health Wellness

On an emotional level, as Ricky already stated, we must know ourselves and own our psychological triggers. When teachers talk about their profession, often they use phrases like "It's rewarding; I love kids; with children every day is different and full of wonder," revealing how much emotion is an integral part of their job satisfaction. But dealing with angry parents, angry students, or angry colleagues drains emotions like water going down a sink. Attending to

Figure 2.1   Socio-emotional needs are equally important for school staff as they are for students.

©Marty Bucella   www.martybucella.com

"I know the kids don't like you and pick on you, but you have to go to school...you're the teacher."

the emotional needs of educators is a necessary part of self-care and whole-staff planning. Triggers are personal. Different events can trigger different responses in each one of us. They bring forth memories, sensations, or flashbacks of our negative experiences that may in turn determine how we respond to others or how we respond in a stressful situation. We all have a past; humble yourself and embrace yours rather than try to deny it or run from it. When we don't acknowledge our own hurts, habits, and hang-ups it can actually make us more vulnerable to stress and the havoc that chronic stress can produce in our lives. By acknowledging and being mindful of our own triggers, they lose their power over us and we can develop self-care practices to keep us at our optimal best. Taking time to learn strategies that develop self-awareness like retreat (what), reflect (why), and review feelings (how) builds resiliency.

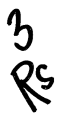

Read, Reflect, Respond

1. Take time to retreat, reflect, and review often. When you find yourself getting upset, being rubbed the wrong way, or irritated, look deeper; remember these 3 Rs:
    o Retreat—What am I feeling?
    o Reflect—Why am I feeling this way?
    o Review—How must I respond so as not to hurt someone's feelings?

2. Use these two scenarios to practice the self-awareness 3 Rs:
   ○ An angry parent calls you a racist because you are calling about his son's misbehavior in class.
   ○ A student makes an obscene gesture with her middle finger after you ask her to remove her earbuds.

Practice for 3 Rs (handwritten annotation)

Mental Health Wellness

Hurt people *hurt* people (Bowen, 2009). School districts across the nation are becoming increasingly aware and engaging in providing professional development to help staff recognize signs of mental distress in students. Teen clinics staffed with social workers and other health care providers are in middle and high schools. But teachers don't get enough help and guidance to mature in the awareness of their own mental health wellness. Who does the teacher, who is developing emotional or sexual feelings for a student, go to without fearing disclosure? How do we begin incorporating a forum for discussing boundary issues, stress caused by concerns outside of the classroom like financial difficulties, and other issues that surface for educators? Inviting professionals practicing in mental health wellness to speak candidly about vulnerabilities that surface in all professions where relationships are an integral part is a good start. Administrators must foster working environments that are safe, supporting, and honor confidentiality. They can also help school counselors free up time to work on activities that support the adults.

School Counselors (handwritten annotation)

Self-Awareness Is a Journey, Not a Destination

Daily movement or exercise, balanced nutrition, adequate sleep, proper relaxation, and fulfilling social connections are vital for a resilient leader. Activities and hobbies that have worked for you in the past can lose their effectiveness. So, don't get stuck in a rut and an ineffective routine; think broadly. Be open, flexible, creative, and intentional as you develop your self-care plan and structure.

From time to time, try a new activity, such as yoga, hiking, new superfood, a spa treatment, sport, or craft even if only once. Just by trying something new, you've provided yourself with an intervention that will help build and stimulate brain cells, open up channels of creativity, and build up your resiliency capacity.

Try New Things (handwritten annotation)

Psychologist W. Richard Walker and colleagues (2003) researched over 30,000 event memories and found that our memories are biased toward happiness. However, mild depression can disrupt this tendency. It's important for educators to find "critical" friends to vent or laugh with. YouTube and TED Talks are great resources for both serious and humorous videos related to teaching. We have listed a few URLs in the resource section. Self-care is about being open to new experiences just as you require your students to do the same when learning new things in your classroom.

our memories ☺ (handwritten annotation)

Caring for ourselves and building self-awareness takes effort and work, maybe even a new mindset. Knowing ourselves, becoming aware of our emotional triggers, and accepting our limitations will build resiliency in

THIS (handwritten annotation)

Role Plays & Simulations help →

Resilient You

Why Self-Care?

ourselves and the work we do. Using hypothetical scenarios to gain self-awareness can be fun, life changing, seem silly, and leave us feeling less vulnerable. Role-plays and simulations are helpful tools for practicing how to respond to duress. Clinicians use them in therapeutic settings to assist patients in building self-confidence and decreasing anxiety. Role-plays and simulations help educators become aware of personal responses and identify triggers before they are in an actual crisis. By having a plan and knowledge of how your body may respond in a crisis brings down your stress level and aids in your ability to bounce back from the encounter and make sound decisions.

The fact is just one behaviorally challenging student in your classroom can easily have you crashing down the spiral of burnout before you even realize it. Without guided practice role-plays led by your school counselor or mental health specialist, you will quickly suffer from hypoxia and be unable to secure your oxygen mask in time to save yourself.

Building a resilient classroom or collaborating with colleagues first requires building a resilient *you*.

I often share with my patients that they are the very best resource that they, their family, job, and community have. If you don't take care of your own physical, emotional, and mental wellness, who will? If self-care isn't a priority and daily practice of yours, what kind of service are you offering when you're not at your best?

Daily practices of self-care make us stronger physically, emotionally, and mentally. When intentional about self-care, we are building resiliency, which gives us the ability to cope with the stresses in our professional and personal lives. Being our best takes work and effort and we must prioritize time for self-care and know what activities, habits, and practices help us to be our best.

As we look to the mental health community for direction and examples of self-care, be mindful that "self-care is any activity that we do deliberately in order to take care of our mental, emotional, and physical health. Although it's a simple concept in theory, it's something we often overlook" (Michael, 2016).

Read, Reflect, Respond

1. Go to https://schools.au.reachout.com/articles/developing-a-self-care-plan and take the self-care assessment.

2. Celebrate the areas in which you are doing well.

3. Consider using feedback from the online assessment to create or revise your current self-care plan. Most importantly put your self-care plan in writing and share it with someone who knows how special you are.

4. Create your self-care plan. Drs. David Rock and Dan Siegel, specialists in brain neuroscience, created the Healthy Mind Platter. Use this link to access more information about the seven essential mental activities for optimal mental health well-being: http://www.drdansiegel.com/resources/healthy_mind_platter/

Sample template: My Self-Care Plan, AKA
Put on My Oxygen Mask First

I. I enjoy my profession because:

II. I want to take care of myself because:

III. When frustrated or upset at work, my critical friend(s) will:

IV. My socioemotional needs at work are:

Physical Health—Based on my annual physical check-up, at work I will:	**Physical Health—At home, I will:**
Mental Health—For my sanity's sake, at work, I will:	**Mental Health—At home, I will:**
Emotional Health—At work, I need:	**Emotional Health—At home, I need:**

Victoria E. Romero, Principal

WWAD?

What would (trauma-informed) administrators do to create a school culture that is safe for teachers to teach and learners to learn?

I was summoned to Mrs. Raider's fifth-grade classroom after the secretary answered her panicked call. As I raced upstairs, not knowing what I would be faced with, I wondered what if I can't physically deal with the situation? Thinking the worst, it must be a fight between two really big fifth graders. Instead, I came upon a scene that makes me cringe even as I recall the incident for this workbook. Mrs. Raider was wagging her finger in this student's face while yelling at her. She was invading this student's personal space to the point the child was leaning back. My first instinct was to get in the middle because of the look of fear on this girl's face. Mrs. Raider began yelling at me, telling me what this student had done—she had stolen candy from her teacher's desk and given it out to her classmates. I was livid and not at the student. I had to look calm and neutral on the outside but inside, my guts were churning.

I told Mrs. Raider to find some place and take an hour to cool down. I needed to deal with the student and her class. I turned to the girl and apologized, not necessarily directly saying anything about her teacher's behavior though, in reality, that is for what I was apologizing. I was apologizing for a memory that would be filed in her fifth-grade brain, perhaps for the rest of her life. She happened to be a Cambodian student who was bussed to my school for English language learning in a school that was 60 percent White and upper middle class. I told her that it was wrong to take things from other people without asking first for permission and that what she had done was wrong even though her intent was a good one because she wanted to share the candy with her classmates. I sent her to the office to lie down.

I went into the classroom to talk to the students who had just witnessed this distressing scene. I could only imagine how they must have felt to see their teacher lose control and humiliate one of their peers. It was one of those moments that I was glad I had a M.Ed. in school counseling and able to use those skills to debrief and talk about reentry for both the teacher and their classmate. I apologized to them as well and said sometimes we adults just lose it. I assured them that their teacher and classmate probably regretted their actions and I asked for ideas on how the class should welcome them back. I was grateful the incident took place in the second half of the day because no effective teaching or learning was going to happen that day. When Mrs. Raider returned to class, I suggested that she do an art activity or play a game for the rest of the day. And I invited her to come and speak with me after school.

One might think I really let her have it in our professional debrief and I may even have felt like it. But I knew that that behavior on my part would have been counterproductive. Instead, I asked her a series of questions to see if she could unpack her feelings and what made her react so vehemently. All of her responses were intellectual and based on her principles that she had been brought up with about stealing. It wasn't until I asked how she felt about creating a negative memory for her student and class that she became emotional and could connect with her heart.

She hadn't thought of her behavior having a negative effect because she was so hung up on *her* stuff.

There were many moments in my first year as a principal in a school where clashes of misunderstanding occurred. The staff was fractured. The teachers felt the 40 percent of students bussed in from families with diverse cultural and ethnic points of view were problematic. When I first started, they even referred to these children as *the bilinguals* or the south-end kids. Some of them couldn't see that they were not taking ownership of their teaching. Teachers blamed these students for pulling down the state scores even though the disaggregated scores of our White students when compared to their counterparts in other schools were significantly lower.

This veteran staff struggled with admitting they were not teaching White students all that well either. But once they got over that shock, they were open to doing whatever was needed to do their best. They were consummate professionals willing to learn new instructional strategies that included teaching their students behaviors appropriate for learning.

Since teachers were willing to try new things, I was willing to take as much off their full plates as possible to free up more time during our school day. With the help of instructional assistants and office staff, I did recess and lunch duties. Their planning schedules were organized so they could meet with their grade-level colleagues. There was an expectation that they work collaboratively to determine what developing, proficient, and exemplary student work looked like and their next instructional steps. I narrowed weekly staff meetings to a monthly meeting. In its place, I organized a leadership team composed of a representative from each grade, the family support worker, the ELL teacher, the nurse, and a parent representative. This group met twice a month to share grade-level updates and discuss school, district, and PTA business. While the leadership team met, the other teachers were expected to use the time planning or evaluating student progress together. The grade-level representatives were switched quarterly to give all teachers equal duty and planning times. Knowing what I know now, I suppose this was my way of helping my staff put on their oxygen masks.

Although the majority of our students quickly responded to our positive discipline values, there were students from both populations, middle class and low income, who needed more socioemotional support. Since I did not have a school counselor, I networked with a community mental health agency that was willing to provide therapeutic support at the school. The parents in the PTA raised funds so that I could pay this person to sit on our student intervention teams when we discussed students struggling with academic or social skills. Having this additional voice and expertise was invaluable. Not only did she deliver therapeutic services at our school, but she shared practical behavior interventions that teachers could try in their classrooms.

The ELL teacher was a brilliant woman who knew her craft. When I asked her how we could accelerate teaching our Level 3 and 4 students (students who understand standard English but still need ELL support) to read and comprehend, she recommended a reading series. I bought all the materials she needed to get that job done. The progress these students made was quickly mirrored in their homerooms. The regular classroom teachers saw the progress and began to call on these students more in class by asking them to read grade-level texts aloud and calling on them to share their interpretation of the text.

At the end of my first year, our state scores increased significantly for all groups, with our ELL Level 3 and 4 students showing the greatest growth. Our school was one of ten schools in the state whose assessment scores had "improved very significantly higher than expected" (Engel et al., 1999) and we were ranked the number one school in our district demonstrating value-added instruction.

Still, I wish I had known then what I know now.

I would have started my first year and every subsequent year helping teachers put on their oxygen masks first. I would focus on self-care and the stress of teaching and managing. In goal-setting conferences at the start of each school year, I would have added questions pertaining to self-care and asked my staff to establish goals addressing their socioemotional needs at work. I would have sought professional development opportunities related to self-care and asked my supportive PTA parents to provide teacher appreciation activities more than one time per year. Perhaps this could have helped Mrs. Raider to realize she needed to adjust to a new normal and look at behaviors as a form of communication. Maybe she would have seen what her student did as trying to make friends to compensate for her not being able to speak English well.

Research about the role educational leaders play in student academic growth and social development is clear. Effective leadership is second to teaching in its impact on student learning, especially in turning around schools with ACEs-impacted students (Leithwood, Louis, Anderson, & Wahlstrom, 2004).

The Professional Standards for Educational Leaders have been updated three times since 1996, when they were first published, in an effort to keep pace with the challenges we have termed in this book as the *new normal* educators face each day. With each revision, there is greater emphasis on principals to

- create and maintain a school culture that is caring and conducive to each student's *and* teacher's learning,
- allocate resources effectively,
- maintain organizational systems, and
- interface with community resources. (National Policy Board for Educational Administration, 2015)

The standards (National Policy Board for Educational Administration, 2015) specifically address the need for principals to have the following skills:

Standard 3 e—Confront and alter institutional biases of student marginalization, deficit-based schooling, and low expectations associated with race, class, culture and language, gender and sexual orientation, and disability or special status.

Standard 5 b—Create and sustain a school environment in which each student is known, accepted and valued, trusted and respected, cared for, and encouraged to be an active and responsible member of the school community.

d—Promote adult–student, student–peer, and school–community relationships that value and support academic learning and positive social and emotional development.

Standard 6 e—Deliver actionable feedback about instruction and other professional practice through valid, research-anchored systems of supervision and evaluation to support the development of teachers' and staff members' knowledge, skills, and practice.

f—Empower and motivate teachers and staff to the highest levels of professional practice and to continuous learning and improvement.

g—Develop the capacity, opportunities, and support for teacher leadership and leadership from other members of the school community.

h—Promote the personal and professional health, well-being, and work–life balance of faculty and staff.

i—Tend to their own learning and effectiveness through reflection, study, and improvement, maintaining a healthy work–life balance.

If my preparation for becoming a school administrator had included opportunity to become proficient practicing and applying these standards, I would not have lost valuable time that should have been focused on instructional systems, scratching my head about how to resolve conflicts between staff members. I probably would have helped teachers unpack their bias toward the students bussed to the school for English language acquisition. Although I brought in therapeutic services to counsel students and families for students whose behaviors made it obvious they were in need, I had no structures in place to meet the needs of the quiet, compliant but troubled child. We used a socioemotional curriculum, Second Steps, but it was not consistently implemented from K–5th grades.

My life was not balanced during my first two years as a principal. A typical day started two hours before the opening bell and ended early evening. I worked Sunday mornings wanting to prepare for the upcoming week, but in reality, I was just catching up with the past week.

We all worked very hard my first year and we were rewarded by the significant academic gains our students made that first year. It buoyed our confidence and commitment to ensure our mission statement started aligning with our data. But we worked harder, not smarter. Smarter to me, as the principal, would have been acknowledging the socioemotional needs of the members of the staff. Although bickering within some grade-level teams planning lessened, some grade-level teams remained hesitant about sharing common assessment data and planning next steps. And a few teachers continued to be reluctant trusting their students being taught by their grade-level colleagues. And as long as our high-stakes test scores continued the climb, I didn't even know what I didn't know at the time. I might have been able to help teachers open their practice for collegial support, understand the emotional roots of resistance, and have a process for staff for restorative conversations when disagreements or misunderstandings occurred. Had Felitti's and Anda's ACEs research been available at the time of my administrative training and integrated in the curriculum, I would have been prepared to work on establishing a working environment with protocols to meet the socioemotional needs of the staff. Administrators need opportunities to learn and develop cultural and socioemotional leadership skills.

Read, Reflect, Respond

1. Standard 6 of the Professional Standards for Educational Leaders addresses minimizing job-related stress. Your superintendent has convened a task force of teachers to help him or her gather ideas and suggestions to help create professional development for principals that address Standard 6, Section h. Using the definition of *compassion fatigue* in the introduction, what would you suggest and why?

   Standard 6 Professional Capacity of School Personnel

   Effective educational leaders develop the professional capacity and practice of school personnel to promote each student's academic success and well-being.

   h—Promote the personal and professional health, well-being, and work–life balance of faculty and staff.

Ability to Promote for Staff and Students	Ideas/Suggestions	Explanation
Personal health		
Professional health		
Well-being		
Work–life balance		

2. Based on your ideas and suggestions, describe the behaviors of a principal toward staff, students, and families who is proficient in meeting Standard 6 Section h.

	Descriptive Behaviors
Leadership style	
Fair and consistent	
Make courageous decisions	
Organized and prepared	
Discerning observer and active listener	

Toolkit Takeaways

1. To be fully present and professionally effective, school employees must care for themselves physically, emotionally, and mentally.

2. Effective administrative leadership is second to teaching in its impact on student learning, especially in turning around schools with ACEs-impacted students.

3. The Professional Standards for Educational Leaders Standards 3f, 5b and d, and 6 e–i relate to skills administrative leaders need to create and maintain a school climate and culture that is physically, mentally, and emotionally safe for staff, students, and families.

4. Today's educators are working directly, and over extended periods of time, with students and families who are under duress. As a result, educators are prone to developing compassion fatigue, which can lead to burnout. In this state, they are no longer able to perform their jobs well. Being in this state may impact their personal lives as well.

5. Online resources are available to take self-care assessments and develop a self-care plan. School administrators should establish ways to encourage staff to maintain wellness by providing onsite opportunities and regular check-ins.

3

It's Easy to Have High Expectations— Hard to Grow a New Mindset

I believe that education is the civil rights issue of our generation. And if you care about promoting opportunity and reducing inequality, the classroom is the place to start. Great teaching is about so much more than education; it is a daily fight for social justice.

—Arne Duncan,
Former Secretary of Department of Education
October 9, 2009

Anticipated Outcomes

Readers will

⊘ be exposed to characteristics of high-poverty, high-performing schools and characteristics of White teachers who successfully eliminated the achievement gap with African American students.

⊘ learn the meaning of transformationist teaching and learning.

⊘ understand that **transformationist teaching** and learning is relational with dimensions of knowing: self, students, and pedagogy.

(Continued)

(Continued)

- o understand that school staff and students need a school climate and culture that fosters socio-emotional development, builds growth mindset, and enhances resiliency.

- o compare concepts (building authentic teacher–learner relationships, implicit/explicit biases, mindset, socioemotional development, and resiliency) to their school or classroom management system.

- o understand and value that as science (e.g., neuroscience, social science, physiology) makes new discoveries, pedagogy must adapt and create strategies to add to its professional toolkit. In education, as in the medical profession, change is a constant.

In 1977, Dr. Ronald Edmonds published a research paper about high-poverty, high-performing schools. *Search for Effective Schools: The Identification and Analysis of City Schools That Are Instructionally Effective for Poor Children* studied 2,500 students in twenty schools located in low-income communities. Effective schools were defined as schools where test scores were above citywide norms. The summary concluded that a family's economic status did not dictate student academic achievement.

During her tenure at the University of Pittsburgh from 1974 to 1992, Dr. Barbara Sizemore researched the attributes of high-poverty, high-performing schools and developed the School Achievement Structures, a model to help other schools replicate (Bradley, 1996; Sizemore, Brossard, & Harrigan, 1983).

Both researchers identified characteristics or correlates these schools had in common. These high-poverty, high-performing schools had

- o effective principals who were able to generate a culture of high expectations for staff and student performance;

- o staff acceptance and belief that academic achievement is the highest priority;

- o schoolwide behavior and attendance expectations that were taught to all students, aligned with classroom management, explained to parents, and visible throughout the school;

- o ongoing observations of teachers and students;

- o consistent monitoring of students' skill mastery;

- o strategies for reaching out and involving parents as a support group: parents were taught ways to help their students;

- o a school office that was family and staff friendly;

- o differentiated instructional groupings to support students who were meeting or exceeding targets or needing more time to meet targets;

- o after-school programs for extending learning time; and

- o exhausted all alternatives before testing for special education classes.

In the four decades since Drs. Edmonds's and Sizemore's groundbreaking research, others have continued to refine and add information. Schools serving significant numbers of low-income students around the nation used the data to change the educational outcomes for their students. The Education Trust catalogued the research findings of over 4,500 high-poverty, high-performing public schools with populations totaling 1.3 million students, of whom 564,000 were African American and 660,000 were Hispanic/Latino (Jerald, 2001).

In 2003, Dr. Johnnie McKinley studied twenty-nine predominately White educators in Washington State who were successful in eliminating the achievement gap with their African American students. She isolated forty-two strategies and contextual features these educators shared (McKinley, n.d.). Now there is a term that would describe them as being *culturally responsive*. According to McKinley, these teachers were able to develop authentic relationships with their students by teaching to and honoring their cultural, social, ethnic, and linguistic differences. They were skilled at aligning instructional strategies to student traits, abilities, and learning-style preferences. Their competencies stretched beyond pedagogy to include knowing who their students were culturally; they used call and response, collaborative learning groupings, and integrated music, dance, and poetry in all content areas. These were strategies that Barbara Shade and colleagues also detail in their 2005 book, *Creating Culturally Responsive Classrooms*.

Child psychiatrist James Comer piloted a program in two New Haven low-performing, high-poverty schools to support the development of students' emotional growth in the late 1960s. Both schools became high-performing schools with scores exceeding the national average. The Comer School Development Program launched what we now know as socioemotional learning (Comer, 1988; Edutopia, 2011). The Collaborative for Academic, Social and Emotional Learning (CASEL) was founded in 1994 with a mission to advocate teaching healthy social and emotional learning (SEL) behaviors as a basic part of education from preschool through high school. In 2003, CASEL published *Safe and Sound: An Educational Leader's Guide to Evidence-Based Social and Emotional Learning (SEL) Programs*. CASEL identified five core competencies for socioemotional development: self-awareness, self-management, social awareness, relationship skills, and responsible decision-making. A well-designed curriculum to strengthen socioemotional skills will have these five SEL components.

Educator Eric Jensen, an ACEs survivor, added another layer to the earlier works of Edmonds, Sizemore, and others when he published *Teaching With Poverty in Mind: What Being Poor Does to Kids' Brains and What Schools Can Do with It?* In this 2009 work, Jensen delved deeper into the biological sciences and social sciences to show how the connection between neuroscience and socioemotional curricula is a vital addition to educational pedagogy. Zaretta Hammond's *Culturally Responsive Teaching & The Brain: Promoting Authentic Engagement and Rigor Among Culturally and Linguistically Diverse Students* adds another dimension to our work.

There are also updated versions of the characteristics of high-poverty, high-performing schools published by a number of other researchers (Kannapel, Clements, Taylor, & Hibpshman, 2005; Parrett & Budge, 2011). Their studies add strategic assignment of staff, dedication to equity and diversity, and regular communication with families.

Kenneth Leithwood (2010) identified thirty-one school districts making significant improvements closing the achievement gaps. The National Education Association (2011) grouped the strategies these districts focused on as culturally responsive competencies, holistic support for students and their families, extended learning opportunities, classroom/school/district cultures that focus on effective teaching and learning; identifying qualified school staff; and effective alignment of resources of the NEA. The NEA continues to publish and make available evidence-based strategies online, literally at the fingertips of today's educators.

Read, Reflect, Respond

Considering the body of research (high-poverty, high-performing schools; **culturally responsive teaching** strategies; socioemotional competencies; and strategies for optimal brain functioning) that began four decades ago and continues to evolve, why do you think more schools and school districts still struggle with closing achievement disparities?

KNOWING MYSELF PRECEDES TEACHING STUDENTS

In his book, *We Can't Teach What We Don't Know*, Gary R. Howard uses a graphic to illustrate what teachers need to know and be able to do to close achievement gaps. His Achievement Triangle (Figure 3.1 on the opposite page) identifies three dimensions of actionable behaviors needed for transformationist pedagogy: knowing myself, knowing my students, and knowing my practice (Howard, 2016). Transformationist practice is educating in a way that the learner develops a growth mindset, is able to demonstrate socioemotional maturity, and knows he or she is resilient.

Transformationist school staff are passionate about equity. They are responsive to the cultural and socioemotional needs of their students. They stay current with the latest research and proven best practices about teaching and learning in diverse populations. They are careful not to let bias affect professional decisions. They are adept at scaffolding tasks to gauge when their students are ready for the next skill and have a number of strategies for teaching the same skill in different ways. They demonstrate high expectations by providing opportunities for their students to analyze, synthesize, and create using the skills they have learned. They hold each student to the same standards. They are on a mission to be their personal and professional best.

Unfortunately, professional development does not begin with school staff exploring *self*. Most initiatives requiring professional development focus on educators knowing my practice and knowing my students. Knowing my practice is more about implementing content. Knowing my students is limited to viewing them as passive receivers of instruction and not about who they are as human beings, with strengths rooted in their cultural and ethnic identities *and* their emotions. As stated previously, our students learn best when they do not have to give up who they are to fit in and are given opportunity to use their innate intellectual capabilities. Opportunity for teachers to know myself and acknowledge where they are professionally or who they are in the equation is usually omitted entirely.

Figure 3.1   Gary R. Howard's Achievement Triangle

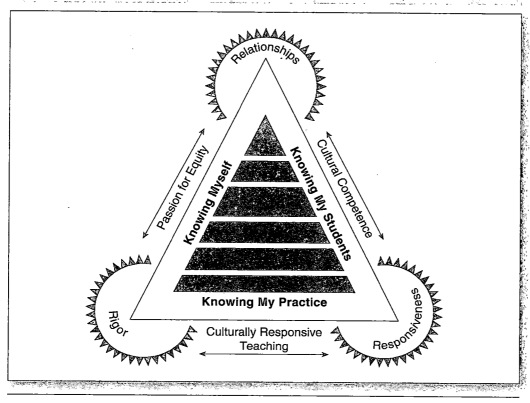

Source: Achievement Triangle: Transformationist Pedagogy, ©2005 Gary R. Howard

The three dimensions of actionable behaviors needed for transformationist pedagogy are connected to one another, and a strong foundation for professional development takes this into account.

Perhaps this omission may be at the root of why many initiatives and innovations are met with resistance or not implemented with fidelity or consistency. This one-size-fits-all approach to professional development assumes that all teachers will receive the information in the same way and be able to implement at mastery level the next day. Master teachers may adapt the new learning if it fits into what they already consider are successful strategies. Good teachers may adapt some of the strategies. Struggling teachers may not understand how or where the new learning fits.

Professional development that furthers employees' understanding of knowing myself should also be a consideration when new initiatives are introduced because it involves change. Adjusting to change is a process. There is an assumption that everyone is ready for change, neglecting the fact that the very act may touch on a bias the educator needs to unpack. For example, when public school districts around the nation had to create policies regarding accommodations for transgender students, some faculty members were opposed (Google "teachers' perspectives on transgender bathrooms"). They should not be judged for having this bias. Instead, they may need to dedicate time to working through their personal feelings, so that professionally, these educators can have and maintain an authentic teaching relationship with the transgender student sitting in their classroom while also accommodating the student's needs.

More professional development time needs to be devoted to supporting school staff with Knowing Self. It needs a holistic approach to support teachers

> *Reduce teaching to intellect and it becomes a cold abstraction; reduce it to emotions and it becomes narcissistic; reduce it to the spiritual and it loses its anchor to the world. Intellect, emotion, and spirit depend on each other for wholeness. They are interwoven in the human self and in education at its best, and we need to interweave them in our pedagogical discourse as well.*
>
> —Parker Palmer

in their socioemotional development, growth mindset, and resilient behaviors.

Courage to Teach

Knowing Myself activities can help employees metacognitively process who they are and unpack their biases and preconceived notions about new initiatives and the students they teach and safeguard against resistance and subjective decision-making. It is human to have preconceived notions or biases but unethical when they influence professional decisions. If the adults who work with youth are not aware of their biases, bad things can and do happen for a child.

Unaware of their biases or lacking confidence about their depth of knowledge about the content, educators may decide a new initiative won't work for their students; they lower their expectations. They remain focused on teaching lower-level skills because they decide their students are not ready to analyze or synthesize content. Bias shows up in their discipline and special education referrals and who gets more teacher time and approval.

Support staff also need to engage in know-myself professional development activities. They are an underutilized human resource in schools because we don't see them as having relationships with students. But many individuals manage to communicate caring and concern for young people. In Chapter 7, there are URL links to videos of school staff and students showing their appreciation for a custodian, school-based police officer, office staff worker, and others because these adults, who have the least amount of contact time, have managed to form strong relationships with students. In the new normal, we need to remember the custodian might be the adult to whom a student living with ACEs turns first.

Bias can be communicated nonverbally too. School staff who work with or around students are always on stage. Our students are always watching us and making judgments. Adults who are not aware of their biases or preconceptions may be sending nonverbal cues that make it difficult to form the needed trusting relationships with their learners. At the same time, students are also biased. Some may have preconceived notions about their teachers. If a student's primary source of information is family, television, or music, a young person's positive or negative biases may be a barrier they create to maintain emotional distance.

For students living with ACEs, observing adult behaviors is tied to their survival. They are hypervigilant and hypersensitive to verbal and nonverbal cues. They are prone to misreading even well-intended verbal and nonverbal signals. If you have ever had a student who was quick to anger because somebody looked at him or her, you witnessed a child that may be living with adverse childhood experiences. Educators who are survivors of adverse childhood experiences may also misread verbal and nonverbal cues when working with students and colleagues. They may not be able to see how their behaviors are problematic and actually put up barriers to having authentic professional relationships.

It has been documented that some students shut down if they feel their teachers don't like them and vice versa (Aspy & Roebuck, 1978). They won't put in the effort to learn. As the late educator Rita Pierson said in her TED Talk, *Every Child Needs a Champion*, teachers will not like every student they teach;

they just can't show it (2013). This is when professional behaviors are essential—you still have to teach so that that student learns.

Imagine a physician with a bias about treating people with red hair. Were it not for the doctor's standard, *do no harm,* and the fact that she can be sued for malpractice, redheads under the care of this doctor would be at risk. Physicians take malpractice very seriously. The lives of the patients are dependent on the doctor's skills and expertise. If we are to turn around the brand school-to-prison pipeline, the added depth to knowing myself must become an integral piece in professional development. The educational lives of America's future are in the hands of all the adults working in a school.

For educators, knowing myself is the awareness that acknowledges humans have bias and bias can show up in decision-making and factor in classroom teaching and professional relationships as well. Transformationist school staff put effort into being conscientious about their biases to avoid discriminatory decision-making. They also want to be prepared to handle negative bias when it shows up in the classroom, as it did in Ricky's class one day. Adults need strategies to address it in that teachable moment. Later in this chapter, Ricky shares what happened to him emotionally and how he handled this moment. Educators who practice self-awareness about their biases are in a better position to teach their students about the nature of bias.

The average classroom teacher will make more than 1,500 educational decisions every school day. In an average 6-hour school day, that's more than four decisions every minute (Fredericks, n.d.). Many of these decisions are made under the pressure of teaching their lessons or pacing to meet calendar guidelines that the grade level, department teams, or districts have established. After participating in professional development focusing on myself, transformationist school staff understand bias is natural but do not let their personal biases affect their professional behaviors and actions.

Read, Reflect, Respond

1. Watch the PBS video about the Implicit Bias Test: http://www.pbs.org/video/2365399552
2. Then consider taking an online test for racial and gender bias on the Understanding Prejudice website: http://www.understandingprejudice.org/iat/index2.htm
3. If you are not comfortable with taking this test, ask yourself why. Then search the Internet for articles about understanding hidden biases:
   http://www.wikihow.com/Overcome-Unconscious-and-Hidden-Biases http://www.tolerance.org/blog/confronting-creepy-crawlies-and-implicit-bias
4. Respond to the following scenario from the points of view of a classroom teacher, paraprofessional (teaching assistant), school counselor, principal, or secretary:
   Four Black boys are sent to the principal's office for disruptive behaviors in music class. Two White boys, involved in the same ruckus, were sent back to the classroom.
   How would you handle this situation?
5. You work in a school where 70 percent of the students have family incomes averaging $90,000. There is a program for English language learners that draws 30 percent of the school's population. These students are immigrants from the Ukraine, Somalia, Marshall Islands, and Mexico. Twenty-eight percent of these students qualify for free or reduced lunch services.

   Your team is reviewing end of the quarter assessment scores in math. The data is showing an achievement gap within the ELL population when equating comparable levels of English acquisition. The Ukrainian students are outpacing their Somalian, Marshallese, and Mexican counterparts. What questions would you pose for the team to consider? What solutions?

Read, Reflect, Respond

1. Do an analysis of the characteristics of high-poverty, high-performing schools and high-performing schools and your school or school district. What do you think should happen in the next steps?

Characteristics of High-Poverty, High-Performing Schools (ASCD, 2005)	Characteristics of High-Performing Schools (OSPI, 2007)	Characteristics at My School or a School in the District (cite evidence)	Possible Next Steps
o The belief that all students can succeed at high levels o High expectations o Collaborative decision making o Teachers accept their role in student success or failure o Strategic assignment of staff o Regular teacher–parent communication o Caring staff and faculty o Dedication to diversity and equity	o A clear and shared focus o High standards and expectations for all students o Effective school leadership o High levels of collaboration and communication o Curriculum, instruction, and assessments aligned with state standards o Frequent monitoring of learning and teaching o Focused professional development o Supportive learning environment o High levels of family and community involvement		

2. What are the demographics of the high-performing schools in your district? What are the demographics of the schools not performing as well? Cite the similarities and differences. What would you do if you were the superintendent?

3. Test your mindset: http://www.londonacademyofit.co.uk/learning-blog/learning/interactive-quiz-fixed-vs-growth-mindset.

   a. Were there any surprises? Explain.

   b. If your bias self-assessment revealed challenges that may be impacting professional choices, stretch your brain and grow new nerve pathways. Unpack your bias, especially if there is a possibility it may be negatively impacting your belief about student behaviors, who will be successful in your classroom, or the value you think your students or their families place on their education.

- Why do I feel this way?
- Is there any evidence that my bias is negatively influencing my professional decisions (review your discipline data, special education or data team referrals, students you are least successful with)?
- Whom do I trust or feel comfortable sharing what I have learned and can help me metacognitively?

c. Review the suggestions for becoming more mindful of dealing with biases mentioned earlier in this chapter. Select one of your challenging thoughts about teaching. Create a plan for yourself that applies the ideals in your personal Educator's Hippocratic Oath, characteristics of effective teaching, and Dweck's growth mindset. Your plan should have measurable outcomes and timelines if needed.

4. How does your practice compare to the characteristics of high-performing teachers?

Characteristics of High-Performing Teachers (Stronge, 2007)	Characteristics of My Practice (cite evidence)	Next Steps
o Assumes ownership for the classroom and students' success o Uses personal experiences to provide real-world examples in teaching o Understands students' feelings o Admits mistakes and corrects them immediately o Thinks about and reflects on practice o Uses humor o Dresses appropriately for the position o Maintains confidential trust and respect o Is structured, yet flexible and spontaneous o Is responsive to situations and students' needs o Enjoys teaching and expects students to enjoy learning o Finds the win–win solution in conflict situations o Listens attentively to student questions, comments, and concerns o Responds to students with respect, even in difficult situations o Communicates high expectations consistently o Conducts one-on-one conversations with students		

(Continued)

(Continued)

Characteristics of High-Performing Teachers (Stronge, 2007)	Characteristics of My Practice (cite evidence)	Next Steps
<ul><li>Treats students equally and fairly; data validates</li><li>Engages in positive dialogue and interaction with students outside the classroom</li><li>Invests time with single students or small groups of students outside the classroom</li><li>Maintains a professional manner at all times</li><li>Addresses students by name</li><li>Speaks in an appropriate tone and volume</li><li>Works actively with students</li><li>Provides tutoring to students before and after school</li></ul>		

5. What are some possible next steps for your practice?

6. If you are not working with students directly, describe a role-model working in your department whom you feel performs his or her responsibilities well. If that person is you, that's OK. Cite evidence.

Characteristics of My Role Model (cite evidence)	Comparison of My Performance (cite evidence)	My Next Steps

KNOWING MY STUDENTS AND KNOWING PEDAGOGY-GROWING MINDSET

Dr. Carol Dweck and colleagues have been studying students' attitudes about failure for three decades. Dr. Dweck wanted to know why some students will continue to put effort in a task until they were successful or not get rattled when they weren't, while other students give up after the first failure or refuse to even try. They discovered the difference was due to the beliefs the students had about themselves. She coined the terms *growth mindset* and *fixed mindset* to describe these dichotomous attitudes or beliefs (Dweck, 2015). Individuals who have a growth mindset believe that through effort, they can always improve.

> *The passion for stretching yourself and sticking to it, even (or especially) when it's not going well, is the hallmark of the growth mindset. This is the mindset that allows people to thrive during some of the most challenging times in their lives.*
>
> —Carol Dweck, Psychologist

Dweck says mindset is not static. Individuals with a fixed mindset can reprogram their internal monologue that tells them not to take risks or passes negative judgment, like, "I told you it was too hard," when they are not successful. Mindset factors into bias. An educator with a fixed mindset makes the decision (and justifies it) that some students just won't get it (Arnett, 2016). The educator with a growth mindset makes the decision (and justifies it) that students will get it because he or she can reteach the same skill differently and will give explicit feedback about their effort.

Before school staff attempt to teach students about growth mindset, they first need to determine their mindset. How can they model a growth mindset if theirs is fixed? They need to know myself first. In the Read, Reflect, Respond section of this chapter is an URL link to an assessment measuring mindset. If your self-assessment reveals you have a fixed mindset, do not worry. Mindset is malleable.

The neurosciences validate that fixed mindset is not a permanent condition. We now know our miracle brains can form new nerve cells after injuries or diseases. *Neuroplasticity* is a medical term used to describe how the brain will regroup and repair itself by forming new nerve pathways (MedicineNet.com, 2017). Imagine the power of teaching students about growth mindset *and* the brain's ability to grow because of their effort.

Dweck's work and the advances in the neurosciences have significant implications for our work. There are short videos of Dr. Dweck explaining the concepts of growth and fixed mindset. Administrators can provide school staff time to reflect, discuss, and role-play with each other using online videos. According to Dweck, when giving our students and colleagues formative feedback, the focus should be on the process and hard work to develop growth mindset. Dweck's research has shown students with a growth mindset are motivated by taking on more challenging work (Blackwell, Trzesniewski, & Dweck, 2007). When teacher performance evaluations are **formative evaluations,** we are encouraging them to apply growth mindset strategies.

KNOWING MY STRENGTHS, KNOWING THE STRENGTHS OF MY STUDENTS FOSTERS RESILIENCY

> *These are the growth capacities which have enabled survival throughout human history. Moreover, they are the very same personal strengths that have enabled each of our own life journeys.*
>
> —Bonnie Benard, MSW
> Resiliency in Action, Inc.

Knowing myself, knowing my students, and having a growth mindset are essential to strengthening resiliency. All humans, regardless of race, nationality, or class, are born with resiliency (Werner & Smith, 1992). It is innate and critical for our survival. Resiliency is the ability to recover or bounce back from difficult challenges. Resiliency builds social competencies.

Social scientist Bonnie Benard developed a framework of four traits with eighteen actions based on long-term studies of children; although born into high-risk families, over half of the participants developed social competence. Social competence is having the social, emotional, and cognitive skills and behaviors needed for positive interactions with others.

Benard identified personal and environmental factors that strengthened the innate resiliency in these children. She warns that the eighteen actions are not *resilient skills* to be taught but are outcomes that can be observed. Socioemotional curriculum that shares examples of what these behaviors look like and provides opportunity for students to role-play, discuss, or observe in action, reinforces their innate resiliency. When classroom, schoolwide, bus, and cafeteria socially competent behaviors are demonstrated and practiced until students can apply them independently, all school staff are strengthening their innate resiliency. Explicit feedback acknowledging a student's effort to use resilient actions helps both teacher and student feel a sense of accomplishment. Humans thrive from a sense of accomplishment (Benard, 1991a).

Benard's research findings validate the professional need for educators to have a growth mindset about the impact they have on student success because it concludes the following:

- o Teachers' beliefs in innate capacity start the change process.
- o Most youth "make it."
- o All individuals have the power to transform and change.
- o Teachers and schools have the power to transform lives.
- o It's how we do what we do that counts.

Traits of Benard's Resiliency Framework

SOCIAL COMPETENCE	PROBLEM-SOLVING
o **Responsiveness**	o Planning
o Cultural flexibility	o Help-seeking
o Empathy	o Critical and creative thinking
o Caring	
o Communication skills	
o Sense of humor	

AUTONOMY	SENSE OF PURPOSE
● Sense of identity ● Self-efficacy ● Self-awareness ● Task-mastery ● Adaptive distancing from negative messages and conditions	● Goal direction ● Educational aspirations ● Optimism ● Faith or spiritual connection

Many of the traits in the Resiliency Framework are already embedded in some of our educational pedagogy (Howard's Achievement Triangle, Dweck's Growth Mindset) and socioemotional curriculum (RULER, Second Step, and MindUp). Effective socioemotional curriculum provides activities that promote caring, empathy, planning, and critical and creative thinking. They also should align with CASEL's Social-Emotional Learning (SEL) core competencies: self-awareness, self-management, social awareness, relationship skills, and responsible decision-making.

CASEL's Social-Emotional Competencies

Self-Awareness	The ability to label emotions and thoughts and articulate how they influence behavior. Having the ability to assess strengths and challenges and a growth mindset that reminds them it's about effort.
Self-Management	The ability to self-regulate emotions, thoughts, and behaviors in different situations. Able to effectively manage stress and control impulses.
Social-Awareness	The ability to listen and understand others, empathize with others, including those from diverse backgrounds and cultures. Understanding behaviors acclimates to fit different settings.
Relationship Skills	The ability to establish and maintain healthy and rewarding relationships with diverse individuals and groups. The ability to communicate clearly, listen well, cooperate with others, resist inappropriate social pressure, negotiate conflict constructively, and seek and offer help when needed.
Responsible Decision-Making	The ability to make choices about personal behavior and social interactions that consider the well-being of self and others. Having the maturity to hold oneself accountable for one's actions.

Educators who take the traits in Benard's Resiliency Framework and transform them into daily actions are supplementing socioemotional competencies.

They have created an effective classroom and schoolwide management system that provides practical conditions for students to apply their socioemotional learning and fortify their innate resiliency. But before they do, professional development activities should help faculty explore their socioemotional competencies and test their resiliency as another way of knowing self. School staff should be given time to learn and explore their strengths and work on resiliency actions that are challenging before modeling and attempting to integrate activities into their daily practice.

Transforma-tive Teaching
1. Know Thyself
2. Know My Students
3. Know what I teach

When knowing myself (aware of bias, having a growth mindset, strengthening personal resiliency), knowing my students (as socioemotional individuals with cultural and academic needs), and knowing pedagogy (integrating socioemotional skills into daily routines, using culturally responsive strategies) come together, instruction is transformative for both the adult and student.

When this support is available at each grade level like English language learner (ELL) or remedial programs, we give all of our students the time they need to learn and practice new ways of *being* when they are with us. When we provide professional development opportunities that are differentiated to meet the socioemotional needs of school staff, our instructional systems become more equitable in every way possible. This is what trauma-informed teaching and building a schoolwide climate and culture that is compassionate is about. When school staff become mindful of and avoid barriers they create because of implicit biases, when they are confident they can do the job, and have the socioemotional supports they need; then teaching becomes a *way of being* every day, all day for 180 days from PreK through 12th grades.

To get a better understanding of what these traits may look like in our practice, Ricky's narrative in this chapter demonstrates Howard's Know Myself, Benard's Resiliency Framework, and Dweck's Growth Mindset.

Read, Reflect, Respond

As you read Ricky's narrative, focus on his teaching and interpersonal behaviors and note how many of the actions in Benard's Resiliency Framework, Howard's Achievement Triangle, and Dweck's Growth Mindset come into play in his actions.

Social Competence (responsiveness, cultural flexibility, empathy, caring, communication skills, sense of humor),

Problem-solving (planning, help-seeking, critical and creative thinking),

Autonomy (sense of identity, self-efficacy, self-awareness, task mastery, adaptive distancing from negative messages and conditions), and

Sense of purpose (goal direction, educational aspirations, optimism).

Look for the times when he models and demonstrates Dweck's Growth Mindset.
Cite evidence of how he strives to follow Howard's Know Self as a person and a professional.

Ricky Robertson, Behavior Specialist

"I CAN'T LEARN BECAUSE YOU'RE WHITE."

I started working in education as a New York City public school teacher. I was fortunate to have the opportunity to teach mathematics at a high school in one of the most diverse school districts in the country, with students from over 100 different countries, speaking dozens of different languages. It was a stark contrast to the suburban school district I attended as a child growing up along Florida's Gulf Coast.

It was the first day of the school year and I was teaching a sophomore geometry class. This day was no different than any other first day of school. Both the students and I were struggling to stay focused, fighting off the restlessness of transitioning from summer's freedom to the routine of the bell schedule. I started class with an activity that I do at the beginning of each school year.

I asked my students, "What gets in the way of you learning math?"

I like to do this activity because it gives us an opportunity, as a class, to see what we are up against, to set goals, and make action plans to overcome the obstacles we can expect to face in the year ahead. On this day, all the responses were similar to ones that I had heard in previous years, the common litany of challenges and anxieties that hinder one's success and confidence in mathematics. Students rattled off everything from not understanding negative numbers to spending too much time playing video games instead of doing homework.

And then one of my students, a quiet, reserved Mexican American young woman who I had taught in algebra the previous year, raised her hand.

She said in all earnestness, "I can't learn because you're White."

As soon as she said this, the class went silent. It was perhaps the quietest my room had ever been or would be. Thirty-four sets of eyes looked at me, waiting for my response.

In that moment, I could feel my skin flush warm and red as it does when I'm nervous.

My throat went dry. My voice quivered, as it does when I'm caught off guard, and I asked, "Why is that?"

She said, "Because White teachers don't like Mexicans."

She went on to share a story about how in third grade she had a White teacher who had said to her, "Mexicans come to America and have too many children that they don't take care of." This racist comment broke this little girl's heart. After school that day, she went home and told her mother what her teacher had said. Her mother decided that each morning they would get up extra early to have more time for getting ready, so that when she arrived at school, her teacher would see how pretty and well-cared for she was. This would be their way of showing the teacher that she was wrong.

When this young woman finished speaking there were tears in her eyes and mine as well. The energy in the room had shifted to one of palpable vulnerability and authenticity. I looked around the room and saw recognition in the facial expressions and head nods of several students. It was evident that many of them had had similar experiences of bias and prejudice.

Read, Reflect, Respond

1. If a student experiences discrimination in school, how do you think it impacts his or her feelings about school? How about the ability to trust current and future teachers?

2. Are you comfortable talking with your students about bias and oppression? Do you think those conversations are valuable? Why or why not?

I can tell you now that her words struck a chord in my heart. They brought up a memory I had not thought about in sometime. One day when I was in fifth grade walking to P.E., my teacher told a group of boys to "rough me up" because it would make me "less of a sissy." And how almost thirty years later as an adult, as a teacher, as a gay man, I still carried that fear somewhere inside of me. It shows up from time to time at work when I worry that a principal, colleague, student, or parent will find out that I am gay and respond with ignorance and hate.

I thought about all the classes after that fifth-grade year where I sat silently in the back of the room. I didn't speak because I was too afraid that the teacher or the other kids would hear that sissy in my voice and I'd suffer for it. This young woman's story made me think about the impact of carrying the traumas and aggressions that we experience from prejudice and systemic oppression, although our experiences were different, and I know that racism and homophobia operate differently in society. I felt connected to her story in ways I hadn't anticipated.

Hearing her story had me realize that there was perhaps a lot more to her being quiet and reserved in class. She may have been protecting herself from more hurt. I could understand how my whiteness could show up for her as a threat, as something not to be trusted, as an impediment to her learning. I accepted that part of living out my commitment to the success and well-being of my students had to involve deepening my understanding of racism, and other forms of oppression, and finding ways to develop myself as a culturally responsive educator. In all these ways, this young woman in her truth and courage, taught me.

My journey in developing my skills as a culturally responsive educator was challenging at first. I had to investigate my own biases and the different forms of privilege I had benefitted from, while having been largely ignorant of the systems of oppression of which they were a product. I grappled with guilt, shame, defensiveness, and anger. I was angry that somehow as a White person, I had grown up in a culture that had caused me to be ignorant of and unempathetic to the struggles of people who were different from me. It felt like harm had been done to my soul. At some point, it made no sense to me to deny my privilege or resist engaging in equity work. To do so would have been to defend the ways that racism had fragmented my psyche and numbed my heart.

Perhaps the most painful part of this growth process was recognizing that at times I had inadvertently sent a message to my students that their cultures and identities weren't welcomed in my class. As a new teacher, I had thought that the demands of the curriculum and standardized testing didn't allow for us to explore how our personal identities impacted learning. I rationalized this point of view by thinking that those opportunities for self-expression were better suited for ELA or social studies, while math was about numbers not personal narratives. I was wrong. I was hiding behind my content. And, I was missing out on an opportunity to motivate and inspire my students.

At first, it was awkward. I started setting aside times in my math classes to have discussions. We talked about our lives, current events, shared challenges that we were facing, and set goals together. We were bonding as a class, but I still felt guilty, like I was deviating from the curriculum. What I didn't realize was that I was forming relationships that would actually fuel learning.

Forming relationships that would fuel learning

With time, I was able to more seamlessly incorporate what I had learned about my students' cultures and identities into our lessons and assignments. We used mathematics to explore topics that were relevant to their lives, hobbies, and interests: topics ranging from sports to gentrification in their neighborhoods. I also began incorporating more paired and group work into my class as a way to honor a more collectivist approach to learning. Finally, I started asking students to team-teach and even co-teach lessons with me, allowing them to then shape both the curriculum and instruction. The results of these efforts were evident in the drastic improvement in their standardized test scores at the end of the year. They were also evident in the profound sense of community that we created in our geometry classroom.

Read, Reflect, Respond

1. Do you think it is important for students to feel accepted and free to express themselves and their culture at school? Explain.

2. If a student feels that his or her culture is valued and accepted at school, do you think the student will be more successful academically and behaviorally? Explain.

3. How do you think your experiences growing up and your culture have shaped how you teach?

Over time, I came to learn a lot more about the relationship between trauma and systemic oppression. I now understand that culturally responsive teaching practices are necessary when working with students who are impacted by ACEs and trauma. One reason is that trauma can be historical and generational. One of the initial studies of generational trauma occurred in the 1960s when Canadian psychiatrists noticed that the grandchildren of Holocaust survivors were overrepresented by 300 percent in referrals for pediatric psychiatric care. The emotional and psychological impact of genocide, enslavement, cultural erasure, forced removal from land, extreme poverty, and long-term abuse can be passed on from generation to generation.

Generational trauma begins when a population endures a mass trauma, such as colonization or slavery, and the psychological and physiological effects of this trauma manifest within the affected population. The symptoms of this trauma are passed onto the next generation, who will exhibit similar behavioral and health conditions. For example, Dr. Bonnie Duran of the University of Washington and her colleagues have established a connection between health disparities among Native Americans and the mass trauma of colonization. Recent epigenetics research is starting to uncover a biological basis for this reality. Researchers have found that exposure to trauma and chronic stress can change the expression of certain genes that impact the body's response to stress. As a result, people impacted by trauma, and their offspring, can be genetically predisposed to develop depression, PTSD, type 2 diabetes, and other deleterious conditions.

Trauma can also be carried out structurally, socially, and politically. Cumulative trauma is caused by repeated exposure to prejudice, structural inequalities, discrimination, microaggressions, and other forms of social and systemic oppression. Students of color, LGBTQ students, students with disabilities, students from families who have experienced generational poverty, as well as students who live at the intersection of these identities, are among those who endure significant cumulative trauma.

Cumulative trauma has an immediate and long-term impact on the health and well-being of our students. For example, research has linked family rejection, as well as experiences of bullying and violence, to self-harming behaviors, substance abuse, depression, and suicide for LGBTQ youth. Nearly 40 percent of our nation's homeless youth identify as LGBTQ, while these young people make up only a small fraction of the general population. Studies about race-based traumatic stress have shown similar outcomes, revealing that repeated exposure to racial discrimination has been associated with anxiety, depression, substance abuse, and other health disparities for people of color. In effect, interpersonal and institutionalized discrimination can be traumatic.

The pain of cumulative trauma is exacerbated by economic and institutional barriers that limit both the access to and prevalence of resources and services (e.g., counseling, health care, safe housing) that could support marginalized youth. For example, across the country, young people of color, especially those who live in poverty, are more likely to be victims of violence than their White peers. Yet there are few programs within education or public health that specifically address the needs of youth of color who have suffered traumatic violence. Racism, poverty, sexism, homophobia, transphobia, ableism, and other forms of discrimination or inequality are at the root of many of the hardships that our students endure and the impact that persists due to limited access to care. Therefore, to best support the young people in our schools, trauma- and ACEs-informed practices must take place within an equity framework.

Culturally responsive teaching affirms and welcomes all our students and all that makes them who they are. This approach to teaching breaks down the isolating and alienating effects of ACEs, trauma, and marginalization, giving students the opportunity to share their experiences, feelings, and histories. When young people feel heard, validated, and valued, there is an opportunity for healing. Inclusive curriculum, culturally responsive teaching, positive behavioral interventions, and restorative practices mitigate the impact of trauma in our classrooms. Individually, we may not be able to change the world, but we have the power to create classroom communities that offer refuge and foster resilience.

Read, Reflect, Respond

1. What could you do to invite students to share more about their lives and their cultures in your classroom?

2. How could you incorporate your students' interests and cultures into your lessons? Are there any opportunities for students to present or co-teach certain topics?

PROGRESS NOT PERFECTION

Jasmin was only in second grade and had already developed a reputation in the school for her notorious meltdowns, which were brought on by a number of triggers, including changes to her schedule, being corrected by her teacher, and negative peer interactions. Her teacher, Mrs. Jackson, had put a considerable amount of effort into establishing a positive relationship with Jasmin and providing her with the supports that she needed to be successful.

Mrs. Jackson and Jasmin checked in every morning to start the day off on a positive note. There was a visual schedule posted in the classroom for Jasmin to orient herself throughout the day. Mrs. Jackson also gave Jasmin verbal reminders before major transitions. There was also a designated cool down area in the classroom where students could take breaks if needed. Mrs. Jackson had even put a few of Jasmin's favorite books in the Cool Down Spot because she knew that reading helped Jasmin to calm down.

Mrs. Jackson's hard work had seemed to pay off. As the year progressed, Jasmin presented fewer and fewer behavioral issues. By March, it had been weeks since Jasmin had had a meltdown in class. Until one day when it all changed. Jasmin got off the school bus and instead of going into the building, she took off running down the street. The school principal and I were eventually able to get her safely into school. We talked with her until she seemed ready to go to class.

Jasmin lasted less than 5 minutes in Mrs. Jackson's classroom before she threw her papers across the room and flipped her desk upside down. She ran over to the cool down area just to rip up one of the books that Mrs. Jackson had put there especially for her. Jasmin spent the remainder of that day in the office, too escalated to return to class. Unfortunately, the rest of the week didn't prove much different. Jasmin's mercurial disposition had returned and with it her meltdowns.

Read, Reflect, Respond

1. Imagine you are implementing a behavioral intervention with a student, seeing great results, and then suddenly it stops working entirely. How would you feel? What would you do?

2. Could challenging behaviors be an opportunity for you to learn more about a student's life?

Jasmin's story presents some key factors related to the importance of a growth mindset for teachers who work with ACEs students. For teachers like Mrs. Jackson, who put a great deal of time and effort into developing and implementing behavioral interventions for their students, it can be incredibly frustrating and disheartening when a student reengages in their challenging behaviors. There have been positive changes in the student's mood and behavior, until suddenly a day arrives when nothing seems to work, and the student's problematic behaviors return full force. When problematic behaviors return, or increase in intensity, it can be tempting for the teacher to feel as though all the hard work has been for nothing. For these teachers, having a growth mindset is key to staying motivated and sane.

For other teachers, a growth mindset will fundamentally change their approach to working with their students. The growth will happen when they shift from a perspective of reward and punishment to relationships and support. For example, I worked with a teacher who had a young man that would get up and walk out of her class anytime he was frustrated. He never asked for her permission or told her where he was going, and this aggravated her to no end. The teacher wanted him to receive a consequence, some kind of punishment, that would make him stop leaving her room without permission. Her growth mindset moment came when she learned that he was going to the restroom and locking himself in a stall as a way to cope with his anxiety.

She set aside her desire for a consequence and began to consider a better way to meet the student's needs. She developed a break system that allowed him to take a certain number of breaks each day. The student had a break card that he put on his desk anytime he was leaving the room so that his teacher knew that he was using one of his breaks. This was a huge shift for her and a whole new approach to supporting her students. As she put it, "I had been looking for a consequence that would make him stop leaving my room, and nothing was working. I was asking myself, 'What can I do *to* this child?' The solution came to me when I started asking, 'What can I do *for* this child?'"

As for Mrs. Jackson, although she was initially frustrated by the escalation of Jasmin's behavior, she eventually shifted into a growth mindset and looked at the situation as an opportunity to learn more about Jasmin, celebrate her progress, and improve upon the strategies that she was using to support her. After meeting with Jasmin's grandmother, we learned that when Jasmin was much younger, her mother had been incarcerated, which was how her grandmother had gotten custody. We asked what time of year this had happened. Her grandmother said, "It was in March," the same time of year that Jasmin's meltdowns had come back. This is a common pattern for many ACEs students, who will exhibit changes in mood and behavior near the anniversary of traumatic events.

Mrs. Jackson acknowledged that although Jasmin's meltdowns had returned, this in no way invalidated all her hard work and the months of progress that Jasmin had made. After all, students with behavioral issues, especially those related to ACEs and trauma, rarely make linear progress. Their path is often marked with setbacks and regressions. Sometimes problematic behaviors will increase in frequency just before they become extinct. When faced with a perceived setback, such as the recurrence of a challenging behavior, it can be tempting for a teacher to give up on the interventions he or she is using and try something radically different. Instead, I suggest adopting a growth mindset and considering ways to improve upon the current intervention plan.

Although our students crave novelty, they also need consistency. ACEs students, who often come from chaotic homes or have experienced the disruptive jolt of trauma, need routines and consistency to establish a sense of trust and safety. Therefore, I recommend modifying an intervention rather than getting rid of it entirely. For instance, imagine that every time a student fails to respond appropriately to an intervention, the teacher changes it and tries something entirely different. In a situation like that, the student is actually learning that their moods dictate the teacher's actions. As a result, the teacher can come across as inconsistent and powerless. So, it is better to continue an intervention, even one with moderate success, in order to firmly establish routines and expectations for the student.

As for Mrs. Jackson, she decided to continue with her classroom interventions and add a visit with the school counselor to Jasmin's daily schedule. During her visits with the counselor, Jasmin could choose to read, talk, or write letters. This was something new that Mrs. Jackson had discovered about Jasmin. She liked to write letters when she was upset. The letters became another way for her and Jasmin to communicate. With time, Jasmin decided that she no longer needed to see the school counselor and her meltdowns gradually subsided.

Read, Reflect, Respond

1. How do you measure improvements in a student's behavior? How do you celebrate the student's progress and your hard work?

2. When planning behavioral interventions, why is it important to think about a back-up plan for the days when nothing seems to work?

3. Do you tend to favor novelty or consistency in your teaching practice? What are the advantages and disadvantages of this approach?

4. When have you experienced a "growth mindset moment," a time when you were faced with a problem and you were able to shift from feeling stuck into a space of inquiry and possibility? What helped you have a change in your thinking?

Read, Reflect, Respond

1. How resilient are you? https://www.academia.edu/5934510/The_Resiliency_Quiz?auto=download

2. What are your areas of strength? What do you need to improve? What do you need to add to your self-care plan?

3. Think about your current practice as you complete the chart on the next pages. What are you currently doing, how can you improve, and what professional development would help support your growth?

(Continued)

(Continued)

Resiliency Behavior	Evidence of What I Already Do	Ways I Can Improve	Professional Development Needs
• Responsiveness			
• Cultural flexibility			
• Empathy			
• Caring			
• Communication skills			
• Sense of humor			
• Planning			
• Help-seeking			
• Critical or creative thinking			
• Sense of identity			
• Self-efficacy			

Resiliency Behavior	Evidence of What I Already Do	Ways I Can Improve	Professional Development Needs
o Task mastery			
o Adaptive distancing from negative messages or conditions			
o Goal direction			
o Educational aspirations			
o Optimism			

4. Read and reflect on the quote to the right. How does it validate or challenge your personal philosophy about your current practice?

5. Use Dr. Diana Stephens's SEL Matrix of Reflective Questions below to assess your strengths and challenging areas. Cite evidence that validates your assessment of your socioemotional competencies. Think of resources and colleagues who can help you with your challenging areas.

> *The major message we want to get across is that perspective really matters. If adults were to stop viewing young people as something to be fixed and controlled, and instead, helped to enable their development, there would be phenomenal change in their lives and society in general.*
>
> —Milbrey McLaughlin
> Emeritus Professor, Stanford University

Socioemotional Learning Competencies	Reflective Questions
Self-Awareness	Guiding Questions: o Who am I in relation to the students and community I serve? How do I become more self-aware and help my students to become more self-aware? o What are ways in which I learn about my culture, and the culture of my colleagues and students? o What are ways I learn about the organizational culture of my classroom and my school?

(Continued)

(Continued)

Socioemotional Learning Competencies	Reflective Questions
Social Awareness	Guiding Questions: ○ How might I increase my own and my students' understanding and empathy for others? ○ In what ways do I demonstrate the value for different perspectives that I hold for my students and their families? ○ What are some activities that I use in the classroom to celebrate and embrace our differences?
Self-Management	Guiding Questions: ○ What does it mean to self-manage? In what ways do I manage my emotions and behaviors and help my students to do the same? What are ways that I facilitate discussions to encourage authentic voices and help one another to develop respect for different views and beliefs?
Relationship Skills	Guiding Questions: ○ How might I increase student interaction, working together, and facilitate conflict resolution skills so we all understand that differences are a natural part of life to be respected? ○ In what ways do I demonstrate adapting to differing cultural experiences? ○ What are ways I can encourage and invite differing perspectives to increase mutual learning and inclusion?
Responsible Decision-Making	Guiding Questions: ○ How might I claim and use my voice to ensure that ALL students in my classroom and in my school receive the support they need? ○ In what ways might I engage additional community partners to adopt inclusive practices? ○ What are steps that I can take to help our school examine policies and practices with the goal of ensuring ALL student voices are included and celebrated?

Source: Adapted from Stephens (2018)

Amber Warner, LCSW

KNOWING MYSELF AND RESPONDING TO CHANGE ARE ABOUT SELF-CARE

You can't change what you don't acknowledge.

—Dr. Phil McGraw
The Dr. Phil Show

Adjusting to change is not an easy process. No matter the age, humans want stability in their personal and professional worlds. Change means things will be different; there will be a new order that requires new ways of behaving and believing. For many, change can feel like a loss. Resistance is natural. But if the benefits of organizational change are not explicit, resistance will continue perhaps to the point of sabotage. Faulty negative biases and preconceived notions are easy to form.

This workbook is about change in Self, change in how school employees work with each other and students, and change in pedagogy. Successful implementation of the ideas that will be presented in later chapters depends on professional development explaining how change will benefit the adults, first and foremost.

Change in the workplace is inevitable, especially in education, and staff need to become comfortable with the reality that there will always be a new normal. Psychologist Tamar Chansky states that when professional development starts with participants visioning what the organization will look like because of the proposed changes, resistance is minimized. Visioning helps to put a realistic time frame on how long implementation may take, allows everyone to see how they fit into the new order, and provides an opportunity for them to determine their own related professional development needs.

Professional development to help school employees adjust to change should include strategies to help them acknowledge and mitigate unconscious biases. However, there are some basic steps to consider immediately.

1. Accept the fact that humans have biases. Some may have roots in your religion or family beliefs. Keep educating yourself about your Self. Get to know your biases so well, you know when your professional judgment may be compromised.

2. Always disaggregate classroom and school discipline and academic data by race, gender, socioeconomic, sexual orientation, learning abilities, or other groups represented in your school population and add to the discussion questions that surface implicit bias. How can you determine if implicit bias is impacting data? Statements like *"When it comes to my students, I don't see color."* or *"I treat all children the same."* or *"His family does not help him with homework assignments"* are really examples of unconscious bias. If we don't see the rich diversity of skin tones, we are asking our students to leave their ethnicity outside the classroom. If we are relying on all families helping the student at home, we are ignoring the possibility they may not be able to do the work. Equal is not equitable. If we are treating all students the same, some students aren't getting what they need to be successful.

3. Administrators can invite speakers representing diverse cultures and ethnic groups to share general cultural and ethnic attributes. Learn as much as you can about how low-income families in all ethnic groups cope with the challenges of being poor. Make this an annual workshop like the yearly review emergency and medical protocols. Even if your school is monoethnic, all learners need to know and understand the broadness and beauty of our country. They are learning other ethnic and cultural groups through the media and some of that imaging needs balance.

4. Working intentionally on developing trusting relationships with colleagues ensures authentic conversations can take place without shame or blame. Administrators and faculty plan annual professional development opportunities to help staff sustain collaborative skills.

5. When asked about a professional decision you have made that involves an individual from a different ethnic, gender, religious, or sexual orientation group, be able to provide an objective, professional *evidenced-based* rationale. Opening a statement with, *I think,* is sharing an opinion. *I know* can be backed up with evidence.

6. Educators may also have in-group biases and can be more critical toward someone who looks like them or had similar childhoods than someone not in that group (e.g., teachers who grew up poor and now teach poor students, White teachers assuming all staff of color grew up poor and vice versa). It's the *I made it; what's wrong with you?* and not the *I made it and I want to help you too.* If you find yourself having *in-group bias,* stop and do some deep self-analysis and work toward seeing yourself at the same age as your student and what you would have wanted a teacher or principal to see in you. A student whose daily home life is full of adversity not only needs you as a role model but needs you to help feed his or her resiliency.

> *We need to open a new frontier in our exploration of good teaching: the inner landscape of a teacher's life.*
>
> —Parker Palmer
> *Courage to Teach*

7. Once you have developed strategies to mitigate your biases, teach your students.

Read, Reflect, Respond

1. Do you think it would make a difference if individual educators, like physicians, could be sued for disproportionally referring an ethnic group to special education classes for behavior, or for their assessment results indicating that females were falling behind male students in math as they moved up in grades? Explain.

2. The medical definition of the Hippocratic Oath:

   One of the oldest binding documents in history, the Oath written by Hippocrates is still held sacred by physicians: to treat the ill to the best of one's ability, to preserve a patient's privacy, to teach the secrets of medicine to the next generation, and so on (MedicineNet.com, 2016). Review both the original translation and a modern version of the Hippocratic Oath at http://www.medicinenet.com/script/main/art.asp?articlekey=20909.

3. Write your personal professional version of a Hippocratic Oath for Educators.

Victoria E. Romero, Teacher

KNOWING MYSELF MATTERS—BECAUSE WHEN NEGATIVE BIAS SHOWS UP, STUDENTS ARE MISEDUCATED

I was teaching in a public school in a middle-class community that included a wealthy gated neighborhood. The last names of many of the students from the gated community were on buildings in the downtown area. The majority of my students were White, four were Black boys, and two were Asian American.

I was returning to my classroom during my planning time and found two of my White students sitting on the floor outside of my classroom. Of course, I asked why they were there and they explained. They had been "horsing" around in music class and named all the boys who were involved. Four were missing. When I asked where they were, I was told they had been sent to the principal's office. The four were my African American boys.

I marched the two White boys to the principal's office so that he could deal fairly with all of them and returned to my room. I knew the principal, an African American male and respected by staff and families, would handle everything in a fair and equitable manner. The four African American boys were the sons from middle-class families. Whatever planning I needed to get done didn't happen. I needed to think and process what I had just witnessed and consider next steps. In my gut, I knew I needed to have a conversation with my colleague and I knew I needed to reeducate my boys—all of my boys! At nine years old, they, Black and White, had learned that race does matter.

After school that day, I met with the principal, shared my thinking, and discussed plans with him. He had called all the families and explained why their sons would be missing recesses the next day and they all accepted and understood. He felt they would be comfortable with my conversation with the boys. I had planned to frame my words around "fairness."

As far as the conversation I wanted to have with this teacher, I just wanted to point out an implicit bias of hers. I wanted, no needed, to think it was a buried subconscious action because I liked her as a colleague and respected her gifts as a talented music teacher. I know she would not have self-identified her actions as racist. This would prove to be true when we met with the principal the next day.

When asked why she sent the Black students to the principal and dismissed the White students back to the classroom, the music teacher was not able to articulate her reasoning about the decision she'd made. In fact, she appeared to register shock that she somehow had seen a difference in the same behaviors along racial lines and her eyes welled up as the realization sank in. When we are unaware of our biases, children are taught bad lessons.

When I met with the six boys, I shared with them why I had taken the two White students to the principal's office. I told them that I thought they would want everyone to be treated the same way and they all vigorously nodded their heads in agreement. One of the African American boys, the son of a prominent Black family, said he was going to tell his parents what had happened but changed his mind when I brought the other two boys in. His father was a lawyer. Then, one of the White students asked a very insightful question: "Should we have told the music teacher we needed to go to the office with our friends?" I smiled and asked him, "Do *you* think that is what you should have done?" And he emphatically answered, "It would have been fair!" Our children know what fairness is and isn't. They are watching us, taking note of our actions, and making judgments about our behaviors.

But the fact remains that six boys were **racialized** that day. With that one incident, six 9-year-old boys learned that race matters. This is a lesson we don't want our students to learn because of the decisions we make. They also learned it would have been okay to stand up and speak out for equitable treatment. I did decide to call all the parents to share with them the meaningful conversation I had with their sons. I didn't name my colleague in the retelling, only the learning and insightful conversation I had had with my boys.

GOOD TEACHING IS NOT ENOUGH—THE NEW NORMAL WARRANTS TRANSFORMATIONIST TEACHING

> *Transformative pedagogy means teaching and leading in such a way that more of our students, across more of their differences, achieve at a higher level and engage at a deeper level, more of the time, without giving up who they are.*
>
> —Gary R. Howard
> *We Can't Teach What We Don't Know*

The process of teaching is one of the most complex professions. Teaching is accomplished only when the learner can successfully use the skill. Transformationist teaching involves added depth that is dimensional in pedagogy, interpersonal style, and cultural awareness (Darling-Hammond, 2006; Howard, 2016). This means educators must not only have thorough knowledge, of curricula content but can affirm their students' cultural and ethnic roots; be able to teach diverse learning styles; maintain a classroom and school culture that supports socioemotional growth and builds resiliency; regularly monitor progress (especially as they teach); and communicate openly and effectively with administrators, colleagues, and families. Transformationist school staff know race, gender, and sexual orientation matter and they do not allow them to become barriers in the work they do. They make no assumptions about the socioemotional needs of their middle-class or wealthy students. Transformationist school staff teach the whole child, no matter who is sitting in their class or where the school is located.

Transformationist educators multitask and constantly make decisions throughout their work day. They use keen observation skills to read nonverbal behaviors to assess if learners are getting it or confused. If they see confusion, they can state or illustrate the learning target in multiple ways. When disciplining or redirecting behaviors, they do it in a way that shows respect for the feelings of the student and the rest of the class. Transformationist educators know all their students watch their behaviors closely, especially when they are dealing with student peers. Words are carefully chosen and specifically address why the behavior is inappropriate. Redirection is spoken in a calm, yet firm tone. They empower students to be problem-solvers, reflective thinkers, and to take responsibility for their behaviors.

Transformationist school staff have *growth mindsets, and model resiliency actions and socioemotional behaviors.* They are open to peer evaluation and see it as ways to enhance and improve their practice. Always wanting to add to their professional toolkit, they are transparent about their teaching strengths and challenges. They take ownership for their own professional growth. Subsequently, they model growth mindset, resilient actions, and socioemotional maturity for their students. They give explicit feedback to their students explaining how effort and hard work equates to learning. Their students know what metacognition means and how to use it to deepen their understanding.

Transformationist school staff have some of the same socioemotional needs as their students. They also thrive in environments that cultivate caring professional relationships and provide opportunities for faculty to sustain their innate resiliency (Baumeister & Leary, 1995). If we are to retain good teachers and encourage them to become strong administrators, we must avoid them succumbing to compassion fatigue and leaving the profession.

Teachers work smarter and more efficiently in systems that honor their professional expertise and provide continuous professional development opportunities, and in school environments that are emotionally safe and supporting. This support helps school staff to value themselves and the work they do. People who feel good about themselves and enjoy the work they do tend to approach others and their work more positively. Students work harder for those teachers they feel like and respect them. They are willing and want to have these teachers and school staff hold them accountable for their academic and socioemotional behaviors (Rimm-Kaufman & Sandilos, n.d.; Zakrzewski, 2012).

Transformationist school staff understand *knowing myself, knowing my students,* and *knowing my pedagogy* are key components for supporting *resiliency* and strengthening *growth mindsets*. They believe they can teach in ways their students will learn to meet or exceed standards (Darling-Hammond, 2004; Howard, 2016). They have a growth-oriented mindset and know educating themselves to keep up with the changing pedagogy and student need is a necessity. For them, in addition to being conscientious about not letting personal biases impact their professional decision-making, they know some of the students in their class may be dealing with adversity. But they do not see these children as at risk. Transformationist school staff place the onus on themselves; they are the game-changers, willing to roll up their sleeves and do whatever is necessary to ensure their students' academic and socioemotional success. They are socially and emotionally competent and model these behaviors with their students and colleagues. Schools are not institutions; they are organisms—living, and ever-changing dynamic entities.

Toolkit Takeaways

- There is a body of contemporary research delineating the characteristics of high-poverty, high-performing schools and the staff who work in these schools that can guide all schools in the process of improving.

- The new normal of today's rural, suburban, and urban classrooms requires school staff who are holistic in their practice. They identify their biases to avoid having them adversely influence their instructional and behavioral actions. They model socioemotional competencies, resilient behaviors, and growth mindset *and* integrate strategies that build resiliency, support socioemotional competencies and growth mindset into their management and instructional routines. They are transformationist educators.

(Continued)

(Continued)

o   Race, gender, and sexual orientation matter. Transformationist educators know and understand that and they guard against letting it become a factor in their professional work and decisions because equity matters more.

o   Change is a constant in education. Professional development must not only address issues associated with change when introducing new initiatives but also place emphasis on teachers Knowing Self first.

o   School staff have the same socioemotional needs as their students. Administrators must be skilled in supporting a school culture that is conducive to meeting the needs of the adult.

The Effects of Trauma on the Brain

There is no separation of mind and emotions; emotions, thinking, and learning are all linked.

—Eric Jensen,
Author of *Teaching With Poverty in Mind*

Anticipated Outcomes

Readers will

o understand how areas of the brain are activated by emotions and affect teaching and learning—in particular, how students who are living in stressful environments benefit from routines and structures that provide opportunities to decompress before and during the instructional day;

o understand the neurological and physiological impact that ACEs may present in the form of defiance, withdrawal, anxiety, or depression, for example;

o understand that new models are needed to teach students the self-regulatory behaviors that will help them be successful learners, specifically students who are impacted by multiple ACEs;

o remember that life-changing events like natural disasters, weather-related storms, sudden homelessness, or house fires are traumatizing for both adults and students. Schools that have a compassionate staff and are caring alleviate duress;

o learn that school counselors and school-based social workers should take the lead in helping school staff understand behavior as a form of communication and how to integrate socioemotional curriculum into their daily instructional practice.

As an educator, you are always preparing for others. In the remaining chapters of this workbook, you will be preparing yourself to consider how you view and manage teaching and learning behaviors. You will read about and practice applying trauma-informed strategies that build resiliency, foster growth mindset, and develop socioemotional competencies. You will be observing and providing explicit feedback when you see your students using these behaviors in class. Be prepared to be comfortable with possible discomfort. You will also be thinking about who you are as a person with serious professional responsibilities. Remember to delve deeper into Self when discomfort surfaces and acknowledge your feelings. Evaluate to determine if the discomfort is negatively affecting your actions.

In his work *Teaching With the Brain in Mind,* educator and researcher Eric Jensen (1998), an ACEs survivor, describes how areas of the brain are activated by emotions and affect learning. Educators who provide explicit and positive feedback when a student is successful academically or manages his or her behavior in new ways are literally energizing the brain. The brain releases hormones, and hormones affect moods and behaviors. The 2015 Disney movie *Inside Out* captures this well and is a student-friendly way to share what happens in the brain when it experiences joy, anger, fear, disgust, and sadness.

Emotional states affect teaching. When professional development does not prepare educators or they don't feel supported with handling the occupational complexities of their role, negative emotions produce hormones that make them sad, angry, fearful, and perhaps forgetful of the ideals that drew them to the profession. They are prone to compassion fatigue and on their way to burnout and making poor decisions about self-care. They will begin to come to work late and leave early. If they have tenure, attendance could begin to be a concern because they have accumulated health-leave days. If they are new to the profession, they will leave.

The status teachers once enjoyed in the community and the positive work that happens every day in classrooms and schools is in the shadows behind negative headlines about achievement disparities, disproportionality in all areas, drop-out rates, and the brand school-to-prison pipeline.

But how long can we keep doing the same things and expecting different results? Einstein said that is the definition for insanity and educators are not insane. We need to change because the needs of our students have changed. We have four decades of information to guide us and as other academic fields like psychology and neuroscience evolve, there's promise of more to come. Education, like many professions, demands a growth mindset for continuous learning because new developments are always happening.

Chapters 4 through 7 are about the innovative changes we can make, in most instances, still using the same human and instructional resources in our existing systems. The activities in the remaining chapters will help with transforming Self, practice, and the way we support students.

The first steps are to make sure all staff members, administrators, teachers, nurses, school counselors, and cafeteria and custodial staff understand the need and are prepared for the transformation. Staff members must have input in planning their professional development and new roles. All need to be included in planning for the transformation.

Read, Reflect, Respond

1. Review the list of ACEs in Chapter 1 and put a check mark by the ones you think affect the students in your school or school district.

2. Based on the ACEs you checked, how can you use the information in your practice?

3. Poverty is an adverse childhood experience. After reviewing your district's data for the students who qualify for free and reduced lunch,

   a. how many are in **self-contained special education** for behavior?

   b. how many are in advance placement, honors, or gifted classes?

   c. how many have attendance problems?

   d. on average, how many of the students who are assigned to self-contained special education exit and how many are assigned to general education classes?

   e. and after reading Chapters 1 through 3, how equitable are your district's procedures?

   f. how does your school and classroom data compare to district trends?

4. If behaviors are a form of communication and some students need to learn a new language, what are your thoughts about the following?

   a. replacing self-contained special education behavior classes with models similar to ELL or remedial programs (Title I)

   b. requiring these new models at elementary, middle, and high school levels. Like their ELL and Title I counterparts, targeted students needing interventions would spend most of their day immersed in general education classes.

   c. using school counselors and special education teachers at all levels to use their expertise to teach intensive, targeted interventions like their ELL and Title I counterparts

   d. school psychologists using intelligence tests that are designed based on modern theories of brain function to identify the intellectual capabilities of students, especially students whose families are low income

   e. creating a job for a paraprofessional or teaching assistant to help families connect with outside social service agencies (e.g., child welfare services, clinics, food or clothing banks)

5. How do you celebrate student behavior progress in your district, school, classroom, office, or cafeteria?

Ricky Robertson, Behavior Specialist

ACKNOWLEDGING THAT TRAUMA IS SITTING IN THE CLASSROOM IS TRANSFORMATIONAL TEACHING

Sofia

Sofia was a fifth grader most days and a cat sometimes. Her cat persona came out when she felt angry or afraid and cornered. Any change in routine was a trigger for Sofia. Her teacher learned this early in the school year when the class welcomed a new student. The sight of an unfamiliar face sitting at her table group sent Sofia over the edge. She kicked off her shoes and went running from the classroom and out of the building. Her teacher alerted the office immediately and all available staff went looking for the student. The custodian radioed on the walkie-talkie that he had found Sofia hiding behind the recess equipment storage shed. The school counselor and two other staff members went to check on Sofia and assist her in returning to class.

As the adults gathered around her, Sofia hissed and spat at them. They spoke softly hoping their words would calm her. The school counselor attempted to reassuringly touch Sofia's shoulders. Her gesture was met with a scratch and a show of teeth. The attention they provided Sofia, all in an effort to help her, caused her to further escalate. The school counselor asked one staff member to remain nearby, in case additional support was needed, and asked everyone else to disperse. The school counselor gave Sofia space and pretended to ignore her for a few minutes. Eventually, she was able to talk with Sofia. At first, the counselor spoke in simple, concrete questions and statements. Finally, she was able to reflect with the student about what had happened and problem-solve a way to return to class.

Nora

Nora was in fourth grade and a star student. She excelled in reading and was a full grade level ahead of the rest of the readers in her class. Nora loved to think about the world, ask questions, and help out. Her teacher had appointed her to be the "class gardener" who was responsible for caring for potted plants in the room. All the other students tended to overwater the plants except for Nora, who gave them the perfect amount of water. Nora did a lot of things perfectly. In fact, she had a very hard time making mistakes. Any grade below an A was certain to bring her to tears and cause her to shut down. Nora's teacher helped her to reframe her mistakes as learning opportunities and, sometimes, this helped. Other times, Nora needed time and space until she could muster the resolve to move beyond her frustration.

Nora and Sofia were wildly different. Sofia was a storm of emotions and reactions. She was impulsive, struggled academically, and had trouble with basic self-care. Sofia struggled with everything from organizing her desk to eating lunch, especially since she preferred to hoard the food rather than eat it. To get through the day, she relied heavily on her teacher, the school counselor, and the service providers who supported her in accordance with her IEP. Nora was a near opposite. Her desk was immaculate. Her academics and behavior were stellar. Nora was well-liked by her teacher but rarely, if ever, asked for help. Yet, these two very different girls were sisters. Only a year apart, they had grown up in a household heavily impacted by poverty, substance abuse, and domestic violence. The impact of their trauma had manifested as uniquely as their personalities.

The realities of the girls' home life had to come to light as a result of the school's efforts to respond to Sofia's behavioral issues. It was after several failed attempts to contact Sofia's parents that the school counselor conducted a home visit and learned that the girls were living in a trailer with no running water and no food in the fridge. The counselor called Child Protective Services (CPS) which ultimately uncovered that the girls were victims of not only poverty but abuse and neglect as well. CPS provided in-home supports to the family and helped them to access food and running water. They also referred the girls to counseling.

Nora's teacher was shocked by the findings of the CPS investigation. She was surprised that this young girl had managed to keep her pain a secret. It was remarkable to her that Nora could focus on school with all she had going on at home, let alone excel academically. Being a model student, Nora could have easily flown under the radar and continued to suffer in silence. Had it not been for Sofia's behavioral outbursts, the school would not have become as involved in the girls' lives and sought support for them.

ACEs AND LEARNING

Sofia and Nora's story shows us that ACEs can impact the learning process differently for each student. I have worked with students like Nora who excel academically despite their trauma. I have noticed, however, that their academic success is often accompanied by anxiety. Their hypervigilance about avoiding mistakes can cause them to be harshly critical of themselves and prone to shutting down in the face of overwhelming pressure. These young people often come from homes in which mistakes are met with condemnation or punishment, or homes that pressure the child to maintain an outward façade of normalcy in order to hide the dysfunction that occurs behind closed doors.

Many of the ACEs students I work with resemble Sofia in their academic struggles. They have difficulty focusing, have a hard time understanding and processing both academic content and classroom instruction, and struggle to remember and recall information. In addition to these deficits, many ACEs students also have a hard time with sequential reasoning and executive functioning. This means they have difficulty making and carrying out a plan, have difficulty understanding multistep tasks, and often fail to grasp cause-and-effect relationships. As a result, they may blame others for their mistakes while not understanding how to appropriately seek help, solve a problem, accept responsibility for their actions, or maintain healthy relationships.

With so many factors inhibiting learning, it is not surprising that students who have experienced multiple ACEs are more likely to be chronically absent, suspended, score poorly on standardized tests, or retained a grade level. These students are also overly represented in special education, at times simply because schools are ill-equipped to respond to their behavioral and emotional needs.

A student with six or more adverse experiences has a near 100 percent chance of being diagnosed with a learning disability and receiving special education services.

In addition to these factors, traumatic stress impacts the brain's ability to effectively respond to stressors and manage emotions. ACEs students can be prone to reactivity and emotional outbursts that further inhibit their learning while also negatively impacting their relationships with adults and peers. These students have a hard time identifying what emotions they are feeling and finding ways to communicate them in a healthy manner. As a result, these young people may be quite good at "acting out" or making demands of others but have a hard time saying what they are feeling, understanding why they are feeling it, and hearing another person's perspective.

Emotional self-regulation skills must be taught, modeled, and reinforced for these students and it may take a considerable amount of time and effort to learn and integrate. This process of emotional maturation is further hindered when our ACEs students live in active trauma. This is the case for the student who sits in class the morning after witnessing his father beat his mother. Or the girl who arrives at school after having slept in a car with her family because they were evicted from their home. These students are expected to learn while managing

Figure 4.1   Impact of ACEs on Humans

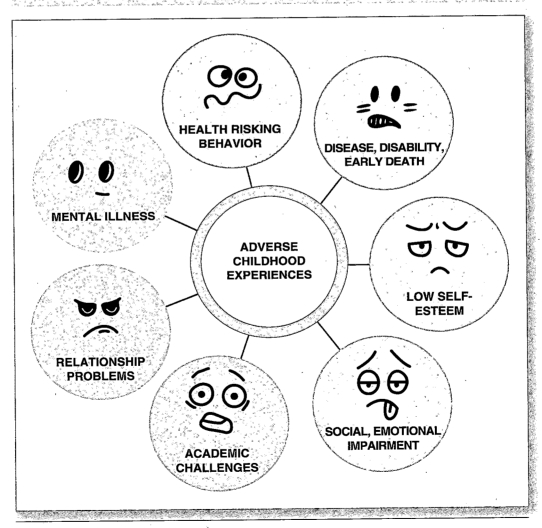

Source: Created by Ashley Pugh (2018)

Understanding the various impacts of ACEs can help teachers better work with students impacted by trauma.

an internal storm of fear and pain. No wonder the authors of *The Heart of Teaching and Learning* liken an ACEs student's efforts to learn in the classroom to playing chess in a hurricane (Wolpow, Johnson, Hertel, & Kincaid, 2009). As educators, we frequently experience the brunt of our students' emotional pain often without full knowledge of its cause. I would add that, without proper supports in place, teaching students impacted by trauma can feel like walking in a minefield uncertain of which move is going to trigger an explosion.

ACEs AND BEHAVIOR

As we saw with Nora and Sofia, students' behavioral responses to trauma can be markedly different. Each of the girls had developed her own way to manage the stressors she faced at home. Nora's people-pleasing and perfectionism were just as much a response to trauma as Sofia's volatility and aggression. One can imagine that in an abusive home, such as theirs, it would make sense for a child to attempt to be a helpful peacemaker while another child might adapt to the volatility of the family by mirroring and reacting to their dynamics. Trouble arose when the girls acted out these same survival traits at school. Nora's perfectionism manifested as anxiety and Sofia's outbursts recreated the chaos of her home life in the classroom. Their story is common for many ACEs students who develop patterns of behavior that help them to survive trauma while sabotaging their success at school.

To further understand the impact of trauma on learning and behavior, it is important to consider the ways that traumatic stress impacts the brain development of children. Research conducted using MRI neuroimaging has shown that traumatic stress can alter the brain and the body's stress response system. When faced with a threat, the limbic system, our brain's fear–response center, is triggered. At this time, brain functioning in more developed regions of the brain is put on hold. As a result, we lose access to the parts of our brain that help us to reason and regulate our thoughts and feelings. In this heightened state of arousal, our heart rate increases, our blood pressure rises, and we react instinctively to find safety.

For children impacted by ACEs and trauma, their bodies and minds are primed for this physiological state of fear and survival. As a result, they tend to overidentify situations as threatening and respond in a state of fight, flight, or freeze, while brain functioning in the prefrontal cortex, amygdala, and other areas of the brain, is altered or impaired. As a result, ACEs children can easily misperceive a situation, such as a transition, a look on a teacher's face, or a difficult assignment, as a threat to their safety. They will often have an exaggerated and impulsive response of fight, flight, or freeze. Fight responses in the classroom can look like the externalizing behaviors that we mentioned such as defiance, impulsivity, and aggression. Freeze and flight responses can appear more like internalized behaviors such as shutting down, withdrawal, anxiety, or depression. Meanwhile, they will not have access to the parts of their brain, such as the prefrontal cortex, that would help them to reason, think flexibly, and respond more appropriately.

As educators, once we understand that trauma and ACEs impact the neurological and physiological functioning of ACEs students, we can begin to have insight and compassion. Their outbursts or meltdowns are no longer simply acts of defiance. Instead they are reflexive, and often ingrained, attempts made by the child to feel safe. Unfortunately, these attempts to feel safe can appear as efforts to control their internal or external environment by shutting down or acting out, neither of which are going to help the child succeed in school or make it easy for us to teach them. Therefore, we are tasked with the responsibility of finding ways to help the ACEs child downregulate their stress response so that they can learn. In the coming chapters, we will explore trauma-informed strategies to foster compassionate, inclusive, and resilient classrooms in which all students, especially those impacted by ACEs, develop skills for academic success and healthy behavior.

Read, Reflect, Respond

1. What challenging behaviors are you dealing with in your classroom? Do you think they could be symptoms of exposure to ACEs or trauma?

2. What role do you think emotion plays in learning? How do you think you could enhance your instruction to support students who struggle with emotional self-regulation?

3. Imagine you are working with an ACEs student and he is being defiant. Recognizing that his oppositional behavior may be coming from a place of fear, how would you handle his behavior differently?

4. To further your understanding of how the brain responds to trauma, use this link to see Dr. Daniel Siegel's Hand Model: https://www.youtube.com/watch?v=gm9CIJ74Oxw.

5. Watch this student-friendly video demonstrating how siblings can experience the same trauma, but have different reactions: https://www.youtube.com/watch?v=cYhRcPZdnBw.

6. Watch this video of children explaining what their brain needs in order for them to learn: https://www.youtube.com/watch?v=lTMLzXzgB_s.

Amber Warner, LCSW

TRAUMA HAS MANY FORMS

I was 750 miles from my home when my husband called to tell me about a wildfire that was burning out of control near our home in Hidden Valley Lake. He first learned about the seriousness of this brush fire when he was not able to return home after a morning of playing golf. It had spread that quickly. There was nothing either of us could do but watch CNN and check online postings on websites we never knew existed like the Incident Information System. InciWeb monitors wildfires and provides updated reports. Later, a neighbor would post a video she made as she drove past our house. On that day, our home was still there.

The Valley Fire that burned in the Lake County area of California from September 12th to October 15th in 2015 destroyed nearly 76,000 acres and threatened 1,322 homes, 27 apartment buildings, and 73 businesses. An additional ninety-three structures were damaged. Four people died and more than 10,000 residents were impacted by evacuations. The Valley Fire would be the largest wildfire for the season prompting Governor Jerry Brown to declare our area a state of emergency. The fire area was larger than the city of San Francisco (Cal Fire, 2015).

Although I did my best to remain optimistic, even philosophical at times—saying to myself things like my husband was safe in a hotel, our dog was with a friend, we can replace things—I was struggling to stay emotionally balanced because there were also depressing thoughts that were hard to push away. My mind would just go there thinking about the things that had sentimental value and could never be replaced—family photos, heirlooms, furniture pieces from my late grandmother's and aunt's home.

A few days after the fire was contained, we were allowed to return to our home, not knowing if it would be there. The drive back through the lowland mountains that lead to some of the most beautiful territorial views in Napa Valley was otherworldly. Healthy green trees had been replaced by black and charred sticks. The exposed soil was blackened. I was trying to fight back tears and the queasy feeling in my stomach.

Driving on our block, there were signs of hope. Most of the homes were OK and then we would pass a burned out space, the house no longer there. When we finally arrived, we saw our home had been spared; the fire was so close a fire hose had been left in our driveway. Three doors down, another home was gone. All total, three homes on our block were destroyed by the sparks from the wildfire. I could exhale but it was a painful breath, thinking about the neighbors who would return to the heartache of loss.

It prompted me to go immediately to the hospital where I worked to see if I was needed. Of course, there was need. Not only was I able to provide counseling support with patients, my colleagues—nurses, doctors, hospital assistants, and administrators—were as distressed. Some of them lost their homes. Sadness and shock were the prevailing emotions. But there was a sense of strength, which our profession as health care providers prepares us for. We take compassionate care of others while caring for ourselves.

I worked with human resources to assess staff needs and I provided time for colleagues to share feelings. A fund was established to help those needing financial support. A boutique was set up where staff could donate items needed by others. Some staff members were allowed to sleep overnight in empty hospital rooms.

Although it has been a few years since the Valley Fire, there is no back to normal or return to regular routines. There is only adjusting to a new normal. Some of my colleagues left the area; others are living in temporary housing until their homes can be rebuilt. There are still three vacant lots on my block where homes once stood. The earth is still blackened but there are sprouts of green. We all are on guard each fire season. Nature can traumatize.

One of the first steps in understanding the need to become trauma informed is to recognize that we are all vulnerable to experiencing it. Trauma can be induced by a wide range of experiences: witnessing a bad accident on the freeway, the sudden death of a loved one or a pet, catastrophic events like 9/11, floods, war, physical pain or injury, or a bad fight on the playground for some children.

Because life experiences are unpredictable and impact ACEs on students and the adults who teach them, the implication for all school staff is to become aware of the effects of trauma and to be prepared to provide supportive care. Supportive care includes knowing which interpersonal behaviors and institutional policies to avoid that might be retraumatizing. Tip #57 of *Trauma-Informed Care in Behavioral Health Services* (Substance Abuse and Mental Health Services Administration, 2014, p. xix) recommends trauma-informed care should include "an understanding of trauma and an awareness of the impact it can have across settings, services, and populations. It involves viewing trauma through an ecological and cultural lens and recognizing that context plays a significant role in how individuals perceive and process traumatic events, whether acute or chronic . . . and upholds the importance of consumer participation in the development, delivery, and evaluation of services."

If your school or school district is assessing and assigning students living with adverse childhood experiences to special education classes, your school or school policies are actually retraumatizing them. The characteristics of high-poverty, high-performing schools prove staff can manage a wide range of behaviors effectively and also educate students living with multiple ACEs. One study of California's high-poverty, high-performing schools noted that none of these schools reported issues with major discipline problems (Izumi, 2002). This proves that when all of the sides, vertices, and angles of Howard's Achievement Triangle are functioning, students living with trauma *do* learn academically and socially.

School counselors and social workers at school and district levels can provide ongoing professional development to help classroom staff with implementing and integrating socioemotional curriculum into their language and daily routines. This frees up time for school counselors or social workers to best support classroom instructors by conducting home visits to assess how a student's family functions and recommend agencies that provide support. A paraprofessional can act as a family support worker to make sure the families follow through. It is important for schools and community agencies like child welfare or child protective services to collaborate since many of them have more authority than schools.

Adjusting the roles of school counselors and social workers can also improve their response time and again, taking some pressure off classroom teachers. They can quickly design a plan of action when a family is displaced because of weather-related storms, house fires, evictions, or death of a family member.

Read, Reflect, Respond

What would you do?

1. You are the art teacher (or custodian or bus driver) at a middle school. You have known Philip since he was in sixth grade and though he is no longer in one of your classes, he still stops by to talk (have brief conversations in the hallways or on the bus) and let you know how well he is doing in school. You always give him positive feedback. You really like Philip. On this day, he shares with you that he is being sexually molested by a family friend. What do you say to him after his disclosure?

2. There is a child in your PreK classroom who is having difficulty adjusting to the routines you have established. Based on your experiences, this child's behaviors are out of the norm for her developmental age. She flops out of her seat and rolls on the floor sucking her thumb. When sitting in a circle for story time, she will often sit just outside the circle and turn her back to face the opposite direction. She is not aggressive toward other children; in fact, she seems like she is in her own little world. Still her behaviors distract her classmates. What would you do?

3. Child psychotherapist Jeanette Yoffe, MFT, has created a version of Dr. Siegel's Hand Model to explain the effects of trauma on the brain. If you are an elementary school staff in the general education, how can you integrate this video into your classroom management plan?

   https://www.youtube.com/watch?v=H_dxnYhdyuY

   Use this video link if you are a middle or high school staff member. How can you integrate this video into your classroom management plan?

   Teaching Mindfulness and Neural Integration by Dan Siegel, M.D. https://www.youtube.com/watch?v=LiyaSr5aeho

4. Use these links to learn more about the effects of trauma and compassion fatigue or secondary trauma:

   Burnout and Post-Traumatic Stress Disorder: TED Talk by Dr. Puelo https://www.youtube.com/watch?v=hFkI69zJzLI

   Drowning in Empathy: The Cost of Vicarious Trauma: TED Talk by Amy Cunningham https://www.youtube.com/watch?v=ZsaorjIo1Yc

Victoria E. Romero, Principal

IF I KNEW THEN WHAT I KNOW NOW

In both schools I administered, there were children living with adverse childhood experiences. Drs. Felitti and Anda were poring over the data they had collected from 17,000 Kaiser Permanente members when I accepted my first principalship. ACEs had not yet been "discovered." If I could have used their research as a principal, I would have augmented some of the strengths I found in both schools and handled many things differently.

The staff at my first school was already using Second Step, one of the first curricula devoted to socioemotional learning, and we created a strong school-wide behavior management plan that reinforced the activities they did in class. That was a strength. We were able to significantly reduce the numbers of students needing to be removed from class or suspended from school for chronic misbehavior. I introduced Second Step and the schoolwide behavior plan at my second school because it lacked both. It was a dysfunctional mess.

Had I understood how trauma affects brain development and learning, I would have provided all staff with the appropriate levels of professional development. I would have them develop goals for a self-care and a trauma-informed strategy to add to their annual evaluation plans. Even though I didn't evaluate the bus drivers or cafeteria staff, I would meet with them and ask them to do the same.

Children with chronic misbehaviors were sent to my office when they should have been going to a Cool Down Spot in the room or to designated rooms to decompress and create a restorative plan with a trained staff member. We had groups for children going through divorce or death of a pet, but we'd return them to the same class without a plan for reentry. There was a special room to allow students time to cool down, but it was not equipped with trained personnel who could help them sort through their feelings. We didn't have a process for helping the adults with restorative steps to repair relationships with colleagues, students, or families.

At the time, my student intervention team met regularly to look at students who were struggling academically, socially, or both. It was composed of me, the school counselor, school psychologist (who was assigned one day per week to my school), nurse (who was there two days per week), ESL and Title I teachers, a family support worker, and parents. I could use district resources to add a reading, math, or science coach to the team as needed.

A classroom teacher would present a student and evidence of their work and behaviors and what interventions they had already tried. We would discuss and decide next steps and create a time-sensitive school–home plan. If there was no progress, our next step would be to look at special education services, our only option at the time.

If I were starting out today as a trauma-informed principal, I would use my student intervention team differently. We would educate ourselves first and then look at our schoolwide behavior management system and envision, then describe, what it should look like now that we are aware trauma is sitting in the classroom and it may not surface in obvious ways.

We would create a two- to three-year strategic plan outlining how to bring teachers and parents on board about trauma. Instead of having the school psychologist assess for special education, they would assess for intelligence. The family support worker would work more closely with our low-income families to make sure their basic needs were being met by community agencies. We would identify students living in foster care, develop relationships and establish regular reporting with their caseworkers to maintain continuity, and try to ensure future placements could remain in our boundaries. We would attend more intentionally to all of our subgroups such as homeless and LBGQT and disaggregate ELL data based on where students were in terms of acquiring a new language.

Teachers would help design our professional development needs, create incremental evaluative checkpoints, and develop steps for sustainability. The intervention team would expand to include soliciting the expertise of social service agencies and health-care practitioners. Together, the team would create a plan of wrap-around support systems for our neediest families and their children. It would also plan self-care check-ins and processes for staff.

Our goal would be to become a compassionate school built on a foundation of resilient teaching and learning.

Read, Reflect, Respond

Professional school counselors and school-based social workers are skilled in socioemotional developmental stages and needs. When preparing a staff to delve deeper into understanding and using trauma-sensitive strategies, these individuals, with principal support, should take the lead. Use these links to get to short videos that can be used in staff meetings or special sessions to open discussion and planning.

Creating Trauma Informed Schools: https://www.youtube.com/watch?v=3om45LrPoC0

Trauma Sensitive Schools: Independence School District: https://www.youtube.com/watch?v=_47YuGeZW7s

Trauma Sensitive Practice in Schools: https://www.youtube.com/watch?v=5ijW0oDDpao

A San Diego Principal Takes on Trauma (Cherokee Point School): https://www.youtube.com/watch?v=dcvQb9e-VLI

Head Start—Trauma Smart: https://www.youtube.com/watch?v=bXzKVpiSzH8

Childhood Trauma: What Every Teacher Needs to Know: https://www.youtube.com/watch?v=VXfsoQMqlyY

Toolkit Takeaways

1. Emotional states affect teaching and learning. School staff working in dysfunctional settings are prone to compassion fatigue and burnout.

2. Students living with ACEs are more likely to have problems with absenteeism, present behaviors like defiance and bullying, may be depressed (which can be mistaken as shyness or compliance), or have anxieties. They may also be overachievers, afraid of making mistakes or letting adults down.

(Continued)

(Continued)

3. Students living with ACEs are more likely to be suspended, to be unable to meet academic and socioemotional milestones, and to be assigned to special education classes for behavior and/or academics.

4. Natural disasters, home fires, and evictions, for example, are traumatic events and induce physiological and emotional stresses.

5. The culture and climate in schools need to meet the socioemotional needs of staff and students. School or district administrators must have the skills needed to create and maintain a compassionate and caring work environment.

6. The roles of the school counselor and school-based social worker need to change. They are the professionals who can teach students emotional self-regulatory skills and help staff learn and practice trauma-informed instructional strategies.

5

Teaching Behaviors, Differentiating Interventions, Changing Pedagogy

Education ultimately depends on what happens in classrooms . . . between teachers and learners. That is fundamental.

—David Perkins,
Author of *Smart Schools*

Anticipated Outcomes

Readers will

o understand students impacted by ACEs want and need authentic relationships based on trust, belonging, and feeling valued. It is safe to assume all students attending schools in rural, suburban, and urban areas benefit from trusting relationships that make them feel they belong and are valued;

o realize school and classroom behaviors can be learned. Instructional models similar to English language learners (ELL) and remedial programs need to be established at every grade level to give all students the time they need to learn new behaviors;

(Continued)

(Continued)

o   learn how trauma-informed strategies like Talk, Feel, Trust, and Repair establish and sustain trusting relationships and give students the sense of belonging and feeling valued;

o   be exposed to several trauma-informed strategies: 2x10, Restorative Practices, Ready to Learn room, Check & Connect, Check-In/Check-Out, Class Circles, journaling, staff greeting students at the doors of school or classroom, school staff making themselves available for students to talk informally, and using a learning taxonomy (i.e., Bloom's) to teach classroom management behaviors that outline teacher and student behaviors needed at each level;

o   be introduced to a trauma-informed response-to-intervention (RTI) behavior model that outlines interventions, school staff responsibilities, and program models at Tier I to III levels;

o   understand that positive behavioral supports are not, in and of themselves, trauma informed and should be informed by and supplemented with socioemotional curricula like Second Step, MindUp, or RULER.

Ricky Robertson, Behavior Specialist

RELATIONSHIPS PRECEDE LEARNING

Ibrahim

Ibrahim was sent to live with his aunt the summer before fourth grade. His aunt met with his teacher, Mrs. Scott, at the beginning of the school year. She explained that she had temporary custody of Ibrahim because he had experienced abuse and neglect when living with his parents. His father had been incarcerated and his mother was receiving court-mandated counseling and parenting classes as part of a plan for her to regain custody. Hearing this news, Mrs. Scott committed to doing whatever it took to welcome Ibrahim to her class and support him during this difficult time.

Mrs. Scott quickly learned that her efforts to support Ibrahim were not as successful as she had hoped. Her warm, enthusiastic demeanor typically won students over, yet Ibrahim remained standoffish. Three months into the school year, Mrs. Scott said that she could not think of a single time she had seen the boy smile. He never raised his hand during lessons. In fact, it didn't seem to matter whether Mrs. Scott was redirecting him or praising him, Ibrahim maintained the same flat affect. However, Ibrahim's behavior revealed that beneath the boy's aloof and detached demeanor, an emotional storm was brewing.

Ibrahim was most successful during highly-structured activities and assignments. His quiet focus helped to keep him on task. However, when it came to less-structured times of the day (e.g., recess, lunch, group work), Ibrahim struggled with impulse control and was prone to physical aggression. His behaviors also seemed to spike in the days before and after he had supervised visitations with his mom. Initially, his aggression would manifest in sudden, reactive behaviors that were small in scale (e.g., shoving in line, tackling during recess).

His teacher made numerous attempts to manage these behaviors; however, Ibrahim seemed unfazed by both consequences and rewards. With time, his behaviors grew to be more significant, until one day, during a math test, a student who was returning to his desk after using the restroom accidentally bumped into Ibrahim's desk. In almost knee jerk fashion, Ibrahim jabbed the student in the hand with his pencil, hard enough to break the skin.

Ibrahim was suspended for the incident. During his absence, his teacher, the school counselor, and I developed an intervention plan to be implemented upon his return to school. As a team, we agreed that Ibrahim would benefit from participating in one of the school counselor's emotional regulation groups. These groups met once a week to learn how to name their feelings and develop strategies to regulate and manage difficult emotions. We also came up with some proactive strategies to support Ibrahim during less-structured times of his day (e.g., an assigned spot in line, a recess routine that specified the games he could play, a class helper job, assigning specific roles for group work). The most important part of his intervention plan had to do with the teacher–student relationship.

Despite Mrs. Scott's best efforts, she and the student had yet to form a positive bond. Her reports of Ibrahim's flat affect, standoffishness, and reluctance to engage in conversations with adults, were all common indicators of a history of ACEs and trauma. To add yet another stressor to their already fragile relationship, Ibrahim had been suspended. Challenging student behaviors coupled with exclusionary discipline practices, such as a suspension, are huge stressors that can fracture and even sever a teacher–student relationship. Therefore, we needed to take a restorative approach aimed at bringing Ibrahim back into the classroom community and strengthening his relationship with his teacher.

I asked Mrs. Scott to implement an intervention called 2x10. Two by ten is a simple strategy in which the teacher talks to a student for 2 minutes a day for 10 consecutive school days. During the conversations, the student has the opportunity to talk about anything they would like to talk about and the teacher just listens or asks questions. This simple intervention has been shown to improve both student behavior and productivity.

At first, Mrs. Scott was doubtful that the intervention would help. Understandably, she had interpreted Ibrahim's standoffishness as a lack of interest in having a relationship with her. I suggested that many ACEs students can appear disinterested or even resistant to forming positive relationships with their teachers. However, this may not be the case. Dr. Claudia Black, an expert on addiction and codependency within families, has identified three norms that shape the interpersonal dynamics of families impacted by substance abuse and family dysfunction: "Don't talk. Don't trust. Don't feel." Many ACEs students internalize a similar set of rules, which in turn create a barrier to forming healthy relationships with adults and peers. Detachment in ACEs students could largely be the result of a history of dysfunctional relationships with their primary caregivers. These students may deeply desire to have a positive, affirming relationship with the adults in their life; however, they may not have the skills or the emotional resources to develop one.

Mrs. Scott agreed to implement 2x10. After about three days, I received an e-mail from Mrs. Scott that said, "He still doesn't want to talk to me. Does a

10-second conversation count?" I encouraged her to continue to check in with Ibrahim each day. Even a simple, "How is your day going?" can be a meaningful building block to creating a better relationship with a student. Also, I knew a secret from having implemented similar interventions with a number of different teachers and students: If the teacher continues to put forth the effort, the student will eventually open up. I also suggested that Mrs. Scott look for opportunities for Ibrahim to be successful in her class and receive positive praise. Having that extra acknowledgment can also help students to feel more confident and willing to engage in positive relationships.

The shift finally happened on day 9 of the 2x10 intervention. Mrs. Scott was having a conversation with another student who happened to sit near Ibrahim. The student was explaining to Mrs. Scott that Ramadan was approaching. Mrs. Scott didn't know much about Ramadan. She asked the student how she and her family observed the holy month. Ibrahim was listening to their conversation and interjected that he celebrated Ramadan as well. He shared about how he loved *iftar*, the meal that his family ate together after sunset. Mrs. Scott realized that this was the opportunity she had been waiting for to connect with Ibrahim.

Over the next few days, Mrs. Scott and Ibrahim had brief conversations during which Ibrahim told Mrs. Scott all about Islam and the different holy days that he celebrated. Mrs. Scott would simply sit and listen, asking questions every once in a while. This was the first time that Ibrahim had mentioned anything about his home life to his teacher, a sign that a bond of trust had finally been established.

Mrs. Scott came up with an idea to support Ibrahim in feeling connected to the culture and faith that he so dearly loved. She decided to incorporate culture lessons throughout the year. Every student in the class would have the opportunity to present about their family's culture and traditions. Ibrahim loved this idea.

Over the next couple months, I checked in regularly with Mrs. Scott. Ibrahim's behavior was continuing to improve. The emotional self-regulation lessons were helping. In fact, Mrs. Scott had started incorporating emotional self-regulation exercises into her whole class instruction. As a result, Ibrahim was now able to name his frustrations and engage in self-management strategies. He still struggled at times with impulse control; however, he was better able to reflect on his actions and take responsibility for them. Ibrahim continued to check in daily with Mrs. Scott, except now *he* initiated the conversations. She also noticed that he was opening up more to his peers and his class participation had increased as well. Finally, Mrs. Scott showed me a picture of Ibrahim on the day that he got to present to the class about his culture. He was smiling ear to ear.

> Relationships precede learning.
>
> —Gary R. Howard
> Author of *We Can't Teach What We Don't Know*

In Chapter 1, we talked about behavior as a form of communication. Through their behavior, ACEs students are often communicating a fundamental need for healthy relationships based upon trust, belonging, and feeling valued. I consider the teacher–student relationship to be the single most important factor when working with all students, and especially students impacted by ACEs. As a Tier I strategy, I recommend the teacher focus on his or her relationship with the ACEs student before they consider any other interventions or supports. The reason is that any additional academic or behavioral interventions will be significantly more effective when they occur within the context of a positive, supportive teacher–student relationship.

Positive interactions between teacher and students have been shown to support learning. These relationships play a particularly vital role in the success of ACEs students. Research has illustrated that positive adult relationships can help ACEs students to build resilience and can mitigate the impact of trauma. For example, a study with adolescents who had been exposed to ACEs and trauma found that the presence of a positive teacher–student relationship made them less likely to abuse opioids as a means to manage their emotional pain. For ACEs students, the teacher–student relationship can disrupt the pervasive alienation of trauma and abuse while providing the emotional nutrients necessary for these young people to develop healthy coping mechanisms.

There are a number of simple classroom strategies that can build positive teacher–student relationships. Certainly 2x10 is an excellent strategy. Meaningful conversations and check-ins are vital for building and maintaining relationships with ACEs students. Classroom acknowledgment circles, class meetings, and other community-building activities also foster a sense of belonging. Additional strategies can include greeting each student at the door at the beginning of class, handshakes or nonverbal cues (e.g., thumbs up, handshakes, spirit fingers) to express belonging, as well as creating academic and nonacademic opportunities for students to feel successful and valued. Teachers can invite students to share about their lives and their cultures in a variety of creative ways (e.g., personal narratives, poems, visual art, collage). This is an excellent opportunity for teachers to model for students how to be open, accepting, and appreciative of all that makes us who we are.

TALK, TRUST, FEEL, REPAIR

As educators, we are not therapists. We cannot fix or solve the problems that our students face in their lives. However, learning is, and always has been, an intellectual, emotional, and relational process. As educators, we can take a student-centered approach to teaching that is rooted in relationships that honor each student and his or her story. In doing so, we enhance and differentiate our relationships with ACEs students in order to lessen the degree to which their trauma interferes with their ability to be successful in our classrooms.

Talk

One of the most important gifts a teacher can give an ACEs student is the opportunity to be heard. This requires that the teacher listens to the student without judgment. This is not an easy task as many of these young people have stories that are difficult to hear. Older students, especially, may have acted out in ways that have harmed themselves or others. I think it is fair to judge the conditions that have caused a young person to suffer but unfair to judge that person for how they have carried their pain.

I was working at an alternative high school with a young man who had been expelled from his previous school after engaging in several instances of gang-related violence. He and I met regularly to talk about his progress in our program. Over time, I got to know him little by little and developed a lot of respect for him—especially after I learned that he worked full time to support his mother and baby sister. I believe that my respect for him became like a bridge of trust between us; and I soon became a person he confided in.

One week, that young man was absent for several days. And, when he returned to school he didn't go to his class but came directly to my office. When I saw him, I could tell immediately that something was wrong. He explained that he had been accused of participating in the gang rape of a young woman. He went on to say very hateful things about the victim, about how she deserved it, about how he hoped she would somehow experience further violence.

I was certainly triggered and upset by what he shared. I did my best to listen past my own judgments, so that I could hear him. I asked him questions about how he felt. As he opened up, he shared first his anger, then his fear, and finally his underlying shame. It was as though the burden of this accusation finally bore down on him. At the end of the conversation, he sunk down onto the floor and got onto his hands and knees. He crawled around my desk, wrapped himself around the chair I was sitting in, and pulled his t-shirt up and over his head, to cover his face as he sobbed. It was in that moment that I understood the tremendous gift of listening with compassion.

In the demands of the school day, it can be challenging for teachers and school staff to find time to talk with students about their lives. In order to effectively meet the needs of ACEs students, schools have to implement programs and practices that consistently provide opportunities for staff and students to connect. Schoolwide programs such as Check-and-Connect, Check-In/Check-Out, or other student mentoring programs are excellent ways to reach large numbers of students. I have seen these programs successfully adapted to meet the needs of students at every grade level, and ACEs students in particular. Programs such as Check-In/Check-Out, which monitors student behavior using a daily behavior chart, can be adapted to better support students impacted by trauma. For example, one school added a socioemotional goal (e.g., show kindness toward another person today, coach yourself through a problem) to the student's daily Check-In/Check-Out behavior chart. Classroom interventions that foster communication and relationships can include class circles, morning check-ins, art, and journaling. I have seen teachers of younger grades supplement their morning check-ins with picture cues that denote different feelings, as well as books and songs that foster socioemotional awareness for young children.

I worked at a high school in Portland, Oregon, where the student support team and administrators greeted the students at the entrance of the school each morning. Students were told on the first day of school that the staff members were not only there to welcome them each morning, but were also available if the student needed to talk about any issues at home or school that were troubling them. Students had the option of talking to the staff members first thing or scheduling an appointment with them later in the day.

Understanding that their school served a high-need population, staff recognized that a number of their students were arriving to school with heavy hearts and minds because of troubles that they were facing at home, in their neighborhoods, and at school. Rather than expecting these students to bottle up these difficult emotions only to have them erupt later in the day, typically in the form of a disciplinary issue, staff made themselves available to talk, listen, and problem-solve at the start of each day. The practice was not only successful in lowering the number of disciplinary referrals but it impacted the school culture as a whole. Students felt part of a family. They knew that they were cared for by every person in the building and were more likely to seek support prior to engaging in a problematic behavior.

Artistic expression can also facilitate communication between teachers and students. A colleague, who was a high school art teacher, proudly told me that she referred more students to the school counselor than any anyone else in her school. From having talked with her students about the inspiration and meaning behind the art that they made in her class, she knew more about the lives of her students than most of their other teachers and was better able to help them. Similarly, a fifth-grade teacher explained to me that her students kept daily journals. She would tell them to write about whatever they were thinking or feeling that day. If they didn't want her to read the entry then they could fold the page in half lengthwise. Otherwise, she would read their journal entries and speak with them if she felt that they needed support. These are just a couple of examples of ways that creative expression can be used to foster communication and healthy emotional expression.

Writing, music, collage, drawing, dance, and other forms of personal and creative expression can be incredibly powerful interventions for ACEs students. Creative projects don't have to directly relate to trauma for them to be effective outlets for students. Simply giving all students an opportunity to engage in a form of creative self-expression each day, or each week, is valuable. Oftentimes, creativity allows a child experiencing abuse and neglect to communicate and alleviate her or his fear, pain, and shame. After all, even the very act of making art (e.g., coloring, drawing) has been shown to lower cortisol levels and calm the nervous system.

Trust

Without trust, there can be no authentic relationship with an ACEs student. These young people are adept at reading people. For many of them, their survival has depended on their ability to read their parents' moods and assess whether a situation is safe. Having had experiences that have shattered their trust, these young people can be slow to open up to an adult. They may even appear suspicious—or in Ibrahim's case, disinterested—when a teacher shows them attention.

There are a number of factors that contribute to building trust with ACEs students. Explicitly teaching and modeling norms and expectations helps them understand the norms of your classroom. This is especially important for younger students who may not understand that the behaviors they see and act out at home may not be acceptable in the classroom environment. I have seen ACEs students in kindergarten and first grade benefit tremendously from social stories that clearly detail appropriate ways to behave at school and interact with peers. Without these social stories, these young students have no context for school-appropriate behavior and simply engage in the behaviors that they have seen at home.

ACEs students will look to see if teachers' actions match their words. ACEs students will often scrupulously evaluate whether or not a teacher maintains consistency, fairness, and integrity in the classroom. Sometimes they will be the first to point out, or rather blurt out, when a teacher has violated a norm or done something they perceive to be unfair or inconsistent with an expectation. Granted no one is perfect, and every teacher is bound to break a promise or contradict one of their own rules from time to time. What matters most to the ACEs student is how the teacher handles these situations. ACEs students often come from homes that are steeped in blame, chaos, and a lack of accountability. Therefore, if a teacher is able to admit when he or she has made a mistake or failed to follow through on a commitment, apologize, and take responsibility for righting the situation, then that teacher is certain to have laid the ground-work for a trusting relationship.

If teachers want to take this a step further, they can even solicit feedback from their students on ways to improve the class. Being able to model for the students how to receive and incorporate constructive feedback is an incredibly powerful tool. For students, this shows that their voices matter and encourages them to advocate in positive, constructive ways. For the ACEs student in partic-ular, it models how an adult accepts criticism in a mature, responsible way.

Many ACEs students will flare up when they perceive the slightest hint of criticism. As a fifth-grade teacher said of one of her ACEs students, "If he hears any hint of criticism in your tone, it's like he runs toward the negativity." Conversely, many ACEs students have internalized an incredible amount of negativity and are victim to an incessant stream of self-criticism and perfection-istic thinking. When these students see a teacher make a mistake, accept respon-sibility, and invite constructive feedback from the students, they are witnessing an adult, perhaps for the first time, model what it means to make a mistake in a manner that is natural and resilient. In essence, the teacher is showing what it looks like to put a growth mindset into action.

I have one caveat pertaining to building trust with ACEs students. It is not uncommon for ACEs students to assess their ability to trust a teacher by sharing a secret with them. Sometimes these secrets can be relatively harmless admis-sions. Other times, these secrets can detail abuse they're experiencing or even criminal activity that they have engaged in. I caution against allowing secrets to become the foundation of the trust bond. Dysfunctional family dynamics, including abuse and neglect, persist because a family develops a culture of secrecy. Keeping secrets can normalize a pattern at home that was established to protect the abuser. Therefore, it is important to be clear with students about your professional responsibilities to support the student, while taking any nec-essary actions to ensure their safety, which may include reporting abuse or neglect. As always it is important when concluding such conversations to ask the student if they feel safe returning home at the end of the day in case immediate action needs to be taken.

Feel

Classroom teachers can embed opportunities to validate and manage emotions within the course of the school day. Mindful minutes, body breaks, deep breathing, yoga stretches, classroom Cool Down Spots, and journaling are just a few strategies that can be incorporated into instruction to support students in managing emotions.

I once observed a middle school ELA class in which the teacher started every period with a mindful minute. She would dim the lights and the class would sit quietly, breathing deeply for one minute. During the remainder of the class, I couldn't help but notice that the teacher had a number of students who struggled significantly with attention and hyperactivity. I had to find out how she was able to get them into the mindful minute routine. She said that at first, she played them YouTube videos about the value of mindfulness for the brain and body. The videos piqued the students' interest and they agreed to give it a try. She said they started with 10 seconds and gradually increased the time until they got to a minute. She also pointed out that a few of her students had fidgets that helped to keep their hands occupied. She also gave a different student each week the job of time keeper. She said that the best part about doing the mindful minutes was that she saw students using the strategy outside of her class. Her students told her about times when they were angry at someone or nervous because of a test and instead of giving in to the emotion, they paused to take a few deep breaths.

Classroom Cool Down Spots are another valuable tool for supporting healthy emotional regulation. A classroom cool down spot is a space in the classroom where students can go when they feel emotionally escalated. This corner of the room may have a comfortable chair or a cushion for the student to sit on. There is usually a timer as well as some sensory tools for the student to use (e.g., fidgets, glitter jar, stuffed animal). The teacher explains to the students that they can access the space when they feel anxious, angry, sad, or upset. Usually, teachers create a cue, such as a hand signal, that the student can give when they would like to use the classroom Cool Down Spot. Once the teacher has given them permission, the student can go to the area, set the timer, and soothe the difficult feelings they are experiencing.

Repair

As we saw in Ibrahim's story, it took Mrs. Scott's consistent effort and unrelenting positive regard to establish a relationship with him. Some ACEs students may appear resistant to forming a relationship with a teacher. It is not uncommon for ACEs students, especially those who externalize, to be highly adversarial and compete with their teachers for power and control. These students benefit from a teacher–student relationship that acknowledges their power while also maintaining expectations and boundaries. A balance of power is achieved when the teacher appropriately manages conflict by consistently rein-forcing expected behaviors while also honoring the student's positive attributes and perspectives. Managing conflict is difficult but, when done successfully, a sense of mutual respect and interdependence will develop between the teacher and the student.

On the other hand, other ACEs students, like those who tend to internalize, may become nervous and timid when a teacher gives them individual atten-tion. These students will need reassurance and positive affirmation in order to connect. Regardless, once these initial barriers subside, there remains the chal-lenge of maintaining a positive relationship with an ACEs student.

Sustaining a positive relationship with an ACEs student is not always easy for the teacher or the student. The student may lack the skills needed to navi-gate healthy relationships or may also present challenging behaviors that repeat-edly fracture the teacher–student relationship, making it harder for the teacher to hold them in positive regard. This places the teacher in a challenging posi-tion. On the one hand, the teacher has to maintain the rules of the classroom and on the other, has to support a student who repeatedly violates those rules.

I have witnessed scenarios in which a teacher has developed a solid rela-tionship with an ACEs student and suddenly the student's behavior worsens. The teacher and student go through a period of push and pull, in which the student seems to fluctuate from attachment to rejection, from compliance to outright defiance. It can seem as though the student is testing the strength of the teacher–student relationship and pushing against the boundaries of inclusion in their classroom community. There are a number of possible reasons for this. For one, exposure to trauma and chronic stress impacts neurological function-ing and dysregulates the brain's response to stress. Therefore, the ACEs student is predisposed to spending much of her time in a neurological state of fight or flight, which inhibits her ability to manage emotions, respond appropriately to stressors, and handle conflict. These neurological factors compound with the possibility that the ACEs student may be reenacting the relationship dynamics she has witnessed at home.

I worked with a sixth-grade student who had developed a positive relation-ship with the school librarian. He loved to help her in the library before school. One day, he was talking loudly to some other students, and she asked him to lower his voice. In response, he unleashed a string of expletives and threatened to kill her before running out of the library. She was beside herself.

A few days later, the three of us sat down and had a restorative conversa-tion. We talked about what happened, the teacher and student shared how they felt during the altercation, and how they imagined the other person must have felt. The student apologized for threatening the librarian and broke down in tears. He said that he was angry at himself because he spoke to her the same way that his dad spoke to his mom. He and the librarian then negotiated a plan for him to regain her trust. He would help every day for five minutes before the first bell. If he communicated in a respectful manner each day and completed the task he was given, then he would gradually earn his time back as her helper. This was an important opportunity for this young man to learn a valuable les-son about healthy communication and accountability.

Restorative conversations are key to maintaining positive relationships with ACEs students. These conversations guide those involved in resolving an issue by identifying the harm, considering another person's perspective (empathy), and, developing a plan for repairing the relationship. Sadly, I have worked in schools where the approach to restorative conversations was simply to have the student think about what they did wrong and apologize. This creates an illusion that apologizing is enough to repair the damage of a harmful act. This approach also implies that the student is incapable of making better choices and being able to repair a damaged relationship. Therefore, having a clear plan for regaining trust and repairing harm is necessary for effective restorative conversations. These conversations restore trust and belonging, two vital nutrients for the health and success of our ACEs students.

Schools that effectively support ACEs students adopt restorative practices as a fundamental component of their schoolwide culture. They train all staff in facilitating restorative conversations and make them a common practice. Later in this chapter, we will discuss a schoolwide intervention, the Ready to Learn room, which dedicates time, structure, and space to the restorative process, in the interest of doing what is best for students and the health of the school community.

An often-overlooked factor in schoolwide restorative practices is the need for community building. Restorative practices are truly a three-tiered process comprised of classroom circles (Tier I), restorative conversations or repair circles (Tier II), and reset circles for students who have been suspended or are at risk for dropping out (Tier III). The Tier I foundation of community has to be established for restorative and repair efforts to be effective. After all, students are more likely to feel a sense of personal accountability to someone they have a relationship with. Also, students are far more likely to internalize the norms and values of a classroom when they are treated as a valued member. When a student feels connected to her school community and a harm occurs (e.g., a fight with another student, an argument with a teacher), that student will be more invested in the restorative process. For students who do not feel valued by their school community, engaging in the restorative process is like asking them to repair a relationship that they never had to begin with.

Therefore, we encourage schools to set aside time each day for classes to have class meetings or class circles. Circles are a format for facilitating classroom meetings in which students and their teacher sit together in a circle. The topic of the daily circle can range from a simple check-in to responding to an open-ended question, or even resolving an issue that has come up within the class. Typically, the circles have opening and closing routines (e.g., reading a poem, ringing a bell, saying a word that describes how you're feeling) as well as a talking piece that is used to bring order to the conversation (see the Additional Resources section for more information). Classroom circles are rich opportunities to foster relatedness, accountability, and healthy interpersonal skills, while laying the foundation for restorative practices.

Even with a great deal of community building and behavioral supports, there will still be instances that challenge a student's relationship with the class and demand an immediate response. For these situations, a Ready to Learn (RTL) room is a valuable intervention for a school to have in place. The RTL room is a space and a process that helps students deescalate, problem-solve, and successfully reengage in the classroom. Teachers can refer a student to the RTL room for emotional or behavioral issues.

To refer a student to the Ready to Learn room, the teacher contacts the office for student support and a member of the student support team (e.g., school counselor, administrator, behavior specialist) accompanies the student from the classroom to the RTL room. In the RTL room, the student engages in a three-step process to deescalate, problem-solve, and reengage. First, the student chooses a deescalation strategy (e.g., yoga stretches, tensing and relaxing muscles, hug a stuffed animal), then the student works with a staff person, who listens without judgment, and helps them process the incident. The final step of the Ready to Learn process is to determine what the student needs to successfully reengage in learning (e.g., complete a small part of an assignment, have a snack if they haven't eaten, prepare for a restorative conversation with their teacher). The student support person then walks the student back to class. The support person may stay in the classroom for a few minutes to ensure that the student has successfully reengaged.

The RTL process is not complete until the teacher and the student discuss the incident and restore their relationship. Having said that, a teacher may not be ready to talk about the event that resulted in the student being referred to the RTL room, especially if the incident was emotionally charged for both parties. The RTL process honors the emotional well-being of both the teacher and the student. Therefore, we advise that the teacher and student have a restorative conversation within twenty-four hours of the incident occurring.

There are a few important considerations for running an effective Ready to Learn room. First, the RTL is a space for students who have exhibited moderate emotional or behavioral escalations that could not be managed successfully by the classroom teacher. The RTL room is not a space for a student who has engaged in a behavior that warrants a major disciplinary action (e.g., attacking a teacher, brandishing a weapon).

Second, the RTL room has limits and these limits should be clearly explained to students and staff. The RTL process of deescalation, problem-solving, and preparation for reengagement, should take approximately ten to fifteen minutes. The RTL room is not a place for a student to avoid class for extended periods of time, nor is it a detention room or space used to complete missing assignments. Visits to the RTL room should be recorded on a sign-in sheet or spreadsheet for data management. It should be noted any time a student is referred to the RTL room multiple times in one day. This information can help the intervention team, in collaboration with the classroom teacher, to develop classroom strategies to prevent the behaviors that are causing the student to be referred to the RTL room.

Most importantly, the RTL room is a schoolwide intervention that is sustained through team effort. The school leadership must identify a student support team comprised of individuals who can process students through the RTL room. The leadership may create a schedule and assign individuals to different time slots. It is wise to have at least two members of the student support team on call at any given time during the school day. Members of the student support team will need to be trained in the RTL process, including deescalation strategies and restorative practices.

Read, Reflect, Respond

1. Meet Mr. Hester, a high school teacher in Richmond, California. As you watch him on YouTube, be thinking about the ways he models or provides opportunities for Talk, Trust, Feel, and Repair. Be mindful; some examples are explicit; some you must infer from the feedback his students share.

   https://www.youtube.com/watch?v=LdF5ry5g5-w

2. Use the **Teacher's Trauma-Informed Toolkit: Talk Trust Feel Repair (TTFR)** to compare your schoolwide and classroom practices. Initial each SW for schoolwide and MP for my practice.

   Feel validated that you and your colleagues are already using trauma-informed practices.

   Think of ways you can incorporate the strategies you did not check into your daily routines.

   Consider starting a conversation with your school's leadership team about the schoolwide strategies they are doing and ways they could incorporate the ones they are not.

   Caveat: this is not an overnight process. Discussion and consensus around what, when, and how to add a new strategy must take place first. Chapter 8 shares suggestions for planning and implementing trauma-informed strategies. This TTFR Toolkit is a good resource.

Talk: Belonging	Trust: Safety
o Greet students at the door. o Use regular class meetings or circles. o Use verbal and nonverbal cues to foster belonging (spirit fingers, thumbs up, handshakes, etc.). o Affirm cultural connections and identities through culturally responsive instruction and learning environment. o Provide multiple opportunities for creative self-expression. o Connect through shared interests (art, music, games, sports, etc.). o Be a coach! Avoid power struggles by coaching a student through challenges. o Listen without judgment. o Set goals and share them with one another. o Practice giving compliments and affirming one another. o Contact parents to share positive news about their child. o Notice when a child is absent and check in when they return. o Close every class by giving students the opportunity to acknowledge one another. o Give students the opportunity to co-teach a lesson or present to the class. o Divide the class into teams and create a points system to reinforce positive behavior and student skills.	o Use clear, consistent expectations and routines. o Teach and reteach behaviors until they become automatic. o Post schedule. o Practice and prepare for transitions. o Get to know the student (2x10). o Maintain teacher integrity (Word/action consistency). o Acknowledge your mistakes and correct them. o Solicit & incorporate student feedback. o Be authentic and selectively vulnerable. o Create opportunities for academic and nonacademic success. o Model interdependence by providing choices and allowing students to share in making decisions. o Break complex tasks and activities into step-by-step instructions that are presented in multiple formats (e.g., a song for going back to your seats and getting out your materials, a graphic organizer for a difficult assignment). o Be self-aware. Periodically notice your mood, tone, and body language. Maintaining a calm, assertive, and respectful demeanor is best.

(Continued)

From Theory to Practice

Transformationist Actions Convert ACEs to Aces

How many effective schools would you have to see to be persuaded of the educability of poor children? If your answer is more than one, then I submit that you have reasons of your own for preferring to believe that pupil performance derives from family background instead of school response to family background.

—Ronald R. Edmonds,
Researcher of Effective Schools

Anticipated Outcomes

Readers will

o review data and concepts shared in previous chapters to understand that what our students need today goes beyond good teaching; they need schools that are transformative;

o compare their current school and school districts with lists describing transformative schools and school districts, instructional staff, school counselors and school-based social workers, school nurses and school psychologists, and support staff (office, food service, bus drivers, custodial, etc.);

o apply SEL competencies and Benard's Resiliency Framework when working with colleagues, self-care plans, students, and their families.

(Continued)

Feel: Emotional Regulation	Repair: Restorative Practices
o Teach socioemotional learning (SEL) lessons. o Designate a Cool Down Spot in the classroom and teach a cool down routine. o Use Mindful Minutes. o Use growth mindset to lessen anxiety and provide encouragement. o Use Body & Brain Breaks. o Use Dr. Siegel's "Brain in the Hand" as a method for communicating emotional arousal. o Acknowledge students for giving or receiving help. o Take the temperature. Have a routine for assessing students' readiness to learn. o Regularly teach and model strategies for calming down (e.g., take deep breaths, tense and relax muscles). o Notice when you are triggered and use a calming strategy.	o Model taking responsibility and making amends. o Problem-solve with the student. o Administer effective consequences that repair rather than punish. o Have restorative conversations. Share what happened. Identify the harm. Listen and empathize. Make a plan to repair and restore the relationship(s).

3. Use the following link to access a video about high school students describing effective teacher–student relationships. Respond to the three questions at the end of the video.

   Taking into account your response to Question #3, what professional development support might be helpful?

   https://www.youtube.com/watch?v=UBP6TtL3miE

4. Watch this video about restorative approaches to discipline published by Chicago Public Schools. PreK through twelfth-grade students and staff share strategies that changed how behaviors were handled. Start and stop (or do what works best for you) the video when you observe one of the actions or behaviors as a form of communication listed below (https://www.youtube.com/watch?v=5r1yvyP141U).

Restorative Approaches	Evidence From Video
Behavior is a form of communication.	
Trust: Teacher to student	
Trust: Student to student	
Sense of Belonging: Teacher to teacher	

Restorative Approaches	Evidence From Video
Sense of Belonging: Teacher to student	
Sense of Belonging: Staff to parents	
Feeling Valued: Teacher to teacher	
Feeling Valued: Teacher to student	
Feeling Valued: Student to student	
Feeling Valued: Staff to parents	
Impact on student's confidence to be successful academically and socially	
Teachers being open and honest	
Students being open and honest	
Unrelenting positive regard for students	

SCHOOLS AND CLASSROOMS HAVE A CULTURE AND CULTURE IS LEARNED

Culture is defined as the set of shared attitudes, values, goals, and practices that characterizes an institution, organization, or group of people. Culture is a mediating factor in all relationships. People get along better when they share the same values, have the same goals, and know how to skillfully maneuver. Schools and school districts are cultural institutions. They have their own beliefs, perceptions, language, attitudes, behaviors, and written and unwritten rules. Culture is learned.

Throughout our lifetime, we live and function in multiple cultural settings like home, community, corporations, and religious institutions. When we understand the "values" each setting requires, we fit in. Sitting in a darkened movie theater, there is a cultural agreement that we will not talk, will silence our cell phones, and never yell "Fire!" as a joke. We don't wear pajamas when we go to the bank for a mortgage loan. At home or in our respective communities, we enter into yet another cultural world.

Teaching our students about the variety of cultural experiences they encounter now and will in their future helps them to begin to understand that behavior is fluid and flexible. They will see the need for adapting behaviors as being multicultural, that it is OK to change behaviors to fit in. Some of our students and their families need to be taught school or school district culture. Schools and school districts must incorporate the cultures of their students and families. They too need to be inclusive, multicultural.

When developing schoolwide or districtwide cultural norms, it is important to recognize that staff and students come with diverse perceptions about school that are shaped by our different identities and experiences. It is important to acknowledge and adapt these differences into shared beliefs, perceptions, language, attitudes, and working agreements for use while in school. Some students, not all, need guided instruction and opportunity to apply school behaviors and language. This includes sharing teacher behaviors. When teachers share what they do, explain why and how it relates to learning, it becomes personal and relevant for the student. For example, at the start of the school year, or new semester, when a teacher shares actual student samples taken at the end of the previous school year, he is letting the students see what they will be doing throughout the year to achieve the same results.

"You will be able to write papers like my student from last year if you give me your attention when I am doing this . . ."

When students see examples of end of the year targets and understand the importance of *learning behaviors*, they are more likely to hit a bullseye.

When teachers teach or ask students to describe classroom behaviors they need teaching and learning, they can articulate what those are—even if they cannot apply them consistently. Explicit feedback is a growth mindset reminder and establishes the expectation, "I know you can and will do better!"

RESPONSE TO INTERVENTION (RTI)

Response to intervention (RTI) is a practical tool to use for differentiating, monitoring, and reteaching students the school's behavior expectations and norms.

Response to intervention (RTI) has its origins in special education as an approach to teach students with learning disabilities at varying levels of intensity. The RTI framework is now used for students in general education to monitor student progress in frequent intervals. Based on these assessments, educators can plan targeted interventions for students as needed.

The framework has three levels: Tier I, II, and III. Tier I instruction begins with teaching and assessing all students after each unit of study. Based on the assessment data, students are then divided into three instructional groups. Depending on a school's intervention procedures, students who master unit skills may move on to the next unit or be given enrichment activities. Interventions are provided at increasing levels of intensity in Tier II and III.

Tier II students receive research-based supplemental interventions from general education teachers or academic specialists and are reassessed usually after a week of reteaching. Students still needing more time to learn new behaviors are then moved to Tier III for intensive intervention.

Scheduling to provide RTI services varies. In some PreK–twelfth-grade schools, instruction times for literacy (reading and writing) and math blocks occur at the same time. All staff members (general education, special education, academic specialists) teach during Tier I to reduce student–teacher ratio. Classified staff or instructional assistants might be assigned to assist teachers in their classrooms if class size cannot be reduced significantly.

Students are reassessed after the unit (or units) has been taught. The schedule is adjusted to accommodate students needing Tier II and III interventions and they are retested after a week or so. Academic specialists and classified staff work with students needing Tier II interventions. For students needing Tier III interventions, special education staff (if possible, regardless of whether student has qualified for special education) and classified staff reteach these students. Tier II and III students are reassessed to determine academic growth. Students consistently needing Tier III interventions become a focus of concern to determine causes for learning delays. Students who have met academic goals can delve deeper into the unit content during the week of reteaching Tier II and III students.

All students remain in general education classrooms for most of their instructional day. Having the same blocks of time for literacy and math ensures that students are with their classmates for other content subjects. In schools that have successful RTI models, educators collaborate. They not only disaggregate the data for each student, they brainstorm instructional strategies to use when working with Tier I to Tier III students. Then the general education teachers decide which groups they can support. Depending on the numbers, they may decide to teach larger groups of Tier I students to allow more general education staff to work with Tier II and III students in smaller groups. The goal during the reteaching cycle is to reduce student to teacher ratio as low as possible.

The RTI model has also been adopted to be used for behavior. Like the RTI framework for academic interventions, the behavior model relies on teaching all students the same core behavior curriculum at the Tier I level. Until standards are created for behavior outcomes at each grade level, schools that have integrated socioemotional curriculum—like Second Step, MindUp, and RULER—in conjunction with **Positive Behavioral Intervention & Supports (PBIS)** are in a better position to create a strong buildingwide management system. Second Step, MindUp, and RULER provide activities for socioemotional learning and PBIS adds the three-tiered framework for behavior interventions. We can use the same resources, but their use and outcomes need to be rooted in a new conceptual understanding:

- Behavior is a form of communication. New ways of communicating can be taught over time using intervention models similar to English language learners (ELL) and Title I remedial models. Like learning to become academically proficient in English, learning a new behavior language may take seven years. It may take some students, especially those living with multiple ACEs, years to learn how to communicate behaviors differently.

- Only 5 percent to 10 percent of a school's population should require an individualized education plan that includes input from medical and mental health agencies. These students may spend 80 percent to 100 percent of their day in self-contained classrooms.

- School staff need to explore Self and become aware of biases or preconceived notions that may result in faulty perceptions and obstruct professional decision-making.

Borrowing medical terminology, we have been *misdiagnosing* the socioemotional needs of students who are exposed to ACEs. As a result, these students are

- o   more likely to fail a grade and fall behind,
- o   disproportionately represented in special education,
- o   prone to higher rates of chronic diseases,
- o   unable to form healthy relationships with adults and peers,
- o   always responding to the world as constant danger,
- o   more likely to engage in criminal activities, and

   more likely to feel marginalized. (Shonk & Cicchetti, 2001)

When every staff member receives professional development and ongoing support to cultivate and apply trauma-informed instructional strategies daily and students are taught the needed cultural norms, schools can provide environments that are professional, relevant, safe, and compassionate at the same time (Roberson, 2013; Wyre, 2013).

LOOKING AT BEHAVIOR MANAGEMENT THROUGH A TRAUMA-INFORMED LENS

An RTI model that integrates behavior outcomes with ongoing socioemotional learning for the adults and students can regulate a school or school district's climate and culture. Professional development and curriculum that teach adults and students ways to Talk, Trust, Feel, and Repair can enable them to develop management systems more capable of meeting the needs of all students and staff. Subsequently, the RTI behavior model is integrated with trauma-informed strategies and interventions. In Chapter 8, we discuss this model, and its implementation, in more detail. For now, here is a brief overview of our three-tiered model of ACEs and trauma-informed interventions and supports.

Tier I

Relationships, along with classroom-based strategies for socioemotional well-being, are the foundation for supporting ACEs students. In Tier I, these relationships provide the context for facilitating academic growth and establishing behavior expectations. The behavior expectations define how each individual interacts when working together—educator to educator, educator to student, student to student, educator to families.

Changing the culture of a school or school district also requires using a different language. Words like *rules* are changed to *working agreements* or *norms.* Detention rooms become "Ready to Learn rooms"—spaces where the adults or students can *talk* and *repair* relationships.

If one of the norms is responsibility, explicit examples of what responsible student and adult behaviors look like are defined, taught, and modeled. Images or word phrases illustrating responsible behaviors are visible everywhere a student might be. Custodial and cafeteria staff reinforce what students are

Figure 5.1   Trauma-Sensitive Response to Interventions for Behavior

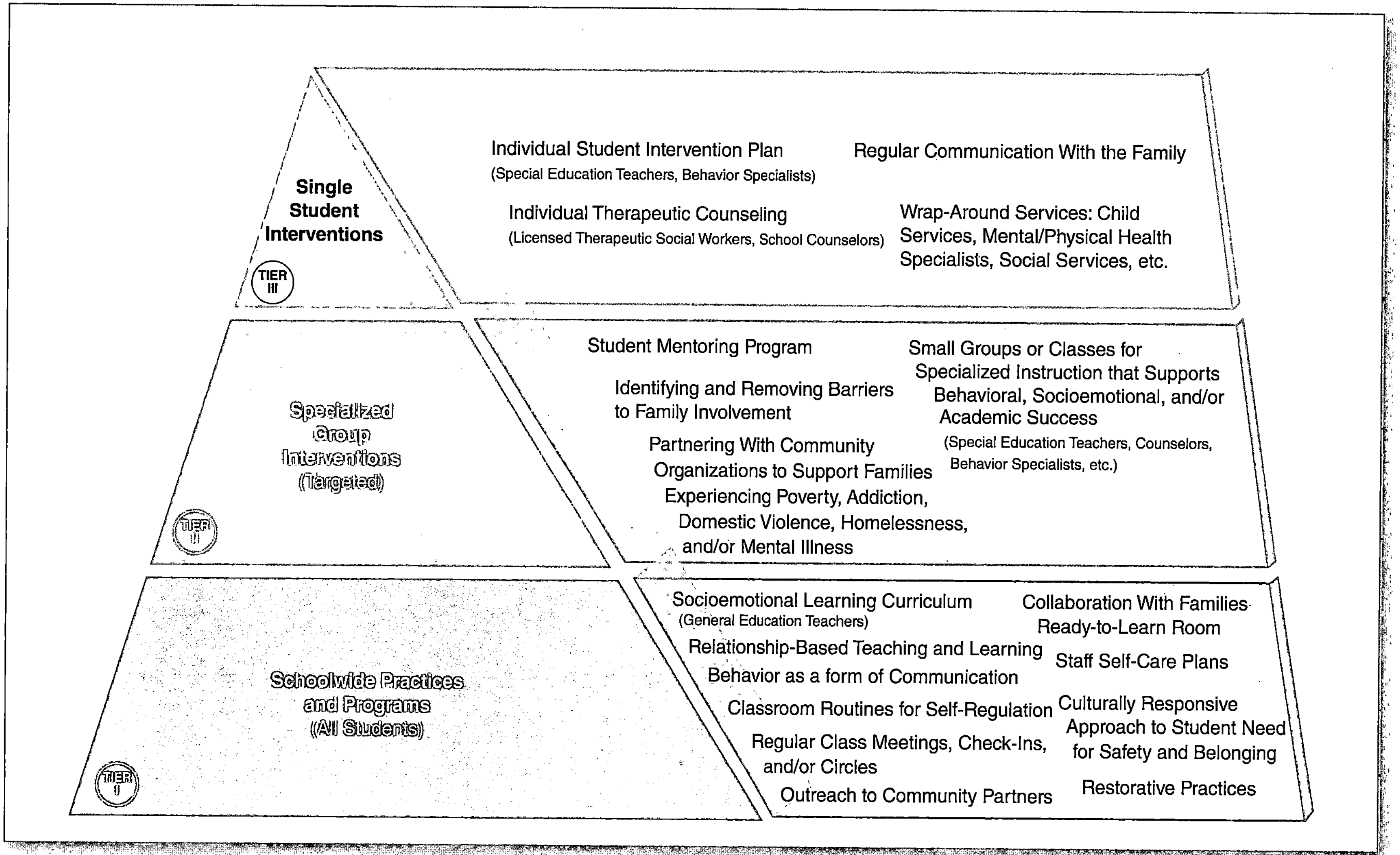

Single Student Interventions
(TIER III)

Individual Student Intervention Plan
(Special Education Teachers, Behavior Specialists)

Individual Therapeutic Counseling
(Licensed Therapeutic Social Workers, School Counselors)

Regular Communication With the Family

Wrap-Around Services: Child Services, Mental/Physical Health Specialists, Social Services, etc.

Specialized Group Interventions (Targeted)
(TIER II)

Student Mentoring Program

Identifying and Removing Barriers to Family Involvement

Partnering With Community Organizations to Support Families Experiencing Poverty, Addiction, Domestic Violence, Homelessness, and/or Mental Illness

Small Groups or Classes for Specialized Instruction that Supports Behavioral, Socioemotional, and/or Academic Success
(Special Education Teachers, Counselors, Behavior Specialists, etc.)

Schoolwide Practices and Programs (All Students)
(TIER I)

Socioemotional Learning Curriculum
(General Education Teachers)

Relationship-Based Teaching and Learning

Behavior as a form of Communication

Classroom Routines for Self-Regulation

Regular Class Meetings, Check-Ins, and/or Circles

Outreach to Community Partners

Collaboration With Families

Ready-to-Learn Room

Staff Self-Care Plans

Culturally Responsive Approach to Student Need for Safety and Belonging

Restorative Practices

learning by giving positive, explicit feedback using the same language students are learning in class. This helps students *feel* they are safe and cared for because everyone is watching and noting their progress.

Classroom and schoolwide celebrations keep students and faculty mindful of Tier I outcomes—positive relationships that create climates and cultures that are safe for teaching and learning. Classroom educators and paraprofessionals who assist in classrooms are responsible for teaching and monitoring socioemotional curriculum, integrating it into classroom management systems and providing opportunities for students to apply new behaviors. School counselors provide ongoing professional development to ensure socioemotional curriculum is being taught with fidelity. Administrators ensure other systems are compatible, manage scheduling, and convene meetings between educators, students, families, and community agencies.

The objective of Tier I instruction is to provide structure and consistency so that 80 percent to 95 percent of the students master new behaviors. To achieve a healthy, functioning culture, all staff members must use the same language, model the same behaviors, and work hard to develop trusting relationships with each other, their students, and families.

Read, Reflect, Respond

1. Think about your current interactions with students. Describe your behavior and your expectations for their behaviors as your lesson moves from basic learning to critical thinking skills.

Bloom's Taxonomy	Teacher Behavior	Student Behavior
Knowledge		
Comprehension		
Application		
Analysis		
Synthesis		
Evaluation		

2. How could you integrate this into your classroom management lessons and daily routines?

Tier II

Supplemental interventions are provided for students needing more time learning new behaviors. A school-based intervention team begins discussions and planning for students. Teams are composed of administrators, staff who work with students, school counselors, school psychologists, and parents. Since poverty is an adverse childhood experience, the school psychologists in low-income schools assess all Tier II students for intellectual skills using performance-based activities to determine how they reason. Assessing the reasoning capabilities identifies Tier II students who have average to above average intelligence, vital information needed to review their academic program for rigor.

Students are assigned to small instructional groups staffed by school counselors or special education staff because of their expertise in mental health therapies and behavior management strategies. The behaviors of students at Tier II are inconsistent. They have good days and then days when they revert to old forms of responding. Instructional groupings are modeled after ELL and Title I pull-out programs. A pull-out instructional model is used where students leave general education rooms for short, scheduled periods at least three to four times per week or are assigned to special elective classes at the middle and high school levels. Students are taught, given guided practice opportunities, and assessed on specific behaviors or needs. Sessions can be designed to target specific traumatizing events such as handling grief, dealing with an incarcerated parent, living in foster care, or family divorce. As they begin to show improvement, their time in these special sessions can decrease and time in general education classrooms increase. It is important for Tier II students to be in general education classrooms for most of their school day. This gives them opportunity to apply new behaviors with their teachers and peers.

Tier III

For the small percentage of students at Tier III, comprehensive individual education plans (IEPs) that engage home, school, and community agencies' supports are needed. These students require wrap-around services because the majority of Tier III students have preexisting mental health issues that impact their behaviors. An intervention team composed of administrators, special education teachers, nurse, school psychologist, school counselor, and parents create and regularly monitor individual education–behavior plans. The forms used by the intervention team should include gathering information from as many resources as needed, including parents, social services, and health care providers.

Whenever possible, Tier III students should be placed in general education classrooms staffed with teachers with endorsements in special education or who are highly proficient in teaching and integrating socioemotional curriculum. By law, these students may qualify for having a full-time trained paraprofessional or teacher assistant with them all day to support as much contact time with their general education peers as possible. There is always a dual focus on academic and social growth.

Read, Reflect, Respond

1. It's the first week of school and you are sharing the school's and your classroom's behavior standards. Create an activity that teaches your students about the concept of culture and the value of being bicultural as you incorporate your needs when students are with you.

(Continued)

(Continued)

2. Several of your school's behavior standards are listed below. Create an activity that teaches and provides opportunities that are interactive for your students to practice what this behavior looks like in your classroom, bus, hallway, or cafeteria.

Accept and appreciate our differences in all areas: skills, learning styles, culture, physical, for example.
Accept the consequences of your behavior willingly.
Help. Be an involved participant in group projects and activities. Work cooperatively with others.

3. There are schools that implement trauma-informed care. Use these links to connect to videos and articles to deepen your understanding of how these schools have moved from theory to practice.

    Pearl-Cohn High School: https://www.youtube.com/watch?v=L6Kxd5Dp6K8

    Fall-Hamilton Elementary School: https://www.youtube.com/watch?v=iydalwamBtg

    http://www.socialjusticesolutions.org/2015/06/01/resilience-practices-overcome-students-aces-trauma-informed-high-school-say-data/

    https://acestoohigh.com/2013/07/22/at-cherokee-point-elementary-kids-dont-conform-to-school-school-conforms-to-kids

4. PBISworld.com is a great resource for adding to your behavior management toolkit. PBIS stands for positive behavior interventions and supports and that is what is available on this website. Use this link, http://www.pbisworld.com/, to click onto behaviors for which you'd like more help using positive support strategies.

5. Describe some special considerations a school intervention team may think about for students who are
    o   experiencing homeless,
    o   in foster care, or
    o   refugees.

We now know there are educators, who themselves are survivors of ACEs, working with students who are living with adverse childhood experiences and know supportive environments help both succeed. There are schools in low-income communities meeting the socioemotional and academic needs of students living with multiple ACEs that we can learn from. We have so many things already in place: curriculum that focuses on socioemotional outcomes, RTI frameworks, PBIS, and more information available online at the internet literally at your fingertips. The neuroscientists say all brains are capable of changing and growing. The social scientists tell us humans are born with innate resiliency. We have the prescription. Why do we continue to wait for our new glasses with trauma-informed lenses?

CHANGE IS HARD AND LEADERSHIP MATTERS

The research about how effective and ineffective principals impact student learning and teacher morale is leaves no room for debate. Principal leadership makes a difference in a school's climate and culture. School climate is about attitude of the staff, while school culture is about their collective personality (Gruenert, 2008; Habegger, 2008).

When considering candidates for a principalship, human resource administrators must ask questions to determine how well this person can build and sustain collegiality and establish authentic relationships with students and parents. Positive school climates decrease student absenteeism and teachers' compassion fatigue (Grayson & Alverez, 2008; Thapa, Cohen, Higgins-D'Alessandro, & Guffey, 2012). Academic achievement increases when teachers and students feel emotionally and psychologically safe (Boccanfuso & Kuhfeld, 2011). School climates that are affirming and constructive mitigate the effects of adverse childhood experiences (Ruiz, 2016). In schools significantly impacted by students dealing with adverse childhood experience, leadership matters. Highly-effective principals can significantly raise achievement levels in a single school year (Branch, Hanushek, & Rivkin, 2013).

Principals capable of modeling caring, trusting, professional relationships are more likely to help create and sustain the needed positive, proactive school climate and culture for improving academic and social growth. They know the pressures that teaching staff face and the importance that positive can-do attitudes and shared understandings can have. Effective principals focus on building healthy collegial relationships based upon trust, belonging, and feeling valued. Something is terribly wrong when the research reveals that teachers love teaching but hate their jobs.

In a survey sponsored by Scholastic and the Bill and Melinda Gates Foundation, 90 percent of the educators responded that they enjoyed what they do; however, only 34 percent felt society valued their work (Richmond, 2014). When asked about their sense of "well-being" in their work environment, teaching ranked 8th out of 14 professions surveyed by Gallup. In the same survey, they were in last place when asked if their supervisor created trusting and open work environments (Richmond, 2013).

According to Leithwood (1994), principals in schools with significant numbers of students living with adverse childhood experiences need to be transformational in their leadership. Transformational principals build and maintain the collective capacity for staff to

- believe in a shared vision,

- build consensus about goals and priorities,

- have high expectations,

- feel professionally supported,

- work in an organized responsive system, and

- teach in a safe environment.

Transformational principals are vested, visible, and committed to the success of their staff and students. In their schools, Talk, Trust, Feel, and Repair is supported in their daily practice at all levels—staff, students, and families.

Talk: Principals set forth directives that are explicitly focused on the needs of each member of the school staff and student. Teachers are empowered to share their professional opinions and encouraged to make decisions. Students know they have access to their principal. Transformational principals cultivate relationships with their staff including custodial and cafeteria workers, students, and parents. They promote collegiality and collaboration. Everyone understands and accepts the vision and mission.

Trust: These principals deliver. When they say they are going to do something, it is done. They are reliable. They are also honest. If they cannot fulfill a professional need or want, they say so. When mandatory directives come from district administrators, they make every effort to mitigate the impact it might have on teaching staff. They maintain a professional neutrality that favors all staff, students, and families.

Feel: Transformational principals understand the demands teaching and learning can have on individuals on any given school day. Policies and procedures for dealing with the stresses of the working environment are in place to support teachers and students. They prioritize goals and objectives and discover ways to integrate professional development that encompass several initiatives.

Repair: The socioemotional well-being of staff and students is a priority. When relationships are strained, these principals mediate or bring in district professionals to heal hurt feelings. They acknowledge emotions come into play in our profession.

Read, Reflect, Respond

1. How would you describe your school's climate and culture? If your district does not provide data assessing your school's culture or climate, there are online surveys.

   http://schoolclimatesurvey.com/surveys.html

2. Education World describes elements of positive and negative school climates. There are also evidenced-based suggestions for steps administrators and teachers can take to turn around negative work and learning environments.

   http://www.educationworld.com/a_admin/admin/admin275.shtml

3. The Office of Public Education in Washington State published *The Characteristics of Improved School Districts: Themes from Research in 2004*. Guiding questions help superintendents and their leadership team reflect on practices and policies at a district level.

   http://www.k12.wa.us/research/pubdocs/DistrictImprovementReport.pdf

But What Can a Teacher Do if the Principal Is Ineffective?

Can we accept the notion that failing schools have dysfunctional systems? You've done your analysis of your school's climate and the results suggest you are working in a system that is not supportive of your efforts and is not meeting the needs of the students. You work in a dysfunctional school supervised by a principal who is ineffective. If you are new to the profession, you are probably thinking you made a serious mistake. You may even be ready to bail out. If you are a veteran, you have probably found ways to "survive" because you have tenure and years to go before retiring. You may have symptoms of compassion fatigue or worse, burnout.

An ineffective principal can demoralize and fracture a staff. You may feel alone but you are not. There are other colleagues who feel the same way. Find *your* people and talk, not vent. Too often, dysfunctional staff will take their frustrations out in the workplace and turn on each other. Use your precious time to further understand what needs to happen and strategize. Be strategic: many a school has been pushed forward because of teacher-leaders.

1. Is your principal approachable? If yes, discuss ways you and colleagues can use your knowledge of the characteristics of an effective school to start a conversation with the principal that is focused on how you want to support him or her, in helping your school turn around. Judging and criticizing in the staff lounge is a waste of your precious working time.

2. If your principal accepts your invitation, begin to discuss how to approach the rest of the staff at a staff meeting. You may want to consider bringing in an outside facilitator or district support to guide the discussion. Meet with the facilitator, share needs, and ask that he or she propose how to achieve your goal of moving staff from venting to voicing for change.

3. If your principal is abusive, consult your union or the appropriate district personnel. Union representatives can help advocate for staff.

Victoria E. Romero, Principal

TALK, TRUST, FEEL, REPAIR: MY ROOKIE YEAR

I thought long and hard when preparing my first opening speech as an administrator for my staff. I had spent my July and early August learning all I could about them and the students I would serve. I read the evaluations of previous principals, talked with my supervisor, pored over the school's performance and school climate data with the director of data analysis. Other principals pulled me aside to share what they knew or had heard. I knew this staff of veteran teachers felt underappreciated. Enrollment was declining, and the district's solution was to place an English language learner (ELL) program and bus students to the school. The school demographics were extreme—60 percent of the students were White and upper-middle class. The rest were children of color, 35 percent eligible for free or reduced lunch. Thirty-eight percent of them were assigned to the school for its ELL pull-out program.

This staff had had a revolving door of principals over a short span of time. Everyone had burrowed into their own world or classrooms. Teachers did their own thing in terms of implementing curriculum. Even within the same grade level, they used different basal materials. Each relied on the materials they felt most comfortable with so there was no continuity in the instructional program. This made it impossible for support staff like the ELL and Title I teachers to align their work with general education staff. And even if everyone was using the same textual materials, the scheduling was based on teacher preference and not student need. There was no time to collaborate within the regular work day because the schedule was built on teacher preference. Some teachers were headed home shortly after the thirty minutes after-school planning time built into their union negotiated schedule.

There was no schoolwide behavior management system. For an elementary school its size, suspensions were high and disproportionately impacting students of color.

To say the challenges facing me as a first-year principal were daunting would be the proverbial understatement. In addition to the inside-the-school work, my school was scheduled for a major renovation. We would be transferred to another school in two years. I had to work with the district's facility personnel to select an architect and then work with him, my staff, students, and the community in a structural redesign of an historic building.

Over 400 students and their parents were depending on me for a good educational year and the entire community wanted to know what was going to happen to their school. In terms of attending to our mediocre test scores, declining White enrollment, and disproportionate disciplinary data, my families and students didn't have the luxury of time to wait for me to figure things out. And as a first-year principal, I knew the clock had already started ticking. I needed a plan, a vision with an approach that could put this school bus back into its proper lane and heading in the right direction starting my day one. I never bought into the *no-big-changes-the-first-year* philosophy that I'd actually heard from professors when I was getting my administrative credentials. The children we serve *only* have one year in their current grade level. For them, every year counts toward high school graduation. This was a value of mine that I planned to share after we looked at our disaggregated data.

After years in the classroom, working in schools administered by effective and ineffective principals, I knew the difference between the two. When I worked for effective principals, I felt empowered. I could voice my opinions (and I was very opinionated) without fearing negative repercussion. The staff was collegial; we worked hard and had fun times together. These principals found ways to make my job easier and enjoyable. They were visionary leaders and able to make all of us feel we could teach gerbils how to read and problem-solve. They mentored me, corrected me, and pushed me to become a better teacher. As a matter of fact, it was one of these principals who sat me down and told me the time had come for me to get my administrative credentials. I never aspired to be a principal. He saw something in me that I did not. Effective principals are like that; they see potential and are willing to push if it means more children will be successful.

On my big day, my first speech with my first staff, I shared my dreams: *I want to be the principal for you that I would want to work for. I know and respect your job and I want to make your work easier.* I also shared my values, what I knew to be true about teaching diverse populations. I shared my experiences of working for effective and ineffective principals. I needed their help to be the former.

And then we reviewed the school's data, most of it problematic. Relying on my group facilitation and classroom teacher skills, I divided them into groups and gave each group a specific data summary to analyze and recommend next steps. We spent the day problem-solving instead of rehashing the problems. What *can* we do instead was the only question driving the agenda, not what are we not doing. As groups reported out, we discussed, debated, and narrowed the recommendations until we had one or two actionable steps to get us started.

When I interjected to share my opinions or proposed alternative solutions, I was careful about my choice of words and delivery. For example, when I pointed out how using the same basal materials would facilitate grade-level and school-wide discussions regarding student progress and allow support staff to align their instruction, the general education teachers were very resistant. That was a battle I was not going to win so, I used a more directive approach when telling them our Plan B. Each grade level would have to align the skills in their textual materials with the standards for their grade. We would administer assessments created by academic coaches every six weeks to make sure students were achieving. I have no idea how difficult that might have been for them but a new schedule was created to give them time to collaborate and plan within their grade level *and* with the ELL and Title I teachers. This was our compromise—keep your basal, but start meeting and planning together to scaffold skills every four to six weeks, assess, and review data in grade-level teams. To start the process, I gave each grade-level team a planning day (with substitute teachers covering classes) every four to six weeks.

I also reassigned playground and lunchroom duty and gave those responsibilities to support staff and myself. This had an added benefit that I had not anticipated; our students were able to develop relationships with school staff they may not have had contact with, including their principal. Walking around and interacting with my students practically eliminated playground scuffles. It's hard to fight or bully when the principal is lurking around. I even had a posse, a group of first graders who thought it was more fun to walk around with their principal. When I told them they should be playing and having fun, I was told they *were* having fun and we continued walking the playground.

I could see firsthand that a lot of our playground injuries and disputes were due to a lack of organization. Working with my PE teacher, we designated and marked off specific areas for certain games and activities so kids wouldn't collide into each other or inadvertently disrupt play for another group. I was able to tell the architect that the new design needed to include benches for children who wanted to read or just sit and talk with their friends. I noticed that some kids used the time to read or talk with playmates.

Since a consistent schoolwide behavior management plan was nonexistent, we started by creating a common vision. How would an effective schoolwide management system benefit teachers and students? Based on that visioning, we decided to focus on rectifying the data that showed we were suspending ELL and the few African American students at a much higher rate than White students for the same infraction. By staffing a classroom for monitored time-outs, we could make every effort to keep students in school. This was a school that used Second Step, a socioemotional curriculum. The idea of having staff in the time-out room review Second Step strategies was a suggestion that came from a teacher.

The visioning conversation was so invigorating, when I asked for volunteers to meet and work on a school management plan that would describe behaviors needed for successful teaching and learning, several stepped forward. When they presented the document they created and how it should be implemented, we were all in awe. It was inclusive and universal. It addressed the socioemotional needs of teachers and students. It was practical because it was relatable and teachable.

Our Core Beliefs for Teaching and Learning

At our school, teachers and students are kind, considerate, and caring because they are

- o respectful of themselves and others,

- o responsible citizens, and

- o reasonable human beings!

This was the preamble to sixteen values spelled out in our schoolwide Tier I management plan. The team had integrated language from Second Step curriculum into the sixteen values we wanted to guide our behaviors. We decided to devote September and October to teach and demonstrate for students what these teacher and student behaviors looked like. Each school week began with my "Welcome back to work" public address sharing three values for our schoolwide focus. After this, I began to share the names of teachers and students I'd seen demonstrating a belief in action. After each long vacation, we'd devote time reviewing the sixteen values and practicing appropriate behaviors before we began the academic program.

The Core Beliefs for Teaching and Learning were posted in every space where a child might be and used by staff to redirect behaviors. We paired them with an incentive program we called GOTCHA. GOTCHAs were script tickets any staff member could give to a student caught behaving appropriately. Students would write their names on the script and put them in a jar in their classrooms. We ended each school week pulling names from each classroom and having students come to the office for a *prize*. I wish I could tell you these were random picks. But no, my administrative assistant would work right alongside with class lists and we would check off names. We wanted every student to have that special moment. When we called names, we could hear children cheering for their classmates.

After the Thanksgiving holiday, we introduced Self-Manager buttons, the second incentive program to augment the sixteen values and GOTCHAs, at a special assembly. Self-managers had privileges: They could leave the class unassisted and be trusted to walk alone to recess, the lunchroom, gym, or library. Self-manager buttons were a student's hall pass. They were first to be chosen by teachers to act as monitors and messengers. Should a new student be assigned to the class, self-managers were assigned as a buddy to help the student get oriented. These privileges were explained to all of the students at the assembly.

When I told them that they would be given a personalized self-manage button when they returned to their classrooms, they cheered. Everyone was starting out as a self-manager. Keeping the button though would depend on their behavior. They could always earn it back by acknowledging and redirecting their behaviors. I had wanted to do this at the start of the school year. But when we discussed this as a staff, the suggestion came from a staff member to wait until after the Thanksgiving break to make sure as many of the students as possible had ample time to learn and demonstrate appropriate school behaviors. I had to agree. It made a lot of sense; taking away a self-manager button too soon for some children could possibly make them give up too soon. It turned out to be the right thing to do. We had inadvertently scaffolded our behavior expectations. We gave ourselves time to teach and reteach our sixteen behavior values. Our students had time to learn, practice, and apply; even if our neediest students struggled, they were getting positive reinforcement daily and time to process their behaviors in our new time-out room (which we actually named the TLC room for tender loving care). Our students were excited and hopeful when told they were all self-managers. And even if it only lasted for that first day after break, the relationship was already established and trusted when we said "Try harder because tomorrow is a new day."

Renovation would be the word that summed up my first administrative year. I worked with an architect to design new insides for an old school while my staff worked at developing relationships with their peers and their students on the inside. The benefit to all was immediate. Our academic scores for all of our students improved significantly after the first year (Engel et al., 1999). And for the entire time I was at this school, I never had a grievance filed with the union.

Amber Warner, LCSW

SCHOOLS ARE IDEAL FOR SOCIAL WORKING

As an elementary school social worker, building relationships with students, staff, administrators, families, and community resource professionals was essential. I can remember my first few days on my new job after finishing my MSW (masters' in social work) as if it were yesterday. My new district had just hired seven social workers to be placed in each of the elementary and junior high schools. I was so excited; this was my dream job. I envisioned interacting with children on a daily basis would be more advantageous than the occasional home visit working for a social service agency. However, it was quite the adjustment and being assigned to a school came with a few challenges.

We were the first social workers this district had hired and there was uncertainty as to how best to utilize us. My principal wasn't sure what to really do with me and I wasn't sure what I could offer. I had just moved from the West Coast to this midwestern town. I had grown up in a city with a million residents; I was moving to a town of 33,000. I wasn't sure what the needs of the school or this community were. But after a few conversations with the seasoned staff, that didn't take long to figure out. Once I explained what social workers did, they voiced their need loud and clear.

"Our school used to not be like this; we were a neighborhood school."

"The bused kids aren't like the kids we are used to."

The bused kids were new to this mostly White, blue-collar community. The *bused kids* and their families had been relocated 145 miles from public housing in Chicago (Popkin, Rich, Hendey, Hayes, & Parilla, 2012). The city of Chicago was demolishing some of its largest low-income projects like Cabrini-Green and the Robert E. Taylor homes and offering these families vouchers to move to other areas in the city, nearby suburban communities, and towns as far away as the one I now called home. The bused kids were poor and mostly Black or Brown.

I must admit, it took a minute or two to really comprehend what teachers were expressing. I was on a thirty-minute bus ride for four years from my middle-class neighborhood to my high school. My experience there was positive. I had teachers who pushed and encouraged me. We were a mini-United Nations. My friends were Ethiopian, Vietnamese, Filipino, Black, and White.

The bused kids the teachers were referring to lived three miles away and yet they did not consider them part of their collective community. The staff was clear about their expectations for me.

"Thank goodness, you're here to help us with *those* children."

Chicago's relocation plans may have looked reasonable and even logical on paper but very little had been done to help the newly relocated families adjust to their small-town community or prepare the community to receive them. Both groups were struggling to figure out this sudden new normal and so were their children.

After showing me to my very first office, which was once a closet in the school's library, the first responsibilities the principal gave me were lunch and recess duty. This turned out to be a good thing. I was able to meet and talk with all of the children. They were confused by my title as well. They knew what the principal, their teachers, and cafeteria staff did, but what was a social worker? Since I was from the same ethnic group as the Black cafeteria staff, the children would call out "Hey, lunch lady" when they needed assistance. We were the only Black staff members at this school.

I soon realized I needed to start with some basic communication and work on developing professional relationships. The students needed to see me doing more things than helping them open milk cartons and my colleagues needed to know me and how my professional skill set could support them. I had to be kind yet set boundaries at the same time. There were some staff members who wanted me to function like a vice principal and handle discipline problems on call. That was not my role. I would tell them I was prepared to create anger-management groups but I was not the new disciplinarian. The most pressing issue was how to let everyone understand what I could and could not do.

I decided I needed to find out who were the teacher leaders, the ones that all of the staff members respected. If I could earn their trust and establish credibility with them, they would be the best ones to help me. They would let their colleagues know I could be trusted and that I was OK.

I started by meeting with teachers during their planning times before and after school and during their lunch times. I asked teachers if I could observe their classes and offered to help them by preparing and teaching lessons to help students with socioemotional skills. I could do home visits and make connections with other social services agencies. There was a sizable poor White population in this school and many of the families of those children were struggling with the same issues as their Black and Brown classmates. The meth epidemic was at its beginning stages and already adversely impacting this town. The needs of the White children were almost invisible to staff. Many of these children were withdrawn; their passivity was seen as compliant. When I observed, these students weren't getting the same teacher time as their White, middle-class peers. For the ones who misbehaved, teachers said it was because they came from families that had acted the same way. It was the Blacks and the Hispanics causing angst.

I was discovering my direction. I gathered names of students who were disrupting learning from the teachers and began connecting with families. I began working with these students and connecting families to other social services. I organized counseling groups around common issues and was allowed in more classrooms to teach socioemotional skills. As the children began to respond positively, cause fewer disruptions in class, and attend to lessons, teachers began to understand how a social worker could support their work. This was also true for the principal. She asked me to join team meetings and to provide her with updates. She asked me to contact families and eventually, she would accompany me on home visits.

I was able to bring back some valuable information to share with staff once I got to know and talk with the families who had been relocated from Chicago. I had thought, and I am sure many others thought the same, that their move to this small town from a major city had been one they were forced to do but this wasn't the case. *They* chose to move to this town because they were trying to get their families as far away from Chicago as possible. This helped all of us have a new respect for our families. I was able to share with staff what this sacrifice really meant. Our families had given up everything they knew to move to a place they didn't know just so their children could have a better life. And even though we were all Americans, for our families, this move was like going to another country where they didn't speak the same language, didn't understand the culture, and they knew they didn't belong. The behaviors of their children were reflecting the same confusion.

I was given time during staff meetings and used it to show the similarities between poor White and Black and Brown children and their families, provide updates as to how the counseling groups and class meetings were going, and ask if teachers were beginning to see and feel a difference. I was always asking for feedback. I signed up for some of the professional development classes designed for teachers. I wanted to understand what they had to do and determine ways I could incorporate those strategies when teaching socioemotional skills.

I started greeting all of the children as they arrived to school in the mornings and telling them "It's a good day to learn." When on the playground and or in the lunchroom, I would ask what did they learn that they didn't know the day before. Because I reached out to all the students, I was able to "check in" with members of my counseling groups without them feeling they were being singled out. They were just other members of a larger school community.

My little closet office became a place where parents felt comfortable, student groups did role-play, and staff stopped by for advice on how to handle a child's behavior or to process an uncomfortable experience they had had with a parent. My closet office, which had felt so uncomfortable and left me wondering how could it become a safe and private space for students or staff, became a safe and private place. All of my professional training was put to good use. I was available for everyone in our school community.

I wish I could say this solved all of the problems this school community was struggling with. It didn't. I took steps to establish trust, relay information between school and families, redirect how teachers judged behaviors, work in large and small student-group settings, and help the principal meet families in their homes; we all knew we were moving to a more compassionate space. Disruptive behaviors began to decrease; families felt welcomed and more engaged as their sacrifices began to pay off.

I was given a second school. This principal and staff had already heard of my work. I was invited into "the circle of trust" immediately. This principal also wanted to get to know and understand the needs of his families from Chicago. We brainstormed ideas and he made things happen. For example, I explained that many of the families were without transportation. They had moved from a city that had buses and subways. He removed that barrier. Families could ride the bus with their children if they wanted to come to school. I would drive them home if that was a need. Any time we had a special event in the evening, he would run school buses to transport families. Our curriculum night, science fairs, and band concerts were well attended by all of the families with children at his school. This dispelled the judgment that some families did not value education. They did. The school also saw that in Black and Brown communities, the entire family attended events—the parents, grandparents, aunts, uncles, cousins, and siblings.

I asked for lunch and recess duties so I could meet and get to know my students. Teachers helped me identify children needing my support. Parents from my first school had already shared my work with their friends whose children were in this second school. When I contacted them, they let me know they had already heard of me. Information travels fast in small communities and even faster in low-income communities.

I was accepted and everyone, in both schools, now understood how a social worker could support their practice. I was able to connect with my peers who worked in social service agencies and help families advocate for their children for services the school could not provide. If case workers wanted to know about a child's attendance or if they were being cared for properly, I could provide that information. This was beneficial for all of the children, regardless of their race, whose families received public assistance.

In terms of dealing with the new normal in today's classrooms, the school community is the best place to have social workers. But according to a 2007 School and Staffing survey published by the National Center for Educational

Statistics, of the 90,760 schools in the sample, only 40 percent of them had a full or part-time social worker. In the same sampling, 78 percent of them had a full or part-time school counselor (U.S. Department of Education, 2017).

There are nearly two times the number of school counselors in the schools surveyed. But they are tasked with a lot of responsibility to track academic progress and help students keep up with their credits, leaving them little time to engage with students, families, or staff in more meaningful ways (American School Counselor Association, n.d.). With the latest advances in technology and easier ways to access this information, perhaps this responsibility can be reassigned to other staff members like a dean or career counselor. For elementary school counselors, they would have time to conduct home visits and counsel staff members.

Felitti and Anda's ACEs research clearly proves that we need to rethink and realign the work of school counselors and social workers with their skill set and give them responsibilities more suited to meet the demands of the new normal. We are both trained in a variety of therapeutic approaches and capable of providing more intensive care to students *and* their teachers. Imagine a school where a teacher could go and debrief with a skilled professional after a traumatic experience with a student or staff member instead of getting depressed or angry and venting in the teacher's lounge. School counselors and social workers could help staff adjust their oxygen masks and take deep breaths. If some of their current responsibilities could be given to others, they could help staff deal with issues like secondary trauma, and perhaps even improve our retention of new teachers.

School counselors and social workers could teach teachers how to use socioemotional curriculum in more effective ways and free up time to work more intensively with the students we have identified in the Tier II and III levels of the RTI behavior model we are suggesting. They would be the "building resiliency specialists" in schools and function more like our ESL staff. Like our ESL programs, counselors and social workers could provide more intensive class time to teach students a new behavior language. On average, it takes a student learning to speak English five to seven years to become academically functional (Hakuta, Butler, & Witt, 2000; Haynes, n.d.). Students living with ACEs may need the same amount of time to strengthen their innate resiliency and become proficient in communicating behaviors needed for learning.

Read, Reflect, Respond

1. What is your reaction to the idea of using school counselors differently in your school? If you are a school counselor, what are your feelings about working with the changes Amber suggests? Are there other responsibilities you think could support your school better?

2. Each of the items on the following page is a step Amber took to develop trusting professional relationships with staff. Read each one and respond by writing how this looks in your practice if you are a school counselor. If you are a member of the staff, how does your school counselor perform?

(Continued)

(Continued)

a. **First be observant of others and your surroundings.** Take time to observe your environment and the dynamics that are at play. By lending a hand to assist my fellow co-workers, I was able to observe their personal style and learned their strengths. I also observed the students in a variety of settings. I soon learned who I needed to check in with and give them that extra support and positive cheerful reminder that today was going to be a great day for them. I was a visible presence—stopping in classrooms to watch them work, walking around the playground and lunchroom. I was there throughout their day to reinforce support.

   How do you (or how does your school's school counselor make himself or herself) observe students in a variety of ways?

b. **Be visible and available.** Although I was taken back a bit at first by "all my assigned duties," I had to learn to leverage these moments to build effective relationships. The playground provided many teachable moments. When conflicts arose, I could help students resolve their problems before situations escalated to a physical fight. There were fewer fights and referrals to the principal's office. In my students' eyes, I must have been very skilled at this as I was soon promoted from being a well-respected lunch lady to be the principal in just a few short weeks. Now when students needed me, they called me "principal."

   If you inform staff or students that you are going to do something for or with them, keep your word, especially with children. So many children have been let down by adults in their life; building a foundation of trust and being reliable is very important. We retraumatize or validate their trauma when we aren't careful.

   How visible are you or how visible is your school counselor throughout the day? Would you be willing to invite your counselor to come and observe your students while you are teaching? Would you be receptive if he or she noted some of your behaviors might be getting in the way?

   Would you be willing to explore your teaching or collegial challenges with your school counselor? Explain.

c. **Interact with the staff often; if you are new to a building, introduce yourself in as many ways as possible.** As teachers began to get to know me, I asked for some classroom time to introduce myself to their students and I explained the role and responsibility of a school social worker. I was someone that students could talk to, someone to help them with solving problems or to stand up to bullies, and to teach about how to be their best self and help them learn the behaviors needed to be a successful student. I was able to get into classrooms and teach a socioemotional curriculum.

   In what ways do you interact with staff or in what ways does your school counselor interact with staff?

d. **Successful relationship building is about verbal and nonverbal communication.** We must be genuine, kind, nonjudgmental, and empathetic and utilize appropriate voice volume and touch. Children know when you are sincere and care about them; they are often looking for positive affirmation and confirmation. The adults have the same need. They need opportunities to be heard and have someone to process with who isn't in an evaluative position. I was the neutral party and because of my training, confidentiality is a given. Make every day filled with meaningful connections; not only will your students benefit from this effort but you will be fulfilled as well. I enjoyed my work and everyone could see and feel it. I was living my dream.

   How do you foster relationships with staff, students, and families or how does your school counselor foster relationships with staff, students, and families?

Toolkit Takeaways

1. The foundations for establishing and maintaining authentic relationships with students and colleagues are Talk, Trust, Feel, and Repair. When school staff are open and listen without judging, students will share their feelings. Consistently applying trauma-informed strategies builds and sustains trust.

2. The response to intervention model (RTI) can easily be adapted to a trauma-informed, three-tiered behavior intervention system.

3. In a trauma-informed RTI behavior intervention model, the roles of staff and how students are served change. Tier I: General Education teachers are responsible for teaching a socioemotional curriculum and providing students with daily practice and application. Tier II: School counselors, school-based social workers, special education teachers, and behavior specialists teach targeted interventions to small groups. Tier III: Special education teachers and behavior specialists teach in smaller ratios; licensed therapists provide counseling. School counselors, school nurses, and school psychologists coordinate services with health care providers and community agencies. School counselors provide ongoing professional development to help teachers implement socioemotional curriculum consistently at each grade level.

4. Trauma-informed strategies like mindful minutes, yoga stretches, a cool down space within the classroom, and deep breathing exercises help students regulate their emotions. A Ready to Learn room is available for students who need time out of the classroom.

5. Schools and classrooms have a culture. Culture is composed of shared beliefs, perceptions, language, attitudes, behaviors, written and unwritten rules, and values. School and classroom culture can be taught and applied daily. Socioemotional curriculum should be the foundation for classroom-management systems. PBIS supplements an effective socioemotional curriculum well.

6. Using a learning taxonomy like Bloom's to explain teacher and student behaviors makes the teaching or learning process relevant. Coupled with school staff giving explicit feedback that supports growth mindset is a powerful trauma-informed strategy because it reinforces school culture is about learning.

7. Administrative leadership matters. If an ineffective principal is approachable, teacher-leaders can lend support and guidance. If a principal is not approachable, pursue the options that are available in your system. Remember, what you do is a major factor in determining the trajectory of a child's life.

Plan With the End in Mind

Visioning a Compassionate School

We can, whenever and wherever we choose, successfully teach all children whose schooling is of interest to us. We already know more than we need to do that. Whether or not we do it must finally depend on how we feel about the fact that we haven't so far.

—Ronald R. Edmonds,
Researcher of Effective Schools

Anticipated Outcomes

Readers will

○ be exposed to a fictional school district's strategic plan to become a culturally responsive and emotionally safe school system for all employees, students, and families,

○ compare their current practice and actions to trauma-informed dos and don'ts,

○ respond to stems asking for evidence of socioemotional actions and reactions in the presence of their students.

THE INNOVATIVE SCHOOL DISTRICT PREK-12TH GRADES

Three years ago, the Innovative School District in Anytown, Anystate, embarked on a bold journey to increase its graduation rates, close achievement gaps, increase academic rigor, and improve working conditions for all employees. The district was determined to align its respective daily practices with its mission and vision statements, which promised to *provide a caring and collaborative learning environment ensuring each student achieves intellectual and personal excellence and is college, career, and culturally ready by 12th grade.*

Using the same financial resources but in different ways and having more intentional engagement with outside **community agencies** and union support, the district created a five-year strategic plan. But, after three years, the data are already showing the district made the right decision. During the first year, district administrators in every department, principals, and school-based staff at every grade level read *Building Resilience in Students Impacted by Adverse Childhood Experiences: A Whole-Staff Approach.*

After much discussion and processing, administrators decided that all employees, in general, and instructional staff in particular, would benefit from being informed about the effects of adverse childhood experiences. Based on their reading and further research, the assumption was there were adult employees who were survivors of ACEs and perhaps struggling in some way that might be impacting their job performance. The teaching and learning department was given the task to create professional development workshops for all of the district's departments like transportation, food services, and human resources. The counseling department, which included **school psychologists**, redefined its job descriptions and identified outside resources to support staff, students, and families. They were also instrumental in developing self-care templates for employees. All employees are now required to add a goal for self-care in their annual evaluation.

Another major decision was to provide professional development for all Innovatives schools regardless of socioeconomic levels or ethnic demographics. Surprisingly, some of the parents in the middle-class and wealthier areas needed persuading. Many changed their opinions when the district shared data about what is happening in comparable schools around the country. The goal was to get at the *heart* of teaching and learning for all students.

Using a **trainer-of-trainer** model, each district department—academic, facilities, human resources, food services, for example—designated one or two staff members whose responsibility was to participate on an equity and access committee. The designee serves as a conduit between his or her department and the newly formed equity and access committee they named Milestones. They selected the name *Milestones* to reflect the change in how they monitored student progress. Now, in addition to monitoring student achievement on academic standards, they use benchmarks to measure socioemotional development.

The Milestones committee is under the umbrella of the special services department. The special services department is the result of merging two departments—counseling and special education. As suggested in *Building Resilience in Students Impacted by Adverse Childhood Experiences: A Whole-Staff Approach*, the roles of certificated **school counselors**, school psychologists, and special education staff, especially those with expertise in behavior disorders, have changed.

School counselors and special education teachers teach Tier II and III students. The school psychologists (and LCSW social workers) provide comprehensive mental and behavior health services for the same groups. At the Tier II and III levels, school psychologists use **culturally and linguistically psychological assessments** that are appropriate for intellectual and problem-solving skills to ensure behaviors do not interfere with academic expectations.

School counselors, school psychologists, and special education staff also provide advisory support for general education teachers on intervention strategies and creating restorative conversations. School counselors, school psychologists, and special education teachers are the primary experts in trauma-informed care. They are in the best position to stay current with the latest research in their respective fields and then work with educators in the teaching and learning department to prepare ways to share with general education practitioners and other staff via the Milestones committee.

Together, combining Bonnie Benard's Resiliency Framework with their district's socioemotional curriculum as guides, this district-level team is responsible for

- providing ongoing professional development about trauma-informed care and building resiliency for all staff (including bus drivers, grounds crews, and food service staff) in all district departments and school buildings;

- providing direct services such as support and modeling for general education teachers needing professional help with implementing trauma-informed strategies;

- maintaining a wellness plan and program for all district employees;

- helping school-based socioemotional teams with intervention planning;

- acting as a resource for school counselors, school psychologists, special education teachers, and **social workers** assigned at the building level;

- networking with community mental health agencies to provide additional services for families;

- monitoring the placement and progress for the district's Tier III students;

- networking with school nurses and community physical health agencies to provide services for Tier III students with preexisting mental disorders (e.g., hypothyroidism, autism spectrum disorder, bipolar disorder, chronic anxiety);

- convening the Milestones committee to monitor the "health" of the new system and reporting to the superintendent;

At the building level, the principal is the primary leader, responsible for making sure the school's culture, expressed in their Tier I socioemotional curriculum, is a culturally responsive and emotionally safe place for teachers to teach and students to learn. The principal is responsive to the needs of all the adults and students. He or she supervises a school-based version of a Milestones team. Members on this team include school counselors, school psychologists, special education staff, grade-level representatives or department leads (at middle and high school), and school nurses.

School counselors and special education teachers serve in three capacities. They teach, provide ongoing professional development updates, and monitor the socioemotional progress of Tier II and III students.

School counselors and special education teachers collaborate with general education teachers to create behavior plans for all Tier II students. Because of their expertise in the behavior health sciences, they now teach socioemotional skills in a model similar to ELL and remedial pull-out classes. They also team with school psychologists and LCSW social workers to create intervention plans for students in Tier III. Intervention plans align appropriate trauma-informed strategies with the behavior need.

School counselors and special education staff follow up on district-directed professional development organized by the Milestone committee and provide ongoing support for the adult learners. Teachers and instructional support staff invite them into their rooms to observe how well they are integrating socioemotional competencies into their language and actions. They use the SEL Data Team/Self-Assessment Checklist to give teachers and instructional support staff explicit feedback.

SEL DATA TEAM/SELF-ASSESSMENT CHECKLIST

How to use:

This checklist can be used several ways.

Teachers can self-assess their respective classroom management and instructional practice.

School counselors can use it to coach instructional staff implementing Tier I socioemotional curriculum. Administrators can use it as a tool to evaluate buildingwide Tier I socioemotional structures.

Data teams and professional learning communities (PLCs) review grade-level or department implementation of socioemotional curriculum.

SEL Standards:

o   Self-awareness (SfA)

o   Social awareness (ScA)

o   Self-management (SM)

- Relationship skills (RS)
- Responsible decision-making (RDM)

Evidence for checklist through:

- classroom observations or walk-thru
- review of lesson plans and materials
- teacher–student interviews
- teacher–student surveys
- observations of schoolwide gatherings (town hall meetings, hallways, etc.)

Questions to consider:

- Are we successfully incorporating SEL standards into the school environment and classroom?
- Are students aware of and meeting SEL standards?
- Are faculty and staff enforcing SEL standards through daily lessons, interactions, and norms?
- Are we preparing students with the social skills and management needed for real-word experiences, interactions, and responsibilities?

SEL Data–Checklist

Teacher/Counselor: _____

Observer: _____

Subject Area: _____   Grade Level: _____   Date: _____

Indicators	Sufficient Evidence	Some Evidence	Little or No Evidence	Notes of Evidence and Ways to Improve
Provides consistent structure and clear expectations for appropriate behavior (ScA, SM, RS, RDM)				
Use of affirming, encouraging language (SfA, ScA, SM)				
Staff uses proximity, choices, deescalation techniques (SM, SfA, ScA, RDM, RS)				
Peer editing and feedback (ScA, SA)				
Upholding school norms (ScA, SfA, SM, RS, RDM)				
Students making personal connections to content (SfA)				
Students write or discuss personal reflections on behavior, content, or work habits (SfA)				
Giving student options (SfA, SM, RDM)				
Students are aware of and track own academic progress (SfA, SM)				
Student reflections based on behavior and decisions (SfA, RDM)				
Calendars and syllabus—students aware of upcoming assignments and expectations (SM)				
Organization systems for students (SM)				
Teaching of group work—norms, roles, etc. (RS)				
Environment open to questions and feedback (RS)				

Indicators	Sufficient Evidence	Some Evidence	Little or No Evidence	Notes of Evidence and Ways to Improve
Students evaluate different decisions (RDM)				
Student equity—engage and involve all students, ensure all students participate (SfA, ScA)				
Students held accountable for actions—reasonable or progressive consequences (SfA, SM, RDM)				
Counselor–teacher communication (SfA, RS)				
Creates a high-quality academic or professional environment and challenges students to act accordingly (ScA, SM) including* ○ Appropriate language (diction/grammar) ○ Students speak in turn and respect the speaker ○ Monitoring volume and movement ○ Appropriate questions and feedback ○ "Looking like a serious student": posture, wearing hoods, feet up, etc. *may be evident through staff's communication and implementation of verbal and physical "code-switching"; students aware of time and place for everything				
Staff addresses school norms outside of classroom ○ hallways ○ lunch ○ outings ○ evening programming				

Source: Graham (2018)

School counselors and special education staff monitor the discipline data and report to the school's Milestone team. The school-based Milestone committee uses data and a flowchart to determine if a student needs to be moved from Tier I to Tier II or III and vice versa as behaviors improve.

Lastly, school counselors and special education staff oversee the operation of the Ready to Learn Room (RTL). The RTL is a welcoming space where students can decompress after a behavior disruption and problem-solve. Students rest first to help return to a calm state so they can reflect upon their thinking. Students will process, with a trained noncertified staff member (e.g., teachers' aide, paraprofessional, instructional assistant), describe the incident from their point of view, what they could have done differently, and what they can do in the future if faced with a similar situation. Before returning to class, RTL staff help students create plans for having restorative conversations if other classmates or adults were involved. All **general education staff** members know, because of the process in the RTL, when students return to their classroom, they are ready to be productive participants. General education teachers also understand they must prepare for a restorative conversation with the student to repair their relationship. After two years of guided practice, many schools in the Innovative School District are finding general education teachers are becoming more skillful and able to have these conversations without the assistance of their principal or counseling staff.

When a behavior disruption involves a staff member, the principal provides an opportunity for them to also decompress. She will have another staff member continue instruction for a brief period of time. The principal and staff member plan a restorative conversation and schedule a time for the meeting. The teacher or student can ask any staff member to observe the restorative conversation. If the incident happened in the presence of other students, the principal will arrange for a school counselor or special education teacher to debrief with the class.

All of the students, PreK–12th grades, enrolled in the Innovative School District are in general education classes. Gone are self-contained special education classrooms for students diagnosed as having behavior disorders. In its place is a strong Tier I socioemotional development program that teaches values or working norms needed for a healthy school culture and climate. These values or working norms are embedded in building and classroom routines and curriculum allowing students to apply positive behavior skills on a daily basis. Tier II and III students, who need more intensive socioemotional instructional time, are taught in small-group settings. Benchmarks are established and special services end once students successfully demonstrate socioemotional competencies.

At the elementary level, principals encourage master teachers to **loop** at least two years with the same students or form cross-grade instructional teams. At the middle and high school levels, principals encourage teachers to team and create extended blocks of instructional time to support developing authentic and supportive relationships with staff *and* students. Middle and high school students receive credit for service projects, mentoring, and tutoring younger students. These instructional strategies are especially successful in schools with significant populations of distressed children like schools in low-income communities.

Students are exposed to careers beginning in PreK. Academic and socio-emotional skills are aligned with their respective career paths. For example, teaching students the skill of comparing and contrasting, a teacher shares with them that developing this thinking skill helps in debates, forensic sciences, and law. People who want to become lawyers or detectives must be able to regulate their emotions to see all sides of a situation and problem-solve. Some teachers have created bulletin boards illustrating how socioemotional and academic skills relate to certain occupations.

Career counselors are assigned to middle and high schools. At the high school level, they help monitor student credits, conduct workshops on complet-ing applications for postsecondary educational opportunities, and organize career fairs. By junior year, each student has a postsecondary plan. During their senior year, they are able to intern or apprentice in a variety of career paths.

In three short years, the Innovative School District (ISD) is well on the way to *providing a caring and collaborative learning environment ensuring each student achieves intellectual and personal excellence and is college, career, and culturally ready by 12th grade.*

As a district, ISD is equally committed to providing a caring and supportive working environment for its staff. The Innovative School District is on a mission to heal itself.

Read, Reflect, Respond

1. Use Benard's Framework for building resiliency and, following the coding, find examples in the Innovative School District that illustrate the descriptors below:

SOCIAL COMPETENCE	PROBLEM-SOLVING
○ Responsiveness—R ○ Cultural flexibility—CF ○ Empathy—E ○ Caring—C ○ Communication skills—CS ○ Sense of humor—SoH	○ Planning—P ○ Help-seeking—HS ○ Critical and creative thinking—CCT
AUTONOMY	SENSE OF PURPOSE
○ Sense of identity—SOI ○ Self-efficacy—S-E ○ Self-awareness—S-A ○ Task-mastery—T-M ○ Adaptive distancing from negative messag-es and conditions—AD	○ Goal direction—GD ○ Educational aspirations—EA ○ Optimism—O ○ Faith/spiritual connection—F/S

(Continued)

(Continued)

2. The Innovative School District (ISD) is a **turnaround** district driven by two values: There are no at-risk students and all staff deserve a stress-free, supportive working environment. Evidence-based policies and procedures are created based on the latest scientific research about the resiliency all humans have. Subsequently, the ISD has created environmental resources to support its staff, students, and their families to align with their innate need for *love and belonging, mastery, power, and meaning,* the building blocks of resiliency (Baumeister & Leary, 1995; Edelstein, 2012; Frankl, 2008; Maslow, Frager, Fadiman, McReynolds, & Cox, 1987). Complete the following chart with examples from the Innovative School District.

Resiliency Building Blocks	Staff	Students
Love and Belonging—innate desire for interpersonal connections		
Mastery—innate desire to feel competent, successful		
Power—innate desire to feel in control of self		
Meaning—innate desire to make sense of situations, need to make judgments or decisions		

Adapted from Maslow et al. (1987), Edelstein (2012), Frankl (2008).

3. Read the following Parker Palmer quote. What's your reaction to his statement?

"If we want to grow as teachers—we must do something alien to academic culture: we must talk to each other about our inner lives—risky stuff in a profession that fears the personal and seeks safety in the technical, the distant, the abstract."

—Parker J. Palmer,
The Courage to Teach: Exploring the
Inner Landscape of a Teacher's Life

Ricky Robertson, Behavior Specialist

CASE STUDY: ISD'S RESPONSE TO BEHAVIOR INTERVENTIONS

Jordan

We will explore the story of one student and how he was supported by his school's three tiers of trauma-informed practice. Our student is Jordan. Jordan was a 16-year-old, multiracial student of Latino and African Caribbean decent. He had a history of gaps in his education due to chronic absenteeism, exclusionary discipline, and incarceration. He had transferred from two previous high schools before arriving at our school.

Fortunately, Jordan was now attending a school whose staff had received extensive professional development on ACEs and trauma-informed practices. Every staff person, from the custodian to the principal, had been trained in a relationship-based response to trauma. They had acquired valuable skills for deescalation, behavioral supports, trauma-sensitive instruction, and ways to connect with students that built belonging and trust. Together they wove this approach into the fundamental culture and day-to-day operations of the school.

Exploring Tier 1 With Jordan

Every morning when Jordan arrived at school, he was greeted, like all of his fellow students, at one of the entrances of the school by a member of the staff. This was an opportunity to both be welcomed into the building and, if needed, talk with an adult. Jordan then went to the cafeteria where his school offered a free breakfast program.

Staff were encouraged to join students for breakfast, not simply to monitor the cafeteria, but also to sit, eat, and talk with students at the start of the day. The cafeteria also had a pool table, piano, chess/checkers boards, and a ping pong table that students could access using tickets that they had earned for exhibiting positive behavior, resiliency, or growth mindset.

The school viewed the free breakfast program, pool table, and games as components of its trauma-informed approach. The breakfast program met the students' physiological needs thereby helping them to be ready to learn. While the pool table and games reinforced positive behavior, they gave students opportunities to have fun in safe and healthy ways. Many of the school's students who had experienced trauma and ACEs had been robbed of such opportunities in their childhoods. For Jordan, he had rarely been on time at his previous schools. However, he now looked forward to arriving at school to have breakfast and play pool.

At the first bell, Jordan would go to class. As was a common practice at the school, teachers greeted their students at the door of their classroom at the start of each period. Most of Jordan's teachers began their classes with a brief warm-up activity or check-in that allowed them to take the temperature of the room and engage their students on a personal and academic level.

Trauma-sensitive instruction and classroom management were common in all classrooms. Teachers had clear, consistent expectations and routines. Teachers used verbal and nonverbal cues to help students redirect their attention, prepare for a transition, or manage their current state of emotional arousal. Space and time were given to practice self-regulation techniques such as a mindful minute, stretch breaks, deep breathing, fidgets, or other sensory supports. To alleviate anxiety and foster motivation, assessments, grades, and other indicators of student progress were discussed using the language of growth mindset, honoring the power of "not yet."

Behavioral challenges were handled in a communication style similar to coaching, which honored students' autonomy while holding them accountable to their goals and the expectations of the classroom community. More significant behavioral issues were addressed using restorative practices such as repair circles. The school fostered culture of accountability that encouraged both staff and students to acknowledge when they had not upheld an expectation of the community, accept responsibility for the impact of their behavior, and make an effort to repair harm, or accept a consequence.

Jordan's teachers had taken time to get to know him and his classmates. They had spoken with him individually, not just about school, but about his life. He had been given opportunities to express himself through different projects and activities. He was shocked and then engaged when his teachers openly spoke about culture, race, differing identities, even bias and discrimination. Jordan felt that he had been racially stereotyped at his previous schools but it had been impossible to confront this injustice when none of his teachers spoke honestly about these realities. Having open conversations about privilege, power, culture, and identity helped him to trust his new teachers.

Jordan most enjoyed his third-period advisory class. Every Monday and Friday, the advisory class had circle time. Everyone in the class sat in a circle while the teacher or a student facilitated a class discussion. Sometimes the circles were lighthearted and positive, like the time when they each complimented the person sitting next to them. Other times, circles were a way to check in about goals for the week, resolve conflicts, or discuss issues that were impacting the school community. The other days of the week usually focused on skills that were needed for success in school and life, which could range from getting organized to managing difficult emotions.

Sometimes issues would arise in a circle meeting that would become a theme for that week—for example, after a number of students were arrested for possession of narcotics at a weekend party. One advisory class spent the week discussing substance abuse, addiction, and harm reduction. They made signs that were displayed around the school raising awareness about substance abuse among teens and ways to seek help. This was a way for the students to process the collective impact of the arrests while fostering self-advocacy.

Each advisory also adopted a community service project each month. The students would participate in raising funds for a charity, volunteering, or any number of ways to lend their help. This empowered many students to see themselves as capable of making a difference. Jordan was proud when his advisory class made cards for children in the cancer ward of a local hospital, which was a project that he had suggested.

Jordan's favorite day at his new school was the beginning of the year field day. The school had partnered with a local nonprofit to host a field day at an outdoor adventure course. The adventure course had a number of activities that required students to work together in teams. The school scheduled events throughout the school year to foster a sense of fun and community. This focus carried over to the schools' outreach to families. Every quarter, the school hosted a family night that included a potluck, childcare, and a presentation for parents on a topic selected by the school's parent advisory council. The school also made its building space available to community nonprofits that hosted events to assist families in matters ranging from parenting classes to learning English.

From the school's perspective, hosting events that were fun, relevant, and community focused strengthened its relationship with students and families, thereby supporting its academic, attendance, and behavioral initiatives. After all, students and families are much more likely to embrace and shape the goals, values, and expectations of a school when they feel valued, cared for, and connected. This is especially true for families impacted by trauma, poverty, and other stressors.

It is all too common for families enduring hardships to experience school as a source of stress and failure rather than a source of support. In Jordan's case, having moved from school to school, there was no way that he would adopt the expectations of his new school and strive to meet them, unless the school did the work of bringing him into their community. The school found that activities like circles, class meetings, and family nights were just as valuable as water balloon fights in helping students let down their guard, connect with teachers and classmates, and embrace the culture and values of the school.

Despite all of these efforts, Jordan's behavior communicated to the staff that he was in need of additional support. The first incident occurred in Jordan's science class when his teacher asked him to put away his cellphone. At first, Jordan ignored his teacher's request. The teacher approached Jordan and made the request again. Jordan snapped. He flipped his desk, got in the teacher's face, and cursed him out before storming out of the classroom and leaving school grounds. Unfortunately, this escalation was the first in a pattern of outbursts that rapidly increased in frequency and intensity. It soon got to the point where Jordan's aggressive outbursts became a daily occurrence, often making it impossible to teach with him in the classroom.

Exploring Tier II With Jordan

Jordan's science teacher referred Jordan to the school's student intervention team. The team was composed of the dean, school counselor, assistant principal, behavior specialist, special education teacher, school nurse, and the student's teachers. Depending on the case, the team may also invite the parents, the student, and any other service providers, community members, or persons directly involved in supporting the student's success in school. Upon reviewing Jordan's case, the team made recommendations for Tier II supports while also determining that, due to the severity of his behaviors, an individualized Tier III plan needed to be developed for Jordan.

Because of Jordan's age, the team felt that it was especially important that Jordan have a say in the intervention process. Incorporating his perspective would be valuable in developing a partnership with him in improving his behavior and addressing the underlying needs that they expressed. As the school's behavior specialist, I met with Jordan. He was initially defensive and uninterested in talking with me. He felt that his teachers and classmates were disrespectful toward him and were ultimately to blame for his aggressive behaviors. However, his attitude changed after I acknowledged that his anger and frustration were completely valid. I also reiterated that our meeting was in no way punitive but an opportunity to talk and, hopefully, to partner in helping him to meet his goals. We then talked about what his goals were and I wrote them down as a way to focus our future work together. I asked his permission to offer suggestions of ways that the school could support him.

I presented Jordan with the recommendations of our Tier II team and asked for his feedback. First, Jordan was invited to choose someone on the staff to act as his mentor. He would check in with this person at the beginning and end of each school day. They would set goals together, celebrate his successes, and work through challenges. Jordan chose the custodian to be his mentor because he enjoyed playing pool with him.

At Jordan's school, the mentorship program was reserved as a Tier II intervention and the student was given the opportunity to select a mentor. At an elementary school that I worked with, every staff person picked five students to take on as mentees. A student could remain as a mentee anywhere from one quarter to the entire school year. If, after a quarter, it was decided that a student could be successful without the support of a mentor, then that student was graduated from the program, awarded with a certificate, and that spot was given to another student. This process embedded the mentorship relationship as part of the school culture and made it accessible to a large number of students. Regardless of how the program is organized, I have found that having some mentorship or relationship-based intervention is vital to supporting student success, especially for students impacted by ACEs and trauma.

Jordan had also been invited to attend a weekly small group facilitated by the school counselor that focused on anger management strategies. Jordan admitted that he had issues with anger but he truly felt that others were to blame, so he declined the invitation. I suggested another group that the school counselor offered on overcoming adversity. From what Jordan had said, it sounded like he was facing a lot of negativity from the people around him. I didn't go into detail but this group was a resiliency-building group that employed trauma-focused cognitive behavioral therapy (TF-CBT). Jordan liked the idea of this group and agreed to attend.

Finally, we discussed electives for the following quarter. When the school had adopted a trauma-informed framework, it redesigned its elective course offerings. The administration asked teachers to think about subjects that they were passionate about and then connect them to the needs of their students. As a result, teachers came up with classes on topics including social justice movements, sustainable living, healthy relationships, and nonviolent communication. They then tailored these classes to be relevant to the needs and interests of the students.

For example, the nonviolent communication curriculum was embedded within a career skills class. In this career and technical education (CTE) course, students learned communication skills to resolve conflicts in the workplace, accept feedback from a supervisor, and incorporate multiple perspectives, while also learning how to write a resume, interview for a job, and uphold standards of professionalism. When discussing his goals, Jordan had mentioned that he wanted to get a job because his family needed an extra source of income. We agreed that this course would be a perfect fit for him.

Since the student intervention team had also recommended Tier III supports, I set aside time in my schedule to observe Jordan in his classes. When working with younger students or with an entire class that is struggling with behavior, I am less likely to let the students know why I am conducting an observation. However, because of Jordan's age, he would certainly suspect something if he saw me in his classes. Therefore, in the interest of building trust, I felt that it was better to let him know the purpose of my observations. I explained to him that, based on my observations, I would offer suggestions to him and his teachers on ways to better work together. In particular, I promised to address his concerns about respect. I wanted Jordan to walk away from the meeting understanding that I was both an advocate for him and a coach encouraging him to be his best self.

Exploring Tier III With Jordan

The Tier III domain is challenging when doing trauma-informed work because there is never going to be a clear path for a school to follow. Rather, it is often a time we have to work together to create the path. The journey may begin with a trauma-informed behavior intervention plan. However, we may then discover factors that require us to extend beyond the school to seek support from other professionals and community organizations.

For Jordan, our first step in the Tier III process was to conduct classroom observations to identify his behaviors and the factors that contributed to them. When I conduct classroom observations, I think of it as a trauma-informed functional behavior assessment. In other words, I look for the antecedent, behavior, and consequence while also considering factors directly related to trauma and resiliency. In making recommendations to teachers, I reflect on Bonnie Bernard's Resiliency Framework (Benard, 1991b) as well as trauma-informed best practices, such as our Trauma Dos and Don'ts.

In my observations of Jordan's classes, I noted a number of highly successful interactions between Jordan and his teachers. There were several times that Jordan's teachers praised his effort, challenged him to do better, and successfully redirected his behavior. I also found areas that we could work on. In some classes, there were simple actions we were able to take that improved Jordan's behavior. For example, Jordan's science class was the one classroom where he sat with his back to the door. I observed that every few minutes Jordan looked over his shoulder at the doorway. For some reason this seemed to contribute to his anxiety. We asked Jordan if he would like to move his desk. He chose a spot where he could view both the teacher and the doorway. His demeanor became much calmer as a result and he was generally less agitated in that class.

For other classes, we needed to do deeper work and focus on the primary point of intervention for ACEs students, the teacher–student relationship. Naturally, Jordan's problematic behaviors had negatively impacted his relationship with some of his teachers. Understandably, it is hard to hold a student in positive regard after he has repeatedly cursed at you or even threatened you.

As Jordan's social studies teachers said, "I can't teach with him in my room." Unfortunately, the teacher's statement is correct. Once we, as educators, have labeled a student as the problem, then there is no way for us to teach that student. Instead, we have to focus on the specific behaviors and the causes of that behavior, otherwise we risk losing the student entirely.

When working with Jordan's social studies teacher, I needed to first give him the opportunity to vent—just like Jordan, he needed an empathic ear to listen to the insults, frustrations, and challenges he had endured. His anger was valid and yet we still had to return to our shared goal: supporting Jordan to be successful in his class. With some effort, we were able to narrow down the specific behaviors that had the greatest negative impact on the class. I learned that Jordan had gotten in the habit of regularly cursing at his teacher and, on more than one occasion, had threatened his life. The teacher admitted that he had acted unprofessionally toward Jordan. At times, he had engaged Jordan sarcastically and made belittling comments that had provoked some of his worst outbursts. We agreed that things had gotten so toxic that perhaps it was best to create an alternative schedule for Jordan.

According to this new schedule, Jordan would attend all direct instruction in class. During independent work, he would have the option to complete his work in the library. Near the end of the period, he would check in with the teacher to review his work. Jordan would have this option in social studies and his other classes, according to his teacher's discretion.

The social studies teacher felt supported by this change in Jordan's schedule, which allowed us to then focus on the most important issue, restoring the teacher–student relationship. The teacher agreed to increase the amount of positive praise directed at Jordan, aiming for a ratio of 5 positives for every 1 redirection. He also agreed to look for ways to redirect Jordan's behavior that avoided power struggles by giving him options when possible and also giving him space after a redirection. Perhaps most importantly, he agreed to self-monitor his own level of arousal in order to determine if he was able to engage with Jordan effectively or if he needed to call the office for support.

The alternative schedule had an almost immediate effect on Jordan's behavior. The opportunity to complete work in the library gave Jordan the space he needed to manage his anxiety. However, we still needed a consistent plan for how to handle his escalations when they occurred. I felt that the best tool for this would be a behavior response script. The script would map out Jordan's escalation cycle and provide suggestions to staff for how to effectively deescalate him at each level of arousal.

In collaboration with Jordan's teachers, we drafted a behavior response script. We mapped the pattern of Jordan's escalation ranging from Level 1 Ready to Learn to Level 5 Aggression. We described what each level of escalation looked like in terms of Jordan's behavior and identified strategies that teachers had found successful in helping Jordan to deescalate. For example, at Level 4 Anger Jordan was usually anxious, fidgety, and making loud negative comments. The best strategies for Level 4 were either a quiet, empathic one-on-one conversation or a nonverbal cue for Jordan to take a break and get a drink of water.

A month after implementation, we saw a significant improvement in Jordan's behavior and decrease in the frequency and severity of his escalations. The behavior response script was successful because it got staff on the same page, thereby improving the effectiveness of the invention by increasing the fidelity and consistency of its implementation. The effectiveness of Tier III interventions is often compromised when staff members respond differently to a student's behavior. Staff can react to a student's behavior in ways that inadvertently reinforce it. As a result, some students will learn to manipulate certain staff members based upon their reactions, which can cause division among staff and worsen student behavior. In Jordan's case, when his escalations became unsafe for him to remain in the classroom, staff now knew the most effective response. And, for Jordan, knowing what to expect from staff helped to reinforce healthy boundaries and provided a consistency that calmed him.

As we worked with Jordan, we learned more about him and the adverse experiences that he had endured prior to coming to our school. One of the most traumatic events occurred during the summer, when he and his best friend were leaving a party. The two young men were confronted by members of a rival gang. A fight broke out between them that ended when one of the rival gang's members shot Jordan's best friend in the head at pointblank range. Everyone dispersed, leaving Jordan with his dying friend.

Jordan admitted that in the weeks following his friend's murder he was unable to sleep through the night. He had nightmares and flashbacks. He was overcome with fear, grief, and rage. He admitted that he had retaliated against the rival gang. He did not tell us specifics but said only that there was now a very real and constant threat to his own life.

We realized that Jordan's behavior was likely a manifestation of PTSD. We began to see how his anxiety, hypervigilance, and aggressive outbursts were all directly related to his trauma and the ongoing threat against his life. This became particularly evident one day when Jordan was walking into his math class and a student accidentally bumped into him. Jordan pushed the student into a row of desks and then threatened to "f-n' kill him." What happened next was unlike what we had seen during his previous escalations. Almost immediately, Jordan stopped, looked around and said, "I'm so sorry. I didn't mean to do that. I know it scared you. I take full responsibility." This incident had us realize that Jordan was not in full control of his behavior and we were not going to be able to manage it on our own either. This put us squarely in the Tier III domain, *having to create the path*.

For Jordan's behavior, we were going to need support outside of school. We invited Jordan's parents to our student intervention team meetings. Working with his family, we connected Jordan to a mental health counselor. The counselor eventually worked with Jordan's doctor, who prescribed **psychotropic medications** to help with Jordan's anxiety and PTSD-related symptoms.

Our staff received a brief training, delivered by a psychiatric nurse, on PTSD as well as related treatments and medications. We had undergone similar trainings when we had students with significant medical conditions. The school administration felt that it was equally important for staff to understand how to appropriately respond to both physical and psychological illnesses, since they can both significantly impact a student's health, safety, and performance in school. The training helped to destigmatize Jordan's struggle and gave staff a valuable opportunity to talk about supporting and respecting the needs of our students who suffer from mental illness.

We also got creative in formulating Jordan's intervention plan. Jordan's family had expressed concern that their son had become increasingly isolated since the death of his friend. They felt that his aggressive behavior was linked to the fact that he now spent most of his time at home alone. When he did leave the house, it was usually with friends who were not a good influence on him. We decided to look for a way to break up this cycle of isolation and negative peer interaction by finding a positive way for Jordan to spend his time. We knew that Jordan loved animals. We contacted the local zoo and enrolled Jordan, with his whole-hearted endorsement, in a volunteer program for teens.

We also reached out to the local community college. Initially, our hope had been to connect Jordan with an admissions counselor who could help him to envision a future beyond gang life. Fortuitously, we ended up talking with an admissions counselor who just so happened to have been a gang member in his youth. Now, he helped undocumented young people navigate the college admissions process.

The admissions counselor came to our school and gave a presentation to our students about community college. He also stayed to have lunch with Jordan. After meeting over lunch, the two learned that they had so much in common that they remained in contact. The admissions counselor became like a big brother to Jordan, checking in with him each week for the remainder of his high school career. Thanks to the collaborative efforts of the school staff, family, mental health providers, and community members, Jordan went on to improve, achieve, and graduate. We had gotten creative and we had created the path.

Read, Reflect, Respond

1. Make a list of your school's trauma-informed practices. Divide them up according to tiers, with Tier I being whole school, Tier II small group, and Tier III individual.
   a) Disaggregate the demographics for each tier by economic status.
   b) If your data is significantly disproportionate at Tiers II and III with students living in poverty, which you now know is an adverse childhood experience, what are some starter steps that you can take to reexamine how you are managing their behaviors?
2. What strategies from Jordan's story could you adopt in your classroom? In your school?

Amber Warner, LCSW

CHANGING POSITIONS TO CHANGE LIVES

It's Monday morning and I am meeting with the school's nurse, school counselor, and special education staff the first period of the day. Every third Monday and Tuesday, we meet to review the IEPs for our Tier III students to monitor their progress or lack of progress. We use a similar process for our Tier II students on the first Monday and Tuesday. Our main guiding question is: Is this student ready for time in a general education class? Fridays are for catching up on paperwork, contacting parents, preparing ongoing professional development tips for our weekly staff bulletin, networking with outside agencies, and rounding to see how well staff is implementing Tier I socioemotional strategies. I use the data to plan future professional development activities, and give teachers feedback. That is also a measure as to how much we trust each other—we assume positive intent and that has helped us become a professional community that values learning from each other. We are a continuous learning community.

We created an electronic rubric for the faculty to add input and this serves as the starting point for our discussion. Our goal is always to support Tier III students and increase their time in general education classes or special classes taught by both a general education and special education team. We no longer have self-contained classrooms for behavior disorders. Tier III students are a targeted group we focus on when monitoring our graduation rates.

In a high school of 1,400, there are seventy students at Tier III with varying challenging behaviors caused by chronic mental disorders. These students have been assessed for intellectual functioning to ensure their academic program maximizes their strengths. A few of these students are in a physics class taught by a general education teacher and special education teacher. The general education teacher delivers content while the special education teacher is there to help redirect behavior. Other Tier III students are taken off campus to work with animals in shelters. We have a dedicated paraprofessional who finds businesses willing to team with our special education staff. These classes are only four weeks in duration and taught by the same special education teacher. It's become very popular with our Tier III students. They must qualify, meaning they must show consistent improvement in their behavior, to be accepted.

For Tier III students on psychotropic medications, the nurse works collaboratively with physicians to monitor them for how well the medication is working and for side effects. I network with case managers at child protective services or welfare agencies to monitor open child abuse cases and our students in foster care.

Second period is planning time for all of us. I teach Talk, Trust, Feel, and Repair, or TTFR, classes for Tier II students at Level A during third, fourth, and sixth periods. Level A students are close to exiting our supplemental intervention and move to Tier I. The special education staff work with Tier II-Level B and III students. Time in Tier II-Level B and Tier III interventions ranges from two periods to four. Their remaining class time is spent in general education classes. Our mission is to increase general education class time, which reflects more of the world students live in when they graduate.

Students at Tier II-Level B are close to moving to Level A. In our previous model, these students were placed in self-contained special education classes for disruptive behaviors we didn't understand. Many would have ended up undereducated or dropouts. We now understand we weren't speaking the same language, that our students needed time to learn a new behavior language, and we needed to work on ours. They were giving up so much of themselves and we punished them for it.

My last period of the day is open for prearranged individual consultations with staff or students. Most times, I am a silent observer to a restorative conversation. Thanks to our principal, we have two dedicated substitute teachers in the building every day to provide coverage for staff who may want some planning or talk time with me.

The positive climate at Innovative High School is palatable. The work is still hard but manageable because we have supportive professional relationships and our students are responding positively. Since we began the process of becoming a trauma-informed high school, our students, their families, and the faculty are driven for success. At one time, we didn't engage our low-income families in ways they could support us or vice versa. When we didn't see them at PTA meetings, we said they didn't value education. We didn't see them as parents working two and three low-paying jobs just to make ends meet and that, in and of itself, *is* parental involvement. Now, there is a dedicated classroom furnished with couches, chairs, computers, and play area for toddlers. Volunteer parents, who are home during the day, walk the halls, sometimes pushing baby carriages, making sure students get to classes on time or they help update bulletin boards for staff. In the evening, community agencies like the YMCA and Goodwill provide classes in English, computer and reading literacy, art, music, parenting, and career development. It seemed once we created ways to support our families, the more they found ways and time to help us.

Our transition did not happen overnight. It took us three years to get to where we are today and based on the data we monitor, there is still room to grow. We spent our first year educating ourselves, like the other schools in our system, while doing our best to continue meeting the needs of our students. During the first year, we did establish a strong, buildingwide management system and taught students the needed classroom behaviors. We shared our vision with our students and families and did a needs-assessment survey. We were also able to focus our attention on our students with attendance and truancy issues.

This year, the number of our Tier I-level students ballooned to its highest numbers because our incoming ninth graders had begun learning from teachers practicing trauma-informed strategies in their middle-school classrooms. According to our most recent data assessing school climate for the adults, 89 percent of the faculty are extremely satisfied coming to work and the remaining are satisfied.

WHAT DOES IT MEAN TO WORK IN A TRAUMA-INFORMED SCHOOL OR SCHOOL DISTRICT?

> All individuals have the power to transform and change. Teachers and schools have the power to transform lives.
>
> —Bonnie Benard
> From Risk to Resiliency: What Schools Can Do

The HIV/AIDS epidemic of the mid-1980s impacted all of the professions where the possibility of direct contact with blood is a factor. Once it was known that the virus could be transmitted via broken skin or an open wound, protocols for protecting health care providers, police, dentists, emergency responders, athletes, and educators were put into place.

For educators, school districts created exposure control plans. Now bloodborne-pathogen training takes place annually and all staff members are required to put on latex gloves when helping the fifth grader with a bloody nose or the high school wrestler with a cut. There is no need to know which student is HIV positive because the change in practice covers all situations and needs.

If each PreK–12th-grade school staff member added trauma-informed strategies to his daily routines and practice, every child in the classroom would benefit. There is no need for all staff members to know which students are dealing with an emotional hardship. All students, from four years old to eighteen, would have an authentic relationship with their teachers and peers, experience academic and social success, engage in activities that build resiliency, and come to understand their education is preparing them for a future they cannot see. Because there are programs in place at each grade level, we increase the odds that they will stay in the system and graduate college, career, and culturally ready to take advantage of the wide array of postsecondary options. If students trust the adults in their schools and they are given examples of inappropriate physical and emotional behaviors, they will disclose.

Staff working in schools with large numbers of students in low-income communities have no choice but to add trauma-informed language and strategies to their daily routines. It is incumbent on staff in these schools to interpret inappropriate behaviors as messages, a form of communication, and create instructional settings modeled after ELL and Title I remedial programs. Poverty is an adverse childhood experience.

Changing the roles of school counselors, school psychologists, special education staff, and social workers to effectively use their therapeutic skills and expertise for redirecting disruptive behavior as an integral part of a student's socioemotional learning is not up to debate. As Ricky stated earlier, general education teachers and **support staff** are not therapists. However, when staff use trauma-informed strategies throughout the day, the number of Tier I students increases because these strategies provide learning environments that are consistent and feel emotionally safe. Everyone in the school, from the bus driver to the teaching staff, takes advantage of contact time with students. When the doors of the bus open, the driver is smiling and welcoming students as they climb aboard. When they drive them home after school, they check in and ask them how the day went. They remind them they will be there for them tomorrow. Teachers occasionally eat lunch with their students or allow them to come into their classrooms during noninstructional times. All staff members are invited to social gatherings. There are regular celebrations to showcase student growth. Everyone is focused on relating to each student and with each other.

The research is clear regarding the positive impact of a strong principal in schools with significantly large populations of low-income students. In these schools, academic outcomes increase under the leadership of effective principals (Branch, Hanushek, & Rivkin, 2013).

In our more middle-class and affluent schools, there is a need for school counselors, school psychologists, and social workers to provide therapeutic instruction for students and ongoing professional development for staff.

Educators who work with our more affluent families need to understand the psychology of behavioral and emotional issues like anxiety, suicide, eating disorders, mass murders, and bullying, which disproportionally affect these students. The ACEs these students bring to the classroom are often masked because our middle-class and affluent students come prepared to fit into school culture. They understand the norms of school culture and behave accordingly. They may perform well academically but mask if they are victims of sexual abuse, living with a drug-addicted family member, managing overscheduling pressures, or witnessing domestic violence. Educators are lulled into thinking these students are fine and attend solely to their academic needs.

Without a foundation of understanding students' emotional needs, our assumptions are shattered when a child brings a gun to school and uses it to harm others, or himself or herself. These students also need to be acknowledged by every staff member from the bus driver to the instructional staff. These students need and should have the same trauma-informed supports from PreK through 12th grades as their low-income counterparts. No child should spend years in our school systems feeling marginalized, as though no one sees them.

> *Actions prove who someone is; words just prove who they want to be.*
>
> —Aaryn Landers Lamb, Esq.
> Child custody and CPS litigation
> Dallas–Fort Worth, TX

When you are trauma informed, you are providing an alternate reality for a student for seven hours each day, 182 days each school year. It is a reality that tells each student *your today is not your future and your education is the most important thing you can do for your future. Each time your students master a skill, you can tell them that that knowledge is theirs to keep. No one can take it away.*

Read, Reflect, Respond

Trauma-Informed Dos

1. The chart shares some trauma-informed strategies and examples. In the second column, identify the closest resiliency descriptor using Benard's Framework. Use the same coding from your analysis of the Innovative School District. In the column on the right, insert how you use this or can use it in your respective role on a daily basis.

Trauma-Informed Dos	Resiliency Builder	Examples	My Practice
Develop caring and respectful relationships.		Share who you are and your goals for working with your students. With student input, define and delineate what respect looks like when teaching or learning and working in teams, for example.	
Do not take the student's behavior personally.		Remember, a student's behavior is a form of communication. Even if the student's anger is directed at you, it's not about you. Stay calm.	

Trauma-Informed Dos	Resiliency Builder	Examples	My Practice
Get to know student's interests, dreams, and gifts.		Create ways and opportunities for 1:1 conferences with students. For middle and high school staff, schedule time for meeting with each student, for example, each Friday. Use bulletin board space to highlight students' aspirations, poems, and raps, for example.	
Identify student's strengths and look for that special hook to connect.		Survey students; ask them to identify strengths. For PreK and K, call families and ask them.	
Always empower.		Learning is about effort and time on task. How long did it take for you to learn how to ride a bike? Use language that enables students to feel a sense of accomplishment.	
Affirm and provide hope for their future.		When you know your students' strengths or gifts, connect them to occupations (e.g., "You always want to know how things work; engineers are like that too!")	
Share what your job is about and the different behaviors students need to use to maximize learning.		Take the mystery out of what you do while sharing behaviors a learner needs to do. Share the dynamics of teaching and learning. Use a taxonomy like Bloom's to delineate teacher and student behaviors for each level of learning.	
Reframe negative language and give praise for making effort and perseverance.		When a student says, "I can't . . ." ask "What have you tried so far?" "Let me hear your thinking; maybe the trouble is there."	
Be consistent.		The consequences for inappropriate behaviors are posted and applied fairly. Students are encouraged to share if they feel they are being treated unfairly.	
Create an environment in which it is safe to take risks and actively participate.		Share with students that many inventions are the results of mistakes. Learning is "trial and error." Mistakes are part of learning.	
Establish routines and structure and prepare students for transitions.		Post daily agendas. Have specific times when students can sharpen pencils or collect homework, for example. Create call and response chants or signals for class attention.	

(Continued)

(Continued)

Trauma-Informed Dos	Resiliency Builder	Examples	My Practice
Deal with inappropriate behaviors by specifically labeling the behavior and why it doesn't work in a school setting.		"It's OK to be upset about something but not OK for you to overturn your desk. Can I get someone to help you clean up and you take a break? We can talk later."	
Know your emotional triggers.		If a student's or staff member's personality irritates you, try to reflect on why. If necessary, meet with a school counselor or school psychologist to help you understand why and how you can best work with this person.	
Be sensitive to cues: body language, unwarranted anger, or lashing out.		Create ways your students can express how they are feeling throughout the day or class period. For example, tape laminated mood expressions on each desk. Incorporate in morning routine, after lunch, and recesses the following question: Let me know if you are ready to learn by circling your Moodlet. For middle and high school students, just ask the question.	
Make learning fun and rigorous.		Know your content well. Throw in fun facts and anecdotal information. Make material come alive. Have students create plays, songs, and raps after history or science unit.	
Be aware of your body language.		Others can read frustration, irritability, or anger in our facial expressions and gestures.	
Don't get into argumentative debate.		Stay calm and actively listen. Acknowledge student's frustration and anger in a respectful way. Invite student to take a break in designated space in the room.	
Give students jobs and responsibilities.		There's much to do in prepping for class: collecting papers, taking attendance. Rotate responsibilities so all students have opportunity.	
Provide a time-out space in the classroom. Let students know they can use it when they feel the need.		Teach students what the space is for and how and when they can use it (whenever they need a break). Have them name the space.	

Trauma-Informed Dos	Resiliency Builder	Examples	My Practice
Create classroom values or norms and consequences with student input.		Use the words *values* or *working norms* instead of *rules*. Invite students to give input on dos and don'ts (for teacher and students) and post. Review values after long holiday breaks.	
Be aware of your biases; question yourself and self-reflect if certain personalities irritate you.		Track your own classroom data. Are you uncertain about managing the behaviors of some students and not others? Do some self-reflection and get support if needed (from a critical friend or a colleague who seems to be able to get along with most students).	
Find a critical friend at school or in your social network.		This is someone who can help you *think about your thinking* and help you process so that you can be a better you and better professional.	
When working with middle and high school students, be aware of professional and ethical boundaries, especially when dealing with students.		If you feel a student is crossing a boundary or you are, consult with guidance counseling staff or private therapist.	
When evaluating student work, give specific feedback on how student can improve.		Students need explicit feedback to correct their work. Vague phrases or plus and minus signs, for example, do not show how to correct.	
Make use of metaphors, similes, and comparisons to help students express feelings.		Integrate emotions as a topic when teaching figurative language. "When I am angry, I feel like _____ (name a fruit or vegetable)." "Happiness is like _____."	
Use the biographies of famous people who are ACEs survivors, such as Walt Disney, Oprah Winfrey, Charlize Theron, Mark Wahlberg, and 50 Cent.		Integrate teaching reading skills using the genre of biography. Create comprehension questions that help students discover resilient behaviors in these survivors.	

Source: Adapted from Wolpow, Johnson, Hertel, & Kincaid (2009)

(Continued)

(Continued)

2. Complete each "How do my students know that . . ." stem with an action-oriented response.

I like them and enjoy their company.	
I respect them.	
I believe they will be academically and socially successful in my class.	
I am upset.	
I am happy.	
I am trying to develop a trusting relationship with them.	
I made a mistake.	
I bring out the best in each student by _____.	
I am a strong academic instructor.	

3. If my colleagues were to describe what it's like to work with me, they would say _____.

Trauma-Informed Don'ts

The chart shares some trauma-informed don'ts and examples. In the column on the right, insert how you manage this or can manage it in the future.

Trauma-Informed Don'ts	Examples	My Practice
Don't give up on your efforts to establish a relationship with a difficult student.	Remember, for some students, trusting an adult is risky. Seek help from a critical friend or school counselor if needed.	
Don't assume middle and high school students can't benefit from positive, caring relationships with their teachers.	Adolescence is a tough stage and being a teenager isn't easy either. Schedule a class period at least twice a month where the focus is on relationship building. Start each class period with a quick-check: "Is everybody ready to work, learn something new?"	
If you are an ACEs survivor, don't assume all students can make it the same way you did or just because you were able to_____.	You have a story you can share but always end it with a question: "What can I do to help you or get help for you?" and a reassuring statement, "I believe you will get through this."	

Trauma-Informed Don'ts	Examples	My Practice
Don't let a student swear you to secrecy.	If a student tells you that he or she needs to share something with you but they don't want you to tell anyone else, let them know that you are a mandatory reporter and what that means. Let them know you will stand by them if it is something that must be reported.	
Don't assume students must respect you first.	The easiest way to get respect is to show respect first.	
Don't enable. Maintain the same work and behavior expectations for all.	If a student isn't turning in class assignments, have him or her work on missing work during their lunch break or before or after school. Make sure they have the skills to do the work.	
Avoid using sarcasm when talking to a student—it can convey contempt or can send a mixed signal.	Sarcasm can be misinterpreted by students or be a trigger, especially for students living in emotionally abusive homes. "I see you didn't bring in your homework again. What happened? The dog ate it?"	
Don't ignore the needs of the whole class when one child has a meltdown or behavior outburst.	Take time to ask if everyone is OK. Reassure them that their classmate will be OK and if necessary, have a discussion about how the class can support the classmate's return.	
Don't abuse personal space when dealing with an angry student.	Part of your classroom management system should include a "safe" out: either a space in your classroom or, an understanding that you and student will have a restorative conversation at a later time. Create your nonverbal signal for your time-out to let students know when they are pressing your buttons.	
Don't minimize a student's feelings. Avoid expressions like "I understand how you feel." "Don't worry." or "You are going to be OK."	"How can I help you right now?" "Could you use a break?" "May I make a suggestion?" "Do you just want me to listen?"	

Source: Adapted from Wolpow, Johnson, Hertel, & Kincaid (2009)

Toolkit Takeaways

1. Schools and school districts can reconstitute themselves from a deficit-based model to one that is strength based when they integrate socioemotional curricula and resiliency-building strategies to help faculty and students develop growth mindsets.

2. School and school district leadership matters most.

3. School counselors, school-based social workers, special education staff, school psychologists, and school nurses need to play a bigger role in this transformation because they have the academic training to provide physical and mental health support to students, staff, and families.

4. A response to intervention (RTI) model can be used to create an intervention system for helping students learn new forms of behavior communication.

5. School psychologists need to use intelligence tests that measure cognitive ability and mental processing. Assessments that are based on brain functioning are better indicators of innate intelligence.

6. Unless a student has a preexisting mental disorder, general education teachers and support staff are the first responders in our system. Students spend the most time in their care. This faculty needs to be proficient at integrating trauma-informed strategies into their language, behavior, and thinking as they collaboratively plan, instruct, and evaluate the socioemotional growth and academic progress of their students.

7. Academic coaches, school counselors, school-based social workers, special education staff, and school psychologists need to work in tandem with general education staff.

8. Schools and classrooms are sacred places.

A scientific theory is based on the conscientious examination of facts and knowledge proven true through experimentation or observation. Practice is the application of facts and ideas. From theory to practice is about taking those facts and knowledge and making them actionable. The research about high-poverty, high-performing schools is nearing its fifth decade. Felitti, Anda, and colleagues' study about the lingering impact of adverse childhood experiences in adults began two decades ago. The connection between socioemotional development and cognitive growth is grounded in a body of research that began three decades ago.

In a standard deck of cards, aces can have the highest or lowest values. Each of these values can be the winning card in most games. We have the facts and body of knowledge to support our students' resiliency and provide the structures and education to turn their short-term ACEs into life changing, long-term aces. This is what it means to be a transformationist educator.

Transformation is a process that has phases a learner passes through. Initially when presented with input or information that cannot be refuted because it is evidenced based, the learner experiences the following:

- cognitive dissonance, a train wreck of the mind

- feelings of guilt or shame

- recognition that others are having the same experience and have ideas about how to change or have changed

- a willingness to explore possibilities: new roles, collegial relations, adopt new actions

- a desire to plan a new course and acquire new skills if necessary

- the satisfaction of new competencies and successful experiences (Mezirow, 1997)

Transformationist educators know it is their belief about their students and how well they teach for mastery that determines academic outcomes (Howard, 2016). The educators in the 4,577 high-poverty, high-performing schools identified by the Education Trust exemplify that when negative teacher beliefs change, students have positive experiences in school. Transformationist teaching and learning is a delicate dance between educator and student. Both must be willing participants and accepting of the fact that the conduit from teacher to learner may sometimes be clear and straightforward and at other times, full of static, confusion, and curves.

Schools and school districts can provide professional development about ACEs, strategies and structures that mitigate the effects of trauma and be intentional about adult self-care for all of the employees in a school system. We know enough to create healing spaces for our children who are experiencing trauma and for the staff who work with them. PreK through12th-grade education is a stressful career choice but we are capable of building systems that foster resiliency for everyone.

Transformationist relationships, educator–educator, educator–student, student–student, and educator–family, are dependent on TALK, TRUST, FEEL, and REPAIR abilities to

TALK—communicate and listen to each other without judgment or bias,

TRUST—build reliable bonding relationships,

FEEL—regulate emotions to help develop strong relationships, and

REPAIR—have restorative conversations to heal relationships.

In this last interactive chapter, you will be processing the **READ**ing, your **REFLECT**ions, and **RESPOND**ing by **APPLY**ing it to your current practice. The guiding questions, online videos, and templates are designed to help you *start where you are, use what you have, do what you can* to infuse trauma-informed strategies into your daily routines. At the end of the chapter is a guide to help you get started with transitioning to a trauma-informed classroom, school, or school district. Don't forget to use the TTFR (trust, talk, feel, and repair) Toolkit in Chapter 5.

For review, the following partial lists summarize what trauma-informed actions can look like at varying levels. What can you add?

> *We want to be able to look back and say to all concerned that we did what we had to do, when we had to do it, and with all the resources required.*
>
> —Arthur Ashe, Wimbledon, U.S. Open and Australian Open Tennis Champion United Nations Address, December 1, 1992

TRANSFORMATIONIST SCHOOLS AND SCHOOL DISTRICTS (ADAPTED FROM NCTSN, 2008)

o reorganize special education classes for behavior disorders and use RTI model to teach behavior expectations to all students. Devise supplemental interventions for Tier II and III students like ELL and Title I programs.

o have plans to support families and school staff after a traumatizing event (e.g., death of a teacher or student, mass shooting, weather-related loss).

o match office and district department staff with middle and high school mentees to help all employees develop relationships with the youth they serve. Mentors can check in by phone and two to three school visits.

o provide stable and consistent schoolwide and districtwide routines so parents can plan.

o provide a dedicated classroom and staff it with trained personnel prepared to deal positively with disruptive behaviors, allow students and staff to "rest and reset" and plan their restorative conversations.

- adjust the school calendar to anticipate times when behaviors may be more disruptive (e.g., before and after long holiday breaks) and restart focusing on classroom and building management routines.

- provide supervision for a teacher's class if she or he has had a traumatic experience with a student or other staff member and plan for their restorative conversations.

- establish ongoing relationships with health care providers, before- and after-school caregivers, and local agencies that support families like child protective services, family social services, and child welfare.

- have special assemblies to recognize student academic and socioemotional progress.

- assign support staff, including district office staff, to mentor or check in with students needing additional support. Every district employee has two to five students they visit during school hours.

- provide ongoing professional development focusing on trauma-informed strategies.

- require all staff to develop their own self-care plans as part of their annual goal-setting.

- provide employee assistance programs for employees needing socioemotional support, smoking cessation, alcohol or drug cessation programs.

- establish a social committee to plan events for staff.

- establish a trauma-informed team or student intervention team that meets and creates plans for supporting difficult cases.

- open buildings to house after-school programs including programs for adult family members.

TRANSFORMATIONIST INSTRUCTIONAL STAFF (ADAPTED FROM ADAMS, 2013)

- create ways to personally connect with each student each day.

- provide stable and consistent classroom, bus, and cafeteria routines.

- provide space in the classroom for students to rest or time themselves out.

- recognize traumatized children may have disruptive behaviors that shouldn't be treated punitively. They correct or redirect the behavior positively.

- anticipate difficult times. For example, a child who has lost a parent or is in foster care might react to making a Mother's or a Father's Day card.

- provide positive and incremental incentives to acknowledge academic and social progress.

o listen. For educators who are able to develop trusting relationships with their students, a traumatized student may seek them out. They may or may not share their personal issues but talk in ways to get the positive reinforcement they need.

o listen and look for cues that a child is behaving differently or has observable bruising.

o seek help and work closely with other school personnel to devise ways to support traumatized children and the other children in the class who are aware of a child's traumatic experience.

o avoid behaviors that retraumatize like disempowering students (e.g., using sarcasm, humiliation, vague feedback), being inconsistent, yelling, and enabling or being too solicitous.

TRANSFORMATIONIST SCHOOL COUNSELORS AND SCHOOL-BASED SOCIAL WORKERS (ADAPTED FROM WOLPOW, JOHNSON, HERTEL, & KINCAID, 2009)

o participate on school and school district trauma teams.

o act as the liaison between school, district support services, and community agencies to establish wrap-around services for students needing intensive supports.

o provide ongoing professional development for faculty, for example, teaching teachers how to implement socioemotional curriculum, which is different from implementing academic curriculum.

o chair trauma-informed team or student-intervention team. They follow up student plans to ensure assigned tasks and timetables are being met.

o provide individual and group therapeutic sessions for staff and students.

o conduct home visits and frequent contacts with families.

TRANSFORMATIONIST SCHOOL PSYCHOLOGISTS AND SCHOOL NURSES

o use intelligence tests based on modern theories of brain function to assess students from low-income families to identify students who may be academically low but have average or above-average intelligence.

o collaborate with school nurses to identify community agencies to work with students and families needing the most intensive mental health services. Monitor progress every six to eight weeks and provide updates to school teams.

o School nurses collaborate with community health care agencies when needed to support students and their families.

TRANSFORMATIONIST SUPPORT STAFF (OFFICE, CAFETERIA, CUSTODIAL, BUS DRIVERS)

- ○ see themselves as educators applying trauma-informed strategies to their work and supporting a climate and culture that is emotionally safe for staff, students, and families.

- ○ greet and acknowledge students and families whenever they encounter them.

- ○ have brief exchanges (2x10 strategy) with students: "Are you learning a lot today?" "How are your classes this semester?" "I like the way you are being responsible." "See you tomorrow, same time, same place. Your big yellow limo will pick you up."

Read, Reflect, Respond

Applying SEL Competencies and Resiliency Framework When Working With Colleagues

1. Describe how CASEL's 5 Social-Emotional Competencies align with Benard's Resiliency Framework.

Social-Emotional Competencies	Resiliency Framework
Self-Management (ability to regulate emotions)	Social Competence (responsiveness, cultural flexibility, empathy, caring communication skills, sense of humor)
Self-Awareness (recognizing and labelling one's emotions, accurate perceptions of self)	Problem-Solving (planning, help-seeking, critical and creative thinking
Social Awareness (understanding and empathizing others, respect for others)	Autonomy (sense of identity, self-efficacy, task mastery, adaptive distancing from negative messages)
Responsible Decision-Making (identifying problem and situation, accepting responsibility, ethical)	Sense of Purpose (goal direction, educational aspirations, optimism)
Relationship Skills (social engagement, negotiating, collaborative, collegial)	

2. Think about a typical work day. What kind of opportunities and experiences do you have that allow you to practice or apply any of these competencies and behaviors with colleagues? Rate your skill levels for all nine categories. What are your strengths, S, and what are your challenges, C ?

3. Watch Jim Tamm's fifteen-minute TED Talk, *Cultivating Collaboration: Don't Be So Defensive*, at http://www.tedxsantacruz.org/talks/jim-tamm/.

   When thinking about your professional behaviors at work and those of your colleagues, what percentage of the staff do you feel are in red and green zones?

   a. If the majority of your colleagues are in the green zone, what are some ideas for increasing the numbers?

   b. If the majority are in the red zone, what are some ideas for decreasing the numbers?

4. Before the Innovative School District began its mission to practice from a strength-based, trauma-informed perspective, they adopted working agreements. All employees gave their input and commitment to adhere. Using the descriptors for socioemotional competencies and resiliency building, explain how their working agreements provide opportunity for all staff to practice these skills.

ISD's Districtwide Working Agreements

o Withhold judgment.

o If you have a deeper, personal reaction to something someone has said, explore your own feelings first, then ask clarifying questions.

o Say "Ouch!" if someone says something that causes you to cringe or feel hurt. Be willing to explain in a way he or she can actively listen.

o Try to understand and learn from a colleague sharing why he or she said "Ouch!"

o Consider language and tone.

o Try to be vulnerable or open.

o Stay present.

o Assume positive intent; discussions and decisions benefit the group.

o Acknowledging and respecting all are not at the same place.

o When at the point of making decisions, think through the ramifications and effect of impact.

o Adhere to the working agreements.

5. What working agreements (written or unwritten) are in place for your department, grade level, district, or school?

   a. If there are no working agreements, do you think creating them would be beneficial to work? Why or why not?

   b. In the following video, a group of educators are planning. As you listen to their interactions, jot down the working agreements that you think they honor. Cite evidence to support your responses.
   https://www.youtube.com/watch?v=_-_Ep4z5RkQ

   c. Using the SEL competencies and Benard's Resiliency Framework descriptors in the first question, identify areas of strength demonstrated by the educators in the video.

(Continued)

(Continued)

    d. Using the same descriptors, identify areas of strength when working with your colleagues (district office departments, school-based departments, or grade-level teams) and cite evidence.

    e. Identify areas you perceive you and your colleagues could use to support strengthening collaborative skills. Brainstorm some ideas, suggestions you can bring to the team to start a discussion. Remember to start with the group's strengths. You are probably not alone in your feelings.

6. Read the article *What Makes Effective Teams Tick*. Outline the changes district and school-based administrators made to support collaborative planning. http://www.educationworld .com/a_admin/admin/admin408_a.shtml

    What comparisons can you make with your team's collaborative planning? What are some differences? What are some challenges? Use the template to think about possible next steps you could take.

CHALLENGES	YOUR SUGGESTIONS	IDENTIFY POSSIBLE BARRIERS	POSSIBLE ALTERNATIVES FOR ELIMINATING BARRIERS

Applying SEL Competencies and Resiliency Framework to Your Self-Care Plan

1. In Chapter 2, *Put on Your Own Oxygen Mask Before Helping Others*, you began work on your self-care plan. Use these links and see how your colleagues around the country circumvent compassion fatigue or burnout. Revisit your plan and revise if you see something beneficial. Thanks to technology, your colleagues around the country are sharing valuable tips. Remember this resource when updating your self-care objectives. You are not alone.

    Avoid Teacher Burnout: Teacher Vlog at https://www.youtube.com/watch?v=uFM46hBkbHg

Good Teachers Don't Quit: 5 Ways to Avoid Teacher Burnout at https://www.youtube.com/watch?v=Ap_LKQzVeR8

Intentional and Radical Self-Care for Teachers at https://www.youtube.com/watch?v=1kletink65M

2. Revisit and revise (if needed) your self-care plan. How will you know if your plan is working throughout the school year?

Applying SEL Competencies and the Resiliency Framework When Working With Students

Before you begin the activities in this section, play this You Tube video, *I Wish My Teacher Knew,* at https://www.youtube.com/watch?v=6k1-KExA9p8.

1. What are the common themes you hear these students expressing and what are the implications for you as an educator?

Complete the chart with at least two examples you hear.

Could Be a PreK–12th Student	Could Be a Student From a Middle-Class or Wealthy Family	Could Be a Student From a Low-Income Family	Could Be a Student Learning English as a Second Language

Explain how completing this chart validates the statement: It is important for all adults working in any school system to be trauma informed.

How can you integrate "I Wish My Teacher Knew" activity into your classroom management plan?

How can you modify the same activity to use with adult staff (e.g., districtwide, school-based staff, grade-level teams, department teams)?

2. Establishing and maintaining positive relationships between students and educators is a robust Tier I behavior ingredient. The links on the next page are to videos demonstrating

(Continued)

(Continued)

how a variety of district employees establish authentic relationships with students and are critical members of a school's educational team. View the video that is closest to your role. Note when socioemotional competencies and Resiliency Framework strategies are applied or reinforced.

a. Cafeteria staff—https://www.youtube.com/watch?v=Gy8DmFNTo-8

b. Paraeducator/Teacher—Assistants—https://www.youtube.com/watch? v=wrHzDtvJTmg

c. Bus drivers—https://www.youtube.com/watch?v=B3XHwk4wgeY

d. Superintendent—https://www.youtube.com/watch?v=HmWpjT 4gRCs

e. Custodians—https://www.youtube.com/watch?v=uV6XHEFsGRo

f. Substitute teacher—https://www.youtube.com/watch?v=B10nXv052Pg

g. School-based police officer—https://www.youtube.com/watch?v=T1u Ap69IJnk

h. Paraeducator or coach—https://www.youtube.com/watch?v=wrHzDtvJTmg

i. Attendance office clerk—https://www.youtube.com/watch?v=335y5St1dGc

j. School secretaries—https://www.youtube.com/watch?v=kRtu1L8-Gu4

3. Describe the attributes or characteristics of the students you are most successful with.

Do the same analysis for the students who are most challenging for you.

What similarities and differences or biases does your analysis reveal?

If you identified a bias, what are some ways you can mitigate its effects?

How can you use this information to help you work more effectively with your more challenging students?

Who can you consult for help or ideas to improve your relationship with challenging students?

4. When preparing for the start of a new school year or semester, what do you do to

a. connect with families?

Additional ideas: Call each family and introduce yourself, share how parents can support you, and ask about student's likes and dislikes about school, for example. For middle and high school staff, use technology (robocalls, e-mail); host a schoolwide event like a back-to-school BBQ.

Go to https://www.responsiveclassroom.org/investing-in-parents-during-the-first-six-weeks-of-school

b. get to know your students before the school year begins?

Additional ideas: Read student accumulative records and identify patterns, check previous grades, and consult with specialists if concerned.

Go to

Elementary—*Summer Letters to My Students: Beginning to Build Relationships,* by Kathy Cassidy

http://kathycassidy.com/2015/08/21/summer-letters-to-my-students-beginning-to-build-relationships/

K–12th Grade—*Winning Strategies for Classroom Management* (Table of Contents) by Carol Cummings

http://www.ascd.org/publications/books/100052.aspx

5. How do you prepare your room to reflect human diversity?

Additional ideas: Bulletin boards with contemporary images of ethnic groups (consider finding images of individuals at work, e.g., Native American astronaut, White male nurse, African American female CEO, Hispanic Supreme Court justice, disabled basketball player).

6. How do you begin to bond with your students on the first day of school?

Additional ideas: Use ice breakers that integrate an academic skill such as student surveys of likes and dislikes to determine mean, median, mode; Sudoku puzzles for teams; visual allegorical puzzles; team projects that rely on problem-solving skills like the Mystery Box (http://seplessons .ucsf.edu/node/387); problem-solving games (https://www.qepbooks.com/Desperately-Seeking-Solutions).

"Five Practices for Building Relationships With Students" by Kelley Clark

http://www.edweek.org/tm/articles/2012/08/07/tln_clark.html

7. How do you teach your students appropriate ways for engaging in civil discourse? https://www.tolerance.org/sites/default/files/2017-06/TT_Civil%20Discourse_ whtppr_0_0.pdf

Additional ideas: Generate ideas from your students first.

Civil Discourse in the Classroom by Kate Shuster

https://www.tolerance.org/magazine/publications/civil-discourse-in-the-classroom

Search the Internet for blogs by teachers around the country.

Teacher Advice: Classroom Management

https://www.youtube.com/watch?v=i7ztQvsptpE

Toolkit Takeaways

1. Transformation is a process. Today's school employees need to be transformationist in their work because true school reform begins with changing the beliefs, providing ongoing professional development and guidance, and meeting the socioemotional needs of the people inside the school.

2. The Internet is today's encyclopedia. Educators, researchers, and consultants are uploading videos and PowerPoints to share their successes and challenges. Most are less than twentyminutes in length, therefore making them great discussion starters at staff meetings or grade-level or department team meetings.

The Process, the Plan, the Transformation

Transformative Learning is the process of using a prior interpretation to construe a new or revised interpretation of the meaning of one's experience in order to guide future action.

—Mezirow, 1996

Anticipated Outcomes

Readers will

○ review their current disaggregated data, policies and procedures, and resources for their strengths and challenges;

○ use the implementation cycle for Tiers I through III 3 to assess capacity, build capacity, implement, and evaluate regularly to plan next steps;

○ understand transformationist school staff must be guided and supported by transformationist leadership: Administrator(s) and school staff leaders.

Ricky Robertson, Behavior Specialist

THE PROCESS

Each school's journey to implementing a trauma-informed framework is unique. It will be shaped by a number of factors including the staff's understanding of trauma and ACEs, the strengths and weaknesses of the school's current programming, the resources available, and the needs of students and families. At the beginning of this journey is the recognition of a necessity for a new approach to supporting learning, behavior, and well-being.

For many schools that recognition takes place during a time of challenge: when a school has exhausted its resources and finds itself failing to fulfill on the promises made to its students and families. I worked with one such school that was reluctant to consider a trauma-informed framework because it could not see how the approach could truly support the behavioral and academic challenges it was facing. This was a high-need, high-poverty school that bore many of the markers that we associate with failing schools: low test scores, high number of suspensions, parent upset, and staff discontent.

The school needed to change, and every stakeholder group had its own perspective as to how. A number of parents had complained to the district that the school was failing their children. Some had even requested waivers for their students to attend other schools, citing concerns about safety and racially discriminatory discipline practices. The parents blamed the teachers for being ill-equipped to teach their children. The veteran teachers claimed that the principal was to blame. They felt that she had failed to galvanize the staff behind a shared vision and was too lax with discipline. From their perspective, the students needed more severe consequences to hold them accountable for their actions. Many of the teachers also expressed frustration with the families, claiming that anytime they called home concerning a student's behavior the families were typically unsupportive. The newer teachers said very little about the school's predicament. Instead, their high turnover rate spoke for them.

The principal and I discussed all of these factors as we reviewed the school's academic, behavioral, and student demographic data. The majority of the students qualified for free and reduced lunch. Poverty is an adverse childhood experience in and of itself, but one that is highly correlated with other ACEs. We also took note of the fact that the school's student population was one of the most racially diverse in the district. Yet, the teaching staff was almost entirely white and female.

When we looked at behavior data throughout the year, we noticed a significant percentage of office referrals for students of color who exhibited "severe disrespect" or "defiance." It was not surprising to find that the student subgroups who had the highest rates of referrals also had the greatest academic achievement gaps. It was becoming easier to understand the perspectives of the families who had complained to the district. At the same time, we could also sympathize with the teachers who felt that their instruction was compromised by rampant behavioral issues. It was easy to see how all of these conflicting perspectives could be valid. And yet, none of them offered a real solution.

I invited the principal to view the data through a trauma-informed lens. A trauma-informed lens considers the students' fundamental needs for physical, academic, and emotional safety and belonging. Through this lens, we saw students coming to school with empty stomachs. We saw families barely making ends meet. Already overwhelmed, these parents only heard from their child's school when there was yet another problem for them to deal with. We saw teachers and students with fractured relationships unable to trust one another and certainly unable to learn from one another. We saw new teachers who were overwhelmed by the needs of their students and overtaken by stress and burn-out. Finally, we saw veteran teachers overworked, frustrated, and unappreciated. They were using strategies to teach and manage their classrooms that were ill-fitted and outdated, but they knew no better.

Through a trauma-informed lens, blame is replaced with compassion. From this perspective, the principal could clearly see the necessity for a new approach that addressed the needs of all students, especially those impacted by trauma and ACEs. An approach that would equip her staff with tools to better teach their students while supporting the well-being of the whole child was needed. I invite you to take a similar journey, by choosing to view your school through a trauma-informed lens and letting compassion guide your next steps.

STEP 1: ASSESSING CAPACITY

Know Your School Community

The first step in assessing capacity for the implementation of a trauma-informed framework is to know your students, staff, and families. Reviewing student behavior and academic and demographic data is a good starting place. Make sure to look at this data through a trauma-informed lens by thinking about the types of needs that students bring to school. Resist the temptation to relegate this approach solely to the field of social work; these issues are at the heart of education. We know that trauma, ACEs, and poverty impact brain development, cognition, emotional regulation, and behavior, all of which play a role in student achievement.

Therefore, as you analyze your student data, ask yourself questions that prompt you to look beyond the numbers and see the human stories. How many students are living in poverty? How many students experience housing instability over the course of the school year? How often have teachers, school counselors, or the school nurse expressed concerns about students dealing with depression, anxiety, substance abuse, suicidal ideation, eating disorders, or other health impairments?

Second, consider forms of quantitative and qualitative data that help you better understand your students' families. Parent-survey data is helpful but think about ways to go beyond that. Ask yourself questions that prompt you to think how and why certain families engage with your school and others don't. How many families attend school events? Are there certain populations of families based upon class or race, for example, that are more likely to engage with the school? What opportunities are there for parents to partner with the school? What services does your school offer to support families experiencing poverty or homelessness?

Finally, you have to know your staff and, more specifically, how they perceive the academic, behavioral, and socioemotional needs of their students. This step is often an informal process of reflecting upon conversations that take place during meetings and in the break room. A brief anonymous staff survey can also be a helpful tool. Ask teachers questions that assess their openness to a trauma-informed approach. For example,

1. Do you believe that students' emotions impact their ability to learn? Why or why not?

2. How could our school improve the ways that it manages student behavior?

3. What role do you think the teacher–student relationship plays in the learning process?

Identify Strengths, Growth Areas, and Barriers

The purpose of this exercise is to identify programs already in place that could be built upon, enhanced, or improved to facilitate the implementation of the trauma-informed framework. Begin by making a list of programs your school currently has in place to support the behavioral, academic, and socioemotional success of students. These programs could include PBIS, an SEL curriculum, special education services, universal free breakfast, and academic intervention programs. Highlight the programs that are having the greatest positive impact on student performance. Then make a note of the programs or interventions that are failing to deliver on their intended outcome. As you continue to grow in your understanding of trauma-informed education, you may have insights as to reasons why certain programs aren't working, particularly if they have failed to account for impact of trauma and ACEs. You may also discover ways to leverage effective programing to meet multiple needs within your school.

The next step is to identify barriers to implementation. Two of the most common barriers are the use of exclusionary discipline and the silos of student support resources. **Exclusionary discipline** is an obvious barrier because it fundamentally disrupts the students' relationship with their teachers and school. The silos of student support resources is an often more complex issue to address. Silos most often take place in schools where students are only able to access small-group and individual socioemotional, behavioral, and academic supports once they have qualified for special education services. This is particularly the case in districts that have yet to adopt a full-inclusion model for special education services.

In the absence of full inclusion, special education students are segregated from their peers, while many general education students, who could benefit from similar supports, are denied access. Our trauma-informed framework seeks to broaden rather than restrict access to student supports. We encourage schools to look for ways to incorporate special education strategies into all daily instruction and classroom management. For example, in our ideal school, we would like to see students receive socioemotional and behavioral instruction in classes that are woven into their daily schedule, without needing an IEP. This is similar to the alternative high school that we mentioned in Chapter 6, which offered electives that taught nonviolent communication, healthy relationship skills, and other topics that supported the overall well-being of students.

Sometimes we, as educators, are the barrier. It may become clear that the stresses of our work have hardened into judgments and biases about our students and their families. It is important to acknowledge these beliefs and the harm that they do to our students and our souls. Oftentimes, our burnout and cynicism disconnect us from the heart of our commitment to help kids learn and grow. And if our colleagues are the cynics and naysayers, then it is important to view them with compassion as well. Underneath their discontent is a frustrated desire, a sense of having failed at the thing they once most wanted to succeed at: teaching. We can't join in their negativity. We can only offer a different approach and hope that they join us on the journey.

As it was stated in Chapter 1, none of us entered this profession because we wanted to send kids to prison. And yet, public education has been branded the school-to-prison pipeline. If we are to change this, then we must adopt a compassionate, solution-focused view of the struggles that we face in education.

STEP 2: BUILDING CAPACITY

Building Our Capacity to Care:
Ongoing Professional Development

The most important step for a school to take on its journey to becoming trauma informed is for the staff to deepen their understanding of the impact of trauma and ACEs on behavior and learning. This includes a willingness to view behavior as a form of communication and an approach to intervention that is relationship based, restorative, and needs focused. As staff begins to see the ways that instruction, behavior management, and school culture can all be enhanced by a trauma-informed approach, they begin to articulate their "why." Why should their school adopt a trauma-informed framework? Why are their students' socioemotional and behavioral needs vital to the learning process? Why is there no time to waste when it comes to helping students who have experienced trauma or ACEs?

The process by which a school community goes about this learning process may vary depending upon the resources that are available. A principal may provide his entire staff with a copy of *Building Resilience in Students Impacted by Adverse Childhood Experiences: A Whole Staff Approach,* to use as a resource and guide. A school district might sponsor a workshop on trauma-informed practices and invite each school to send a team. A number of the schools that I have worked with have allocated professional development funds, or acquired grants, that have allowed their staff to receive training and coaching. The most important thing is that the professional development process is ongoing. The learning process must be sustained over multiple years by infusing trauma-informed language into conversations about learning and behavior, incorporating trauma-informed interventions into the school's improvement plan, and, most importantly, developing systems that implement trauma-informed practices within the day-to-day operations of the school.

At the heart of this effort is teamwork. For a school to effectively serve its students through the implementation of a three-tiered trauma-informed framework, the school staff must work collaboratively in teams. The first team to be created is the leadership team. The leadership team is the organizing force behind the trauma-informed programming that will shape the school's culture. This team is most effective when it comprises of a broad representation of individuals who share a strong commitment to helping children. The school counselor, school nurse, instructional specialist, behavior specialist, general education teachers, special education teachers, and an administrator should be on the leadership team. The school is also encouraged to invite parents and representatives from relevant community organizations and mental health agencies to participate as well. Beyond the leadership team, the school will also need to create intervention teams for each of the three tiers. Members of the leadership team should act as team leaders for each of the tiered intervention teams. The intervention team leaders will help the school to coordinate efforts across the three tiers of intervention (see the Implementation Guide for more information on the teams including the frequency of their meetings).

Implementation Action Plan: Identifying Priorities

The leadership team, in collaboration with the school staff, should identify three to four priorities for implementation during the upcoming school year. To determine priorities for implementation, the staff may wish to collaboratively identify the school's areas of greatest need (e.g., behavior management, student engagement, instruction). Then consider ways that the trauma-informed framework can address those needs. The staff can refer to the three tiers of the trauma-informed framework as well as the Implementation Guide to facilitate this process. A good starting point for a school in its first year of implementation is to focus on deepening their staff's understanding of trauma and ACEs, while incorporating strategies from the Teacher's Trauma-Informed Toolkit in Chapter 5 and a SEL curriculum into daily instruction and classroom management.

I worked at an elementary school that identified one priority for the leadership team and one for each of the tiered intervention teams. These were their four priorities for implementation:

1. The leadership team will provide the entire school staff with ongoing professional development that will deepen our school's understanding of, and response to, the impact of trauma and ACEs on learning and behavior.

2. The Tier I team will support the incorporation of self-regulation strategies, derived from the SEL curriculum, into daily classroom instruction and behavior management, by creating Cool Down Spots in every classroom and teaching students how and when to use them.

3. The Tier II team will develop culturally responsive young men's and young women's leadership groups that will address the behavioral and socioemotional needs of Tier II students, while supporting character development and positive peer bonding.

4. The Tier III team will seek to reduce the use of exclusionary discipline with Tier III students through the implementation of a Ready to Learn Room, which will be used for deescalation, problem-solving, restorative conversations, and reengagement in the learning process.

Remember to Leverage Strengths

When developing its priorities for implementation, a school may find that it has multiple areas of concern and the capacity to better address some more than others. I recommend that schools identify their areas of greatest need while also considering ways that they can leverage their strengths to address them. For example, I worked with a middle school with high rates of both suspension and chronic absenteeism and low rates of parental involvement. One approach would be to develop three separate intervention programs for each area of concern. Realistically, this would have put added pressure on a school whose resources were already stretched thin. Instead, I asked the school's leadership team to consider which of the school's strengths we could build upon to better address behavior, attendance, and parental involvement.

In *Step 1: Assessing Capacity*, the leadership team had identified that the school had a successful homeroom advisory program. In advisory, students set goals, caught up on assignments, learned study skills, and discussed their weekly progress with their advisor. The advisory program set the foundation for us to create a more formalized mentoring program that could address our three areas of concern.

We trained the advisory teachers on the roles and responsibilities of becoming mentors including the purpose and frequency of check-ins, goal-setting, relationship-building, supportive accountability, and family outreach. Each advisor agreed to take on up to five students to mentor each quarter. The mentees were students who were identified as Tier II or Tier III students due to behavior or attendance. These students had a formal check-in with their advisor once a week and informally checked in every day. The advisors also became the primary contact person at school for their mentees' families. The advisors made weekly phone calls to update families on their student's progress and to check in about attendance. Building upon the advisory program, we were able to develop a mentoring intervention that improved attendance, behavior, and family involvement. We had successfully leveraged a strength to address multiple needs.

STEP 3: IMPLEMENTATION

While the leadership team provides support and guidance, the tiered intervention teams really drive the implementation process. It is essential that each tiered intervention team formulates a vision, goal, and action plan for their work. The intervention team's goal should align with the priorities that were identified in Step 2. Their action plan should delineate the steps they will take to achieve this goal over the course of the school year. I encourage intervention teams to consider how their action plan can address these issues: schoolwide policies and practices, classroom interventions and strategies, family collaboration, community partnerships, and staff self-care.

For example, earlier I mentioned an elementary school that sought to implement young men's and women's leadership groups that would provide behavioral and socioemotional support. The Tier II team decided to pilot these small group interventions over the course of a semester. The school counselor selected six boys and six girls to participate in the pilot. A number of the students that were chosen to participate had presented significant behavioral issues. The school counselor was aware that students who tend to internalize the impacts of ACEs and trauma often fly under radar even though they still suffer and

Figure 8.1   Implementation Cycle for Tiers I to III

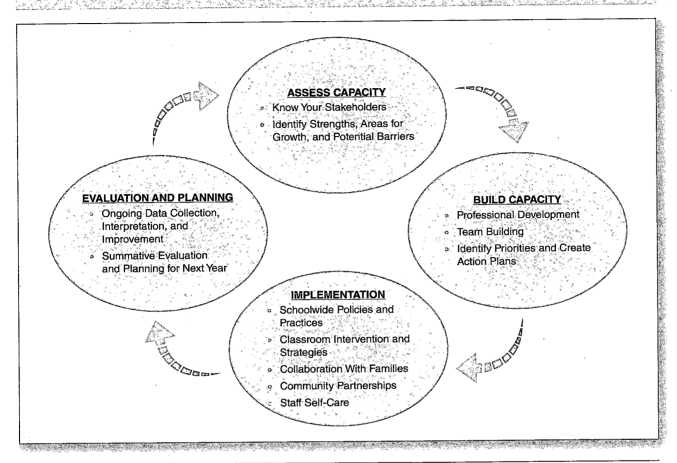

ASSESS CAPACITY
- Know Your Stakeholders
- Identify Strengths, Areas for Growth, and Potential Barriers

BUILD CAPACITY
- Professional Development
- Team Building
- Identify Priorities and Create Action Plans

IMPLEMENTATION
- Schoolwide Policies and Practices
- Classroom Intervention and Strategies
- Collaboration With Families
- Community Partnerships
- Staff Self-Care

EVALUATION AND PLANNING
- Ongoing Data Collection, Interpretation, and Improvement
- Summative Evaluation and Planning for Next Year

Source: Created by Ashley Pugh (2018)

need support. Therefore, she also selected students to participate in the groups who displayed appropriate behavior but struggled with either difficult emotions or social skills.

Over the course of the semester, the students engaged in group discussions, played games, completed service projects, and participated in a variety of other activities. A diverse group of guest speakers were invited from throughout the community to meet with the students and share their unique stories. The groups culminated in a luncheon and award ceremony that was hosted for the students and their families.

The team learned a number of valuable lessons from the pilot program. First, they realized that they needed to devote more time to building trust and establishing norms within the group sessions. Some of the internalizing students had a difficult time opening up and trusting their groupmates, while some of the students with behavioral issues had a hard time managing impulses, waiting their turn, and speaking respectfully. Moving forward, the meetings would start with modeling and reviewing group norms. They would also include more games and affirmation circles as a way to build trust.

Second, the Tier II team realized that they had not linked the small-group intervention to classroom strategies and the larger school community. During the second semester, they devoted a bulletin board to displaying photos of the leadership group completing service projects. They also sent these photos to the students' families through e-mail and apps. The group facilitators also sent an e-mail each week to the students' teachers to let them know what topics or activities the groups would be engaging with that week. The e-mails included suggestions for ways that teachers could reinforce the valuable work that was taking place within the groups.

Finally, the group facilitators realized that they needed a plan for how to follow up with individual students who shared about traumatic events during the group sessions. It seemed inappropriate to return a child to class right after sharing something that was emotionally upsetting. Moving forward, the team decided that the groups would be facilitated by two staff members rather than one. This way both the students and facilitators would have more support. The team also decided that each group session would close with mindful breathing, followed by a snack, as a way to naturally calm the level of emotional arousal. The school counselor agreed to follow up with any student who shared about his or her trauma during a session.

I share this example because it exemplifies a number of important markers of effective program implementation. The Tier II team started with a pilot program that gave them the opportunity to problem-solve and adapt the program so that it could effectively serve a larger number of students. The Team found ways to include the larger community through guest speakers and community service projects. They also remained mindful of the impact of running a group alone by adding a second staff person to assist with group meetings. Teachers and families felt included in the process thanks to regular communication. Overall, the action plan successfully implemented the intervention in a way that connected it to the classroom, schoolwide practices, family outreach, community partnerships, and staff self-care.

STEP 4: EVALUATING PROGRAM EFFECTIVENESS

Data-Informed Decision-Making

Once a month, the tiered intervention teams review data to monitor the need for, and effectiveness of, their programs and interventions. The use of relevant and specific data is important for creating targeted interventions. For example, I was working with an elementary school's Tier I team. We were looking at monthly referral data. For our intervention to be effective, we needed to know not only how many referrals were being given each month, but what behaviors were the most prevalent and where and when these behaviors were happening the most. We dug deeper into the data and learned that the majority of the referrals were being given for defiance, disrespect, or physical aggression in the classroom. We also learned that it was not uncommon for a student involved in such behavior to leave the classroom without permission following an incident. We found that third grade had the highest number of these referrals.

The Tier I team met with the third-grade teachers and developed a plan to create a Cool Down Spot in each of the third-grade classrooms. When students were escalated, they could ask for permission to go to the Cool Down Spot, where they would set a timer and choose from a menu of calming activities (e.g., taking deep breaths, playing with a fidget, squeezing a stress ball). When the timer was up, students would return to their desk and resume work. The school counselor delivered mini-lessons in each of the classrooms to help students understand when and how to appropriately use the Cool Down Spot. The teachers reinforced the use of the space in their daily classroom management.

A month later, the Tier I team reviewed the referral data and found a sharp decline in the number of classroom referrals generated for third-grade students. A couple of the third-grade teachers agreed to present at the next staff meeting and share their experiences using the Cool Down Spot intervention. Following the presentation, the staff voted to make Cool Down Spots a component of every classroom in the school. Their work provides an excellent example of the use of relevant and specific data to guide the implementation process.

Monthly Leadership Team Meetings

The monthly leadership team meetings are an opportunity for the team leaders from each of the tiered intervention teams to share about their team's goals, actions, and needs. They are also an opportunity to review quantitative and qualitative data to determine the impact of the tiered interventions and plan next steps to support implementation. The leadership team has a unique "mountain-top view" of the implementation process, in that it is able to see the ways that the tiered intervention work coalesces to cultivate a compassionate, trauma-informed school. As a result, the leadership team plays a vital role in sustaining the implementation process, particularly when things do not go as planned.

I was working with a high school that was in its third year of implementing a trauma-informed framework. The school's leadership team had made family partnerships a priority across all three tiers. The Tier I efforts to increase family engagement were proving to be successful. The leadership team had applied for a grant that allowed the school to provide food and childcare at school events. The team had also created a calendar of events throughout the school year that were relevant and fun including a volleyball game, potluck, college financial aid night, and hosting a nonprofit that provided evening classes for parents getting their GED. The number of families attending school events had significantly increased from previous years. However, the school's Tier II and Tier III efforts were flailing.

The Tier II and Tier III teams had decided to conduct home visits as a way to build relationships with disengaged families. Thus far, the visits had been a disaster. A number of the families had called the principal about the visits. Some said they felt "harassed" and "insulted" when they were "ambushed" by a school staff person showing up at their front door unannounced.

Equally challenging were the situations in which the families had welcomed the school staff person's visit. One teacher arrived at a family's home in the middle of an eviction. She ended up comforting crying children and moving boxes out onto the street corner. Another teacher arrived to a crying mother who begged him to drive her to the city utilities office so that she could plea with them to turn her water back on. The family's water had been shut off for weeks and they were going to the bathroom in buckets.

These staff members were in no way prepared for these situations. The school had not anticipated that they would be encountering families in the midst of crisis. As a result, they were unable to respond effectively. When this occurs, the school's response risks being inconsistent and reactive, inadvertently sustaining the chaotic nature of the adverse experience. In other words, the school begins to embody the impact of trauma and ACEs.

The leadership team intervened and put a temporary halt to the home visits. It redirected the school's efforts to focus on building their capacity to work with Tier II and Tier III families. The leadership team tasked the Tier II team with doing research on effective outreach to, and communication with, families experiencing trauma and poverty. The Tier III Team shifted its efforts from home visits to building a family outreach committee. The committee included school staff, a parent, and representatives from local community organizations and agencies that specialized in working with families impacted by poverty, substance abuse, domestic violence, and mental illness. The team compiled a list of agencies that the school could refer families to for support.

The Tier III team also reached out to the agencies and established at least one staff person at each agency that was willing to be a point person for the school. Too often social service agencies are revolving doors. When staff reaches out for support, they speak to someone and a week later call back and learn that that person has moved on to another job, quit due to burnout, or they were an intern whose position was never permanent to begin with. As a result, families fall through the cracks. Having a point person at each agency, especially one who had seniority, helped to provide comprehensive wraparound services.

The following school year, the school informed all families that home visits were a part of the school culture. The staff made sure to schedule the visits in advance and made reminder calls on the morning of the visit. The visits were now conducted by two staff members rather than one. The Tier II team equipped staff with an outline of topics to cover during a home visit, including the list of community organizations that the family outreach committee had compiled. The staff also role-played different home visit scenarios and coached one another to improve their communication. The Tier II and Tier III teams were now prepared to have conversations with families about barriers to education and provide referrals to relevant agencies.

The teams also established a protocol for reaching out to an agency when a referral was made to let them know to anticipate a call from the family. A follow-up call was also made a week after the referral to see if the family had made contact; in this case, securing a Release of Information was sometimes the next step, if the services impacted the student's performance at school.

In the ideal school, school counselors and social workers are providing professional development for staff members to help them understand the need for establishing boundaries as part of their self-care plans. They are also well-suited to be liaisons with community agencies.

Some families would much prefer to turn to a familiar face at their school rather than follow through on a referral to an agency. As a result, a codependent dynamic can evolve if the school attempts to fulfill needs that would be better met by a social service agency. In these circumstances, school staff should uphold appropriate boundaries while encouraging families to access support. School counselors and school-based social workers are a good resource for staff since they are trained to maintain boundaries while serving clients.

Other families may be outright resistant to all forms of help or intervention. When working with resistant families, school counselors and social workers can act as liaisons to support these families in establishing contact with community agencies, especially if the family's circumstances could evolve into abuse or neglect.

I share this school's journey because it illustrates how responsive leadership supported the effective implementation of tiered interventions. The leadership team understood that the school could not continue in its initial course and needed to shift the focus of its efforts. Instead, the school developed a protocol for scheduling, communicating, and conducting family outreach with staff who were now prepared to respond to families in crisis. Their story is true for many schools that quickly find themselves in over their heads once they begin working more closely with students and families impacted by trauma. Again, I recommend that a school pilot a Tier II or Tier III intervention for a quarter or a semester before expanding it to serve a larger number of students and families. A pilot gives the school the opportunity to build the capacity of the program to better respond to the need.

Summative Evaluation

At the end of the school year, the leadership team conducts a summative evaluation of the implementation process. The purpose of the summative evaluation is twofold. First, the team assesses the progress that has been made with regard to each of the implementation priorities that were identified at the beginning of the year. Behavior, academic, and attendance data are useful sources of information when conducting the evaluation. The team should also consider data that is specific to each tier. For example, they may wish to include data from the behavioral charts of students who were served in a Tier II Check-In/Check-Out program. They may also wish to review data that was collected through Tier III student intervention plans. Parent communication logs; the number of students processed through the Ready to Learn Room; the number of teachers incorporating the S.E.L. curriculum into their daily instruction; and staff, student, and parent surveys are just a few of several different sources of data that can be helpful in assessing a school's implementation of a trauma-informed framework.

The second function of the summative evaluation is to plan for the following school year. It is helpful for the leadership team to revisit the three tiers of the trauma-informed framework and identify the school's strengths and growth areas. Using the lessons learned over the course of the school year, the team should identify ways to improve and sustain the interventions and programs that have been put in place. They will likely see new areas of need that may become implementation priorities for the upcoming school year.

WHERE IS OUR SENSE OF URGENCY?

The Transformationist School Counselor or Social Worker and Family Support

I started working in a school setting in 1993, seven months after receiving my bachelors' degree. I had the privilege of returning to the high school where I graduated to serve as a community outreach worker. In this role, I was providing case management services for at-risk students. I now know they were not at-risk but living with adverse childhood experiences.

Even though ACEs research was in its infancy, I was learning while on the job about trauma-informed strategies. I learned immediately that I needed to establish a meaningful relationship with the students and their families. If I made a commitment, I had to follow through. I had to learn how to maintain a professional boundary, yet still convey respect, interest, and caring.

I had office space at the community agency where I worked and on the school campus. I made sure each space was comfortable and welcoming. There were pictures of diverse family groupings reflecting the children and families I served. The images reflected the rich ethnic diversity that is America. Although there was a desk in the office at work, I'd arranged the chairs so that I would sit on the same side as the parents or students. In the space at the schools, I used round tables.

But I sometimes found myself struggling with teachers who didn't understand or had little feeling or empathy for students and their families. There were parents who didn't trust anyone at their children's schools and were unwilling to hear any feedback about their child. I found myself literally translating conversations for the two points of view that, at times, were polar opposites. In the meantime, while the adults were busy berating each other, the children were acting out their frustrations in the classrooms and sometimes in their communities. At best, I was a human bandage trying to cover up the wounded on all sides.

Children have no choice but to come to school and, in most states, remain there until they are at least sixteen years old. It may take years for a school to transform itself from an adult-centric institution to a child-centered compassionate school, just as I learned more was needed than just creating a comfortable space or working on relationship building to help students, families, and teachers understand each other. But schools can change when the adults change.

At the elementary level, school counselors spend a lot of their time teaching socioemotional curricula in classrooms. Middle and high school counselors spend a good portion of their time as intermediate disciplinarians or providing time-out space, doing career counseling, and monitoring credit acquisition. Instead, as mentioned earlier, they can begin working on becoming transformationalist school counselors by designing instructional models to deliver therapeutic counseling and support directly to students impacted by ACEs, providing professional development activities to help classroom teachers integrate socioemotional curriculum into their daily routines, facilitating restorative conversations between teachers and students, and do **rounding** with administrators to observe how well students are applying socioemotional strategies as they work in their classrooms and make adjustments in future professional development for teachers.

Transformationalist school counselors and social workers can be instrumental in helping school staff develop cohesion around changing how they deal with disruptive behaviors so that everyone is an expert and a consumer simultaneously. Working in silos is not emotionally healthy for anyone in today's school setting.

Transformative school counselors and social workers can help schools engage families and families engage with school more effectively. Our current definition of *family involvement* is very narrow and like most school cultures, only fits middle class and wealthy families. When parents help the school raise money, attend PTA meetings, host school carnivals, or give teachers special gifts on National Teachers' Day, we say they are involved. We need to appreciate and reframe parent involvement as it relates to our families who are low income. These families are working two and three jobs just to clothe their children and provide them with the basic necessities of food, shelter, and love. They are raising them in neighborhoods that are not safe. Still, they get their children to school with the hope they will get the education to better their lives. These parents get their children involved in sport teams and community organizations like the YMCA or Big Brothers Big Sisters programs. They take their children to worship services. This is the parent involvement schools overlook.

Transformative school counselors can help school staff understand that dysfunctional families are in every American school, regardless of ethnic or economic status.

Newtown, Connecticut, a small community sixty miles from New York City, is 96 percent White based on 2017 data. The median income is $110,852, and the "excellent" schools were not prepared to network with outside agencies to support Adam Lanza or help his mother with viable options that would have kept him in school. Although Adam showed signs of developmental and mental health issues at an early age, he had a relatively good experience in elementary school. As he got older, however, his socioemotional development worsened and his mother withdrew him from school when he was in eighth grade. It is not clear how well his home schooling was going. A year later, his mother had him evaluated at the Yale Child Study Center. They recommended that Adam needed to be enrolled back in a school setting or else isolation would worsen his anxieties. When Adam was twenty years old, he murdered his mother and then went to Sandy Hook Elementary and killed twenty-six people before taking his own life. Twenty of the shooting victims were children ages six and seven years old. In a report released by the Office of the Child Advocate, there were a number of missed opportunities indicating that communication and coordination between Adam's physicians, educators, and mental professionals may have prevented this tragedy (Griffin & Kovner, 2013). Schools and community resources need to develop ways to communicate and update each other. Unfortunately, a similar situation happened in Florida in the case of Nikolas Cruz. There were many warning signs that he was a troubled young person. His mother died, he was expelled from school, he had a fight with the son of the family who took him in and calls were made to 911. A neighbor videotaped him holding a gun in his backyard. Surely we have the technological capability of developing software for all of these agencies to input and share information. In states where it is legal for an eighteen-year-old to purchase any weapon, information should be available for law enforcement officials to monitor and follow up with parents and school officials.

Transformative school counselors, school-based social workers, and psychologists are integral supports in the changes needed to close the achievement gap and open an opportunity gap for students. They have the therapeutic and psychometric skillsets to integrate psychology with cognitive behavior to build resiliency in staff, students, and families. In the transformative school or school district, they can be the liaison between school and school district and physical and mental agencies.

When students like Adam Lanza are identified as needing Tier III interventions and their parents decide to home school, transformative school counselors and school-based social workers can maintain contact with them and increase contact with physicians and mental health caregivers. Most police departments conduct well-child checks and all states have agencies that handle child abuse. In this case, perhaps all of the stakeholders could have designed a plan that supported both Adam and his mother better. Had his middle and high school continued the good work his elementary teachers started, Adam would have remained in school as recommended by the Yale Child Study Center.

The field of education is expanding to include the latest research in neuroscience. School psychologists can assess the intellectual abilities of Tier II and III students using tests that are based on the latest research on brain functioning and multiple intelligences (Gardner, 1993; Sternberg et al., 1995).

Changing the roles of school counselors, school-based social workers, and psychologist will change policies and procedures that now merely validate a student's eligibility for special education and end the isolation schools are in. When they can use the skills they were trained for, they are in a better position to help create academic and social behavior plans, support the implementation process, and bring community agencies to the intervention table.

THE PLAN: IMPLEMENTATION GUIDE TO TRANSFORMATION

Assessing Capacity

o **Know your students.** Review student data (academic, attendance, behavioral, free-reduced lunch, etc.) to assess the potential impact of ACEs and trauma.

○ **Know your staff.** Assess staff perceptions of students' needs and behaviors as well as satisfaction with the school's current approach to addressing these issues.

○ **Identify strengths.** Identify programs currently in place that support the behavioral, socioemotional, and academic success of students (PBIS, SEL curriculum, universal free breakfast program, etc.). Identify staff members who already provide exceptional support to struggling students.

○ **Identify growth areas and barriers to implementation.** Review the three tiers of trauma-informed response to intervention in Chapter 5. Identify gaps in your school's current programing. Also, consider which programs your school has in place that are failing to produce desired outcomes. Identify staff members who struggle with meeting the academic or behavioral needs of students. Identify barriers to implementation such as exclusionary discipline practices, racial disproportionalities in student achievement and behavioral data, and lack of parent outreach.

Build Capacity

○ **Establish the foundation.** Professional development at the start of the school year must lay the groundwork for a trauma-informed school. This foundation includes viewing behavior as a form of communication, understanding the impact of trauma and ACEs on learning and behavior, adopting a relationship-based approach to trauma, an introduction to trauma-informed classroom strategies, and an overview of the three-tiered model. As the year progresses, additional techniques and strategies from the Trauma-Informed Toolkit will be presented to the staff to build upon this foundation.

○ **Offer intensive training for leadership team.** Provide additional training to specialists (school counselor, special education teachers, instructional specialist, family liaison, school nurse, behavior specialist, administrators, dean, etc.) on tiered trauma-informed interventions and supports. These individuals will be working directly with staff, students, and families to build a trauma-informed culture in your school. They are your leadership team.

○ **Develop tiered intervention teams.** Invite staff to participate on Tier I, Tier II, and Tier III intervention teams. Assign at least one member of the leadership team to lead each of the tiered intervention teams. These team leaders will guide their intervention team in implementing the appropriate interventions for their tier.

○ **Establish maintenance structures.** Designate regular meeting times and protocols (agenda, review data, action plan, etc.) for the leadership and intervention teams. The leadership team should meet monthly, while the intervention teams should meet weekly or biweekly. In addition, schedule time for members of the leadership team to meet once a month with each grade-level team to discuss trauma-informed interventions and supports.

IMPLEMENTATION

Leadership Team: Ongoing Support and Development

○ **Ongoing referral process.** Prior to the start of the school year, develop a process to identify students for tiered interventions and supports. Your school may already have a process for identifying students for tiered support (i.e., PBIS's Universal Screener) to build upon. If not, the leadership team will need to design a referral process (see a sample Tiered Intervention Referral Process below). Information gathered from student data, grade-level team meetings, intervention team meetings, caregiver requests, and teacher referrals may be used to inform your referral process.

Tiered Intervention Referral Process

A student remains in Tier I when

○ trauma-informed schoolwide practices and classroom strategies are sufficient in supporting the student's academic, socioemotional, and behavioral progress.

A student is referred to Tier II when

○ despite the documented and consistent implementation of Tier I classroom strategies, the teacher refers the student to the Tier II Team for additional support.

○ a parent contacts the school because his child needs additional support, which can be provided through mentoring or small group.

A student is referred to Tier III when

○ a student's behavior is a significant threat to safety and requires an intervention plan.

○ the student has shown no improvement in behavior after receiving Tier IUI supports (mentoring or small group) for a minimum of four weeks.

○ a parent discusses significant emotional or behavioral issues that suggest the need for an individualized intervention plan.

○ a parent authorizes her child's health care provider or mental health counselor to contact the school, and the professional provides information that suggests the need for an intervention plan.

○ school staff and community agencies monitor student progress on a regular basis.

○ **Trauma-informed grade-level team meetings.** When members of the leadership team meet once a month with each grade-level team, they will collaboratively develop classroom interventions and socioemotional supports. These meetings are an opportunity for teachers to plan interventions, request support, share successes, and provide encouragement.

Tier I Team: Building a Trauma-Informed School Culture

o **Schoolwide Policies and Practices**

  o Teach and model positive behavioral expectations and restorative practices schoolwide. Students must understand that school has clear and consistent values or norms and consequences that are upheld with care and respect.

  o Create a welcoming environment. Decorate the school with messages and images that reinforce positive behavior, represent diverse identities, and promote achievement. Consider personalizing this approach by having members of the Tier I team greet students at the entrance to the school each morning.

  o Designate a deescalation area in the school, such as a Ready to Learn (RTL) Room. Stock this room with resources that address the first rungs of Maslow's Hierarchy of Needs (e.g., snacks, water, sensory materials). Design and disseminate a plan for how and when students can access the RTL Room. In the Ready to Learn room, students need to reflect, analyze their behavior, and plan a restorative conversation to repair the relationship.

o **Classroom Interventions and Strategies**

  o Tier II team reviews the Trauma-Informed Toolkit in Chapter 5 and chooses one strategy per month to present to the staff.

  o Once a month, time is set aside at a staff meeting to introduce a Strategy of the Month from the Toolkit. Invite staff to try the strategy and report back the next month on how they made it work for their students. Teachers may also invite colleagues to visit their classroom and observe the strategy in action.

o **Collaboration with Families**

  o Adopt an ACEs-informed approach to family engagement by identifying the barriers to family involvement and the supports that are needed to remove them.

  o Choose one action step to implement as a component of your school's ACEs-informed family outreach process. For example, consider providing food or childcare at school events.

  o Parent outreach must be culturally responsive, so utilize translation services, consider multiple modes of communication (text messaging, parent–teacher apps, etc.), and have events that encourage participation and community.

o **Community Partnerships**

  o Make a list of community organizations and social service agencies in your area. Contact relevant organizations and inquire about the services they provide to children and families. Share this list with the school staff.

  o Invite community organizations to host an information table at a school event.

o **Staff Self-Care**

  o Provide time during a staff meeting at the beginning of the year for staff members to draft a self-care plan.

- o Set aside time at the end of each quarter for staff to review and revise their plans. Encourage staff to partner with a colleague to support one another in taking a self-care action each week.

Tier II Team: Mentoring and Small Group Support

- o **Schoolwide Policies and Practices**
  - o Student Mentoring Program
    - □ Provide all staff with an introduction to the mentoring program.
    - □ Explain to teachers the process for which students can be referred for Tier II mentoring.
    - □ Recruit a team of teachers and support staff to be mentors for Tier II students.
    - □ Provide mentors with training on the mentoring process, including frequency and focus of check-ins, types of data to be collected, and the process for recording and reviewing data. To guide this process, the mentoring program can be modeled after research-based programs such as Check-In/Check-Out or Check & Connect. However, the program can also be built from the ground up, if that better suits the needs of your school.
    - □ The first year of implementation is a pilot year. Mentors should meet biweekly to problem-solve and adapt the program to best fit the needs of staff, students, and families.
  - o Small-Group Interventions
    - □ Students who are identified for Tier II supports may be matched with a small-group intervention that addresses a specific need (e.g., emotional regulation, self-control, conflict resolution).
    - □ Small groups meet weekly and are facilitated by the school counselor, behavior specialist, special education teacher, or another appropriate staff person.

- o **Classroom Interventions and Strategies**
  - o Once a student has been assigned a mentor or a small group, a member of the Tier II team must notify the teacher.
  - o Teachers honor the change in the student's schedule to allow for meeting with the mentor or small group.
  - o Teachers are encouraged to provide feedback to the Tier II team to support the intervention process.

- o **Collaboration with Families**
  - o Families are informed that their child has been selected to participate in the school's mentoring program or to attend a small group.
  - o Mentors are encouraged to reach out to families and introduce themselves.

- o **Community Partnerships**
  - o Tier II students and their families often need additional support with clothing, food, shelter, or mental health counseling, for example. Referrals to community agencies are a need.
  - o Contact Child Protective Services if necessary.

o **Staff Self-Care**
  o Administrators should give incentives and awards to honor the demanding work of their staff, especially their mentors.
  o Mentors often provide emotional support and guidance to students who are recovering from, or living through, a traumatic life event; as a result, mentors may experience secondary trauma or compassion fatigue. Encourage mentors to reach out to colleagues, including the school counselor, if they experience vicarious trauma stemming from their relationship with their mentees.

Tier III Team: Student Intervention Support

o **Student Intervention Plan**
  o Tier III team meets weekly to develop intervention plans for Tier III students. The Tier III team may invite the student's teachers, family, related service providers, and, if appropriate, the student to attend the meeting.
  o The behavior specialist, special education teacher, school psychologist, or another appropriate staff person should conduct classroom observations to draft the student's intervention plan. The plan should be presented to the Tier III team for revisions. Teacher, parent, and student input should be included in the plan as well.

o **Schoolwide Policies and Practices**
  o Ensure all staff who work with the student are informed of the intervention plan.
  o Provide staff with copies of the plan and any supplemental materials.

o **Classroom Interventions and Strategies**
  o Adjust classroom practices and routines to support the implementation of the plan.
  o If an alternative schedule is part of the student's plan, ensure that the student and teachers are made aware of the changes and determine the new transition routines.

o **Collaboration with Families**
  o Include the family, as much as possible, in drafting and implementing the intervention plan.
  o Determine how and when the parent and teacher will communicate on the student's progress.
  o If possible, work with the family to create a plan for reinforcing the intervention plan at home:
    □ talking with their child about their day at school
    □ using similar behavioral intervention strategies at home
    □ providing reasonable and consistent consequences and rewards at home based upon the student's behavior at school
  o Assess the family's need for additional support and provide referrals to community agencies and organizations as needed.
  o Schedule a follow-up meeting in six to eight weeks.

- **Community Partnerships**
  - Refer student and family to relevant community organizations or social service agencies. Contact the agencies to inform them that a referral has been made.
  - Connect student with a mentoring, volunteer, or other youth development program as needed.
  - Contact Child Protective Services if necessary.

- **Staff Self-Care**
  - Staff who work with a Tier III student are encouraged to adhere to their self-care plan.
  - If the student has a significant escalation that poses a threat to safety, a member of the leadership team should follow up with any staff members who were involved. The primary purpose of the follow-up is to problem-solve, to prevent a future occurrence, and to offer support to the staff members involved. These incidents can be exhausting and triggering for staff; therefore, it is important that the leadership team member listens and offers meaningful support. Following the incident, adjustments may need to be made to the student's intervention plan. The incident must also be documented according to your district's policy.

EVALUATION AND PLANNING

- **Leadership Team Monthly Meetings.** Leadership team reviews quantitative (student data, intervention team data, etc.) and qualitative (feedback from meetings, general perceptions, etc.) data regarding program implementation. At the monthly meeting, the intervention teams' leaders will share about their teams' current priorities, action steps, and needs. The leadership team will use this information to determine next steps in providing staff support and coordinating efforts to strengthen implementation.

- **Summative Evaluation.** End-of-year analysis of schoolwide behavior, academic, and attendance data, along with feedback from a staff survey, is used by the leadership team to determine strengths, growth areas, and program needs for the upcoming year.

Read, Reflect, Respond

Select the template that works best for your next steps. Use the Implementation Guide, the TTFR Toolkit, and all that you have read to complete the template. This needs thoughtful time and plan out for as many years your leadership team or your grade-level team feel is needed. Start at any point that meets your current need. Align this template with your strategic district or school improvement or professional goal-setting plan. We encourage you to have one document.

District Implementation Guide—Goal to Transform Special Education Services for Tier II and III Students

Assessing Capacity	
Know Your Students	Review records of students from low-income families and students in self-contained special education classes for behaviors. Students with Tier II behaviors should be reassigned to classes using an ESL/Title I pull-out model, spending more time in general education classes. Tier III students should have documented evidence from medical or mental health specialists. Special education teachers with expertise in behavior disorders teach these students. Students should be mainstreamed in general education classes based on their capability.
Know Your Staff	Identify your most effective principals, teachers, and support staff. Reassign them to high-poverty schools. If possible, offer financial compensation or other tangible incentives (more planning time, sabbatical leave after five years, paying for college courses).
	Identify most effective school counselors and social workers and create a Tier I–III resource team to mirror structure at the school level. These teams will provide ongoing professional development for school-based teams, monitor transformation process for fidelity, help all schools plan transformation based on demographics of school, and provide feedback to superintendent's executive committee.
	Create procedure for staff to observe other staff members (demonstration teachers) who are effective in classroom management, using effective socioemotional strategies integrated with the classroom instructional process and skilled in evaluative approaches as they are presenting content (e.g., observation, constructing questions, monitoring individuals as they teach).
Identify Staff	Identify paraprofessional staff for new positions, monitor credits and on-time graduation needs at the high school level, act as family support workers in low-income communities, staff Ready to Learn rooms.
	Now that you know some of your employees may be survivors of ACEs, help employee assistant programs develop activities, add new protocols to provide services for those requesting, or those you have discovered because, for example, alcoholism has impacted work.
Identify Strengths	Use TTFR Toolkit to analyze current systems and practices.
	Have district Tier I–III teams research states that have developed standards for socioemotional development and make recommendations.
Identify Growth Areas	Based on research Tier I–III conducted, create your own or ask permission to use their socioemotional standards.
	Work with community agencies to add adult literacy, English, parenting classes for after-school programs.
	Work with community agencies (welfare, mental and physical health clinics, foster and adoption agencies, police, etc.) to create protocols for collaboration.
Build Capacity	In Years I and II, school board, union representatives, and district executive committee (superintendent, assistant superintendents, department supervisors [e.g., human resources, facilities, payroll, food services, transportation]) receive extensive training using *Building Resilience in Students Impacted by Adverse Childhood Experiences* to determine how to implement within their areas.
	In Year III, districtwide rollout begins.

School Implementation Guide—Goal to Transform Special Education Services for Tier II and III Students

Assessing Capacity	
Know Your Students	Review records of students from low-income families and students in self-contained special education classes for behaviors. Students with Tier II behaviors should be reassigned to classes using an ESL/Title I pull-out model, spending more time in general education classes. Tier III students should have documented evidence from medical or mental health specialists. Special education teachers with expertise in behavior disorders teach these students. Students should be mainstreamed in general education classes based on their capability.
Know Your Staff	Identify your most effective teachers and support staff. Reassign them to high-poverty schools. If possible offer financial compensation or other tangible incentives (more planning time, sabbatical leave after five years, paying for college courses).
	Work and plan with school counselors and social workers and create Tier I–III resource teams. These teams will monitor transformation process for fidelity, plan transformation based on demographics of school, and provide feedback to superintendent's executive committee.
	Create procedure for staff to observe other staff members (demonstration teachers) who are effective in classroom management, using effective socioemotional and resiliency building strategies.
	Monitor for compassion fatigue and burnout and attendance or emotional outbursts disproportionate to situation; be prepared to ask critical questions and direct employee to support services.
Identify Staff	Identify paraprofessional staff for new positions, monitor credits and on-time graduation needs at the high school level, act as family support workers on low-income communities, staff Ready to Learn rooms.
Identify Strengths	Use TTFR Toolkit to analyze current systems and practices.
	Have school Tier I–III teams research states that have developed standards for socioemotional development and make recommendations.
Identify Growth Areas	Based on research Tier I–III conducted, create your own or ask permission to use their socioemotional standards.
	Work with community agencies to add adult literacy, English, parenting classes for after-school programs.
	Work with community agencies (welfare, mental and physical health clinics, foster and adoption agencies, police, etc.) to create protocols for collaboration.
Build Capacity	In Years I–II, principal, department chairs, school counselors, special education staff, union representatives, bus drivers, and cafeteria staff receive extensive training using *Building Resilience in Students Impacted by Adverse Childhood Experiences* to determine how to implement within their areas.
	In Year III, districtwide rollout begins.

Classroom Implementation Guide—Goal to Transform Special Education Services for Tier II and III Students

Your school is not ready to implement recommendations, but you are because you found *Building Resilience in Students Impacted by Adverse Childhood Experiences* for your own professional growth. Consider forming a professional learning community with your grade-level colleagues or critical friends who think like you.

Assessing Capacity	
Know Your Students	Review records of students of your incoming classes with school counselor and identify students with behavior, attendance, or medical needs.
	Select a way you can communicate with all of your families before the start of school year or new semester: call parents and care givers, send letters, make robo-calls, for example, to introduce yourself and provide times you are available for conferencing.
	Use the TTFR Toolkit to analyze your classroom management procedures.
Know Your Staff	Use TTFR Toolkit to create plan for working with grade-level teams or academic department colleagues, identify each individual's strengths—classroom management, socioemotional strengths—and arrange observation times.
	Ask teachers to self-assess where they are in terms of processing and using strategies suggested in *Building Resilience in Students Impacted by Adverse Childhood Experiences* and create steps for continuing feedback from them to plan next steps.
	When teams meet to discuss student progress, add the categories socioemotional growth, attendance, and successful interventions to forms. It is important to document successful interventions for future staff who will work with the same student and to give feedback to students and parents that attendance is a positive correlate to academic achievement.
	Select a grade-level team leader (rotate throughout the year) who is responsible for connecting with staff and a support staff member (e.g., nurse, counselor, family support worker) responsible for networking with community agencies, monitoring attendance.
Identify Staff	Create working norms for team meetings and processing.
	Find a critical friend you can turn to for advice who will listen and not judge when you are frustrated by a situation.
Identify Strengths	Use TTFR Toolkit to analyze current systems and practices.
Identify Growth Areas	Use TTFR Toolkit to identify areas of growth in current systems and practices.
	Identify possible barriers and solutions since you are implementing this within your school system.
Build Capacity	Determine what you can reasonably do, when, and how, considering your circumstances.

Figure 8.2 Trauma-Sensitive Response to Interventions for Behavior

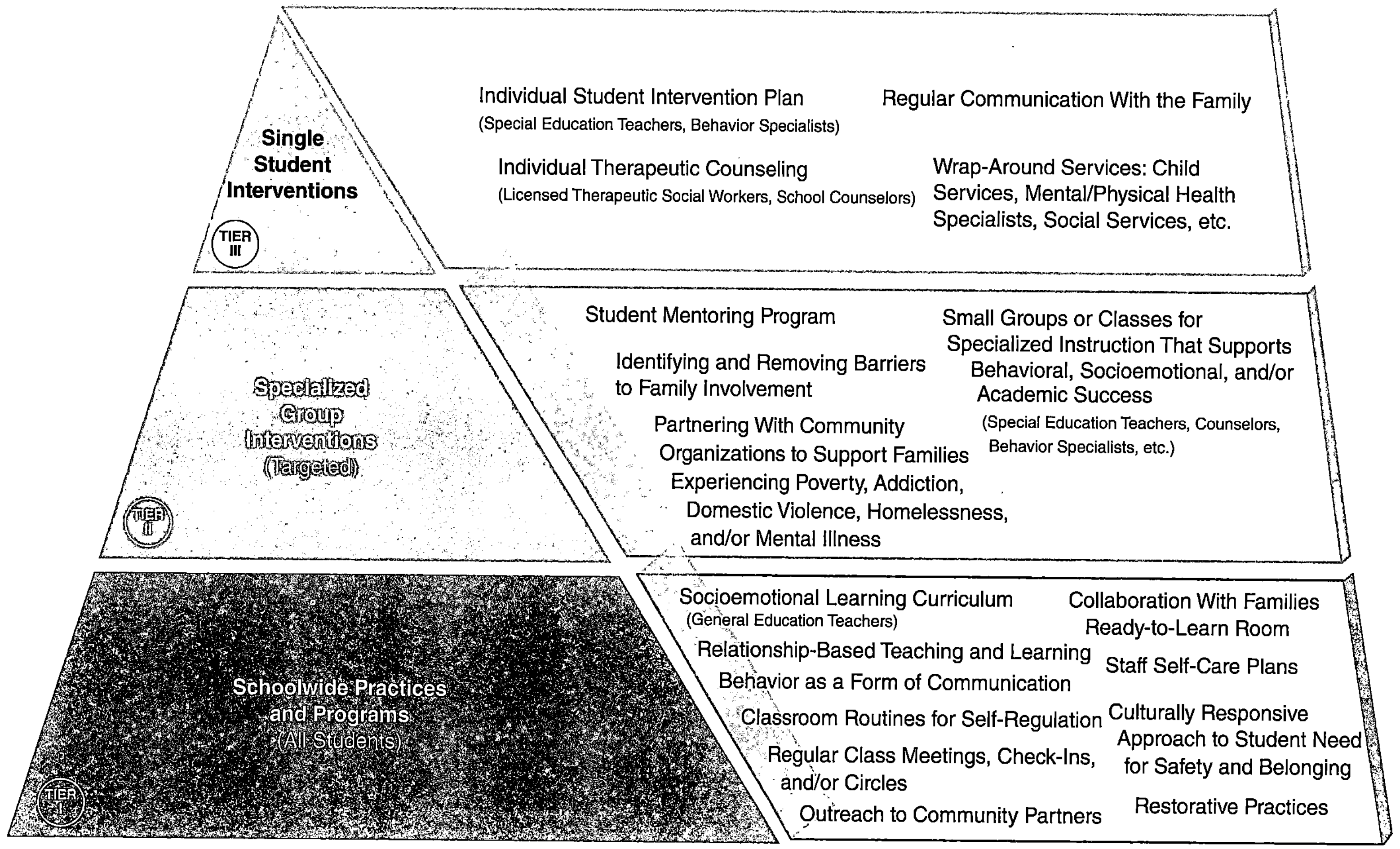

TIER III

Single Student Interventions

Individual Student Intervention Plan
(Special Education Teachers, Behavior Specialists)

Individual Therapeutic Counseling
(Licensed Therapeutic Social Workers, School Counselors)

Regular Communication With the Family

Wrap-Around Services: Child Services, Mental/Physical Health Specialists, Social Services, etc.

TIER II

Specialized Group Interventions (Targeted)

Student Mentoring Program

Identifying and Removing Barriers to Family Involvement

Partnering With Community Organizations to Support Families Experiencing Poverty, Addiction, Domestic Violence, Homelessness, and/or Mental Illness

Small Groups or Classes for Specialized Instruction That Supports Behavioral, Socioemotional, and/or Academic Success
(Special Education Teachers, Counselors, Behavior Specialists, etc.)

TIER I

Schoolwide Practices and Programs (All Students)

Socioemotional Learning Curriculum
(General Education Teachers)

Relationship-Based Teaching and Learning

Behavior as a Form of Communication

Classroom Routines for Self-Regulation

Regular Class Meetings, Check-Ins, and/or Circles

Outreach to Community Partners

Collaboration With Families

Ready-to-Learn Room   Staff Self-Care Plans

Culturally Responsive Approach to Student Need for Safety and Belonging

Restorative Practices

Read, Reflect, Respond

Use the graphic Trauma-Sensitive Response to Interventions for Behavior to analyze your school's policy and procedures. What are some possible next steps your school could take to implement?

Toolkit Takeaways

1. *Start Where You Are. Use What You Have. Do What You Can.* (Arthur Ashe quote)

2. Classrooms, schools, and school districts can transform to meet the needs of today's students.

3. Moving forward to a transformative pedagogy is needed for American students to be active participants in the global workforce.

4. The process of moving forward to a transformative pedagogy is one of continuous learning and adapting.

In Their Own Words

Meet Antwone Fisher, Cleressa Brown, Conor Black, Maria Gonzales, and the Salomon Martinez family. Antwone, Cleressa, Conor, and Maria have had to figure out how to live their adult lives as survivors of adverse childhood experiences. The Martinez family are currently parenting two beautiful young boys who were living with adverse childhood experiences.

Each contributor was asked to share his or her memories of their PreK to 12th-grade experiences. As you read their stories you will see how they at times felt supported by the adults in their schools and times when they did not. Maria Gonzales cannot remember much of her PreK to 12th-grade years that was positive with the exception of the day her kindergarten teacher read a story about a zoologist and she decided that she wanted to be one. In the case of the Martinez family, they would not have been able to make the tremendous strides with their sons were it not for a trauma-informed staff.

If you are starting to read the last chapter first as suggested in the preface, please be thinking about the following guiding question:

> What would their experiences have been like if there were trauma-informed interventions coupled with rigorous academic instruction at every grade level of their PreK to 12th-grade experience?

As you begin to read *Building Resilience in Students Impacted by Adverse Childhood Experiences*, please be thinking about why it is taking us so long to do the best things for all American students.

ANTWONE FISHER

Antwone Fisher lives in Los Angeles with his wife, Lynette, and their two beautiful daughters, Indigo and Azure. He is a screenwriter, producer, poet, and author. His autobiography, *Finding Fish: A Memoir*, is a *New York Times* best seller and was made into a movie, *Antwone Fisher*. The movie, directed by

Academy Award winner Denzel Washington, was Antwone's first screenplay. The movie won nineteen awards and was nominated for another twenty-two. Antwone's gifts as a screenwriter were recognized by the American Screenwriters Association's Discover Screenwriting Award, Black Reel Awards, and the Christopher Award. *Antwone Fisher* was the American Film Institute's 2003 Movie of the Year and the Humanitas Prize's featured film. Denzel Washington won several awards and nominations for directing and acting. The movie launched Derek Luke's acting career and he won several awards for best actor. Derek Luke played the counselor in Netflix's *13 Reasons Why* (2017) and Gabe Jones in *Captain America: The Avengers* (2011).

Antwone made his film directing debut with *My Summer Friend* (2009), which won the Audience Award Best Short Film at the Los Angeles Jewish Film Festival. His collection of poetry, *Who Will Cry for the Little Boy?* was a national best seller. Other poetic works are featured in Nikki Giovanni's *Hip Hop Speaks to Children*. His third book, *A Boy Should Know How to Tie a Tie and Other Lessons for Succeeding in Life*, won the 2011 NAACP's award for best literary work.

> *No child should spend all of his life in foster care.*
>
> —Antwone Quenton Fisher

Antwone received an honorary doctor of humane letters degree from Cleveland State University. Always willing to share his story, he is a motivational speaker. In 2013, he testified before the Committee on Finance of the 113th Congress at a hearing on ways to reform the foster care system. This special session was titled *The Antwone Fisher Story as a Case Study for Child Welfare*.

The Antwone Fisher Story as a Case Study for Child Welfare

I know a lot about my life from birth to my 17th year because of notations all of my caseworkers wrote in my files. I spent my entire childhood and teenage years in Ohio's foster care system. I learned my mother's and father's names from these recordings. I learned that I had a middle name, Quenton, when I was sixteen. That my mother named me Antwone after her favorite blues singer, Antoine 'Fats' Domino. No one should spend their entire lives in foster care without some professional adult monitoring the placement and ensuring each child is being nurtured and cared for properly. Without due diligence, a child's experience as a ward of the state is an adverse childhood experience.

I was born in a prison hospital to a teenaged mother. Two months before my birth, my father had been murdered by another young woman who'd had two of his children. My first weeks of life were in a Cleveland orphanage before I was placed in my first foster home. According to the written records chronicling my life, this first placement was a good one. My foster mother loved me, nurtured me and according to her, spoiled me! She did what all good mothers do—she met my every need, made me feel wanted, she loved me. In this first placement, I learned to crawl, stand up and walk. I said my first words and I smiled a lot. By the time I was two, the records reveal my foster mother was conflicted about her feelings toward me. According to the social worker's documentation, she felt she was becoming too emotionally attached to me. She wanted to give me up for an older child. In the next notation, she would change her mind. On one visit, the social worker noted that my foster mother held me like an infant even though I was a big two-year old. Evidently, I was okay about it because I nestled in her arms like a younger baby. This notation actually documented the social worker telling my foster mother that she shouldn't encourage a strong emotional bond. According to another entry, they were waiting for my mother to take more interest in me and come to get me. The latter didn't happen and at some point, someone made the decision to remove me from my first foster home.

At age 2½, I was placed into my second foster home. My new foster parents were middle-aged and had grown children and grandchildren. According to my records when I realized that I was no longer going home with my first foster mother, I cried until I was too tired to cry. The caseworker wrote that I cried until I couldn't cry anymore.

But I found more tears once I was left with these strangers and I refused to let anyone take my coat off. This is when my suffering truly began because I would come of age in this home, come to understand that I was a ward of the state, come to know how powerless and vulnerable a child can be in a system where the social workers who are charged with my well-being changed so often, connecting the dots was impossible. They weren't able to read my subtle and later, in my teen years, not-so-subtle cues. I had been placed in an emotionally, physically, and sexually abusive foster home where I braved myself for the next twelve years.

So, I daydreamed a lot. I made up my early childhood life. I imagined that my real parents were looking for me. Then I imagined that they knew where I was and would come and get me—soon.

I dreamt about my future self. I have a memory of my young self, telling people that I was going to be somebody. I begin to imagine myself as a grown-up, able to take care of myself. Art and music became my personal refuge.

I learn to be quiet and observant. I would shut down my reality and escape more and more into my daydreams, made up stories, art and music. At night, I would dream about being with people who cared about me and for me. In one recurring dream, a beautiful couple feed me pancakes and tell me not to worry, that I am not alone. When I think about those dreams now, it must have been my brain's way of helping me cope with my distress. These dreams instilled in my mind that I was somebody and I did belong—somewhere, some day. They literally gave me hope I would have a better tomorrow.

School was a haven. My kindergarten report card read "Antwone is a good citizen!' I earned a 'B' in conduct, a 'B' in effort and an 'A' in appearance. This would change by first grade. I was seen as very shy, not withdrawn. I walked with my head down and stumbled on words whenever I had to recite out loud. I couldn't focus and my daydreaming was cause for reprimand from my teacher. Looking back at my 6-year-old self, I was probably depressed, couldn't speak out and I was afraid of making mistakes. In my foster home, speaking up was not allowed. Making a mistake at home would land me in a dark basement kneeling on my knees, tied to a pole after a whipping.

By 3rd grade, school was becoming as repressive as home. I distinctly remember a teacher standing over me and pointing at my hair. She teased me about the zigzag part I'd tried to make in my hair. It felt like the entire class laughed with her. It's around this time that I notice my daydreams no longer made me happy. I began to lose interest in school and started playing hooky. I was developing a definite stutter. At 8, it seemed like learning was something that other kids did.

When my next caseworker learned that I was skipping school and constantly fighting with another foster kid in the same home, she decided to have me tested by a psychologist who concluded that I had above average intelligence but was not working to my full potential. The tests also revealed I had a great deal of fear and anger. The psychologist picked up on some of my anxieties but never asked me questions about my foster placement. Subsequently, she drew the wrong conclusions.

(Continued)

(Continued)

This caseworker followed through with one of the recommendations of the psychological evaluation. My foster brother and I started seeing a therapist. However, this did not last long as my foster mother wouldn't take us there. Evidently, our caseworker didn't insist that she should follow through.

I was failing academically and socially. My report card says I was "normal but a loner." In physical ed, music, and art, I earned 'B's". The only 'C' I earned was in social studies. I got 'D's' in everything else. I did well in art and classmates started asking me to draw things for them or asking me to show them how to draw something. I remember this time as my first experience that I could do something that made other people happy. It made me feel good.

And then a miracle happened. I changed schools and my 4th grade teacher was amazing. She was more than a teacher, she was a nurturer. She had a way about her that made every student in her care feel welcomed and wanted. By this age, I am adept at reading people and I knew by the end of my first day that she was fair and for real. She works hard to make sure we understand what she is teaching us. We have responsibilities and jobs to do. Our class runs smoothly and unlike my other school, we all get along. No one wants to upset her. She is a calming presence and it settles us and makes us want to behave in a calm way. The environment is peaceful and positive. I liked coming to school.

Our desks are in groups of four. We are face to face and side by side. Gone are the solitary seating arrangements and rows for the 'good' kids and rows for the 'bad' ones. I am making new friends—girls and boys. I am beginning to talk more and without fear.

My 4th grade teacher always greeted each of us at the door. Throughout the day, she complimented us, often. When she needed to discipline us or correct our work, she was specific. Her criticism was always constructive and well received because we knew it made us smarter or encouraged us to behave more appropriately. We had a ritual and routine. After our breakfast program was finished, we had a five-minute quiet time. She told us that we could meditate, think about something meaningful or silently pray. I would mentally recite the Lord's Prayer. Eventually, I began to talk to God—asking when was the good part going to come at home?

She rewarded the whole class with impromptu parties, field trips, and other celebrations. We celebrated when one classmate made huge gains and when we did well as a group. We were truly a family, a functional, loving family.

Sometimes her husband would come to class. We could see they really loved each other. They were the first couple I had ever seen in real life that were affectionate with each other with just a look or a smile. I would hold an image of him looking at her with love and respect in my daydreams for many years.

My academic grades were so bad that she waivered about promoting me to fifth grade. And then another miracle happened—she moved up to fifth grade keeping our school family all together. She would do this for my 6th grade year too. I had three solid years of great education. I worked hard to improve my reading and math. I distinctly remember the day I read out loud and didn't feel the panic I normally did. I didn't stumble over my words. It was during the middle of my 5th grade year. As I read, I managed to use the phonetic skills she'd taught us to decode a difficult word. When I finished reading, I look up and she had the biggest smile on her face. She tells me out loud so that my classmates all hear, how proud she is of my improvement and the effort I am putting into my work. There are more smiling faces all around me. I work even harder just to receive this collective warmth more and more. It is the first time I realize that by simply working harder, I can improve. In my foster home, I was always hearing what I couldn't do or that

I was no good. In school, under the guidance of my teacher and the encouragement from my classmates, I was learning that my foster parents were wrong. I could be successful just by working harder. My classmates wanted me and my teacher valued me. School gave me breathing room.

When I started telling my school friends stories about my foster mother and imitating her, they laughed. I was learning another good defense—I was cultivating a sense of humor. I could make people laugh and it made me feel good.

My junior high years at Roosevelt were uneventful. Many of my friends from the neighborhood and Parkwood Elementary also went there. And school remained my sanctuary away from my foster home. I enjoyed learning new subjects and thanks to the three years with a strong teacher, I understood that when learning, I needed to take risks and put in effort for decent grades.

All of this would change when I went to high school. Most of my friends from junior high were going to another school but because of where I lived, my school was John Hay. The sense of self I had been given during my fourth–sixth grades and had lasted throughout junior high was gone. Most of the friends I knew and trusted were gone. School was no longer my happy place. My love of learning slowly ebbed away. I was failing academically and falling emotionally into the deep.

Living in my foster home became increasingly more difficult and on a rainy morning, my foster mother told me to pack my clothes in two large paper bags and gave me bus fare. She told me to "go back." Not knowing what that meant, I went to the Child Welfare social service office and met my latest caseworker for the first time. She had been trying to contact my foster family for months.

I spent the next two years in a reform school. I was declared an emancipated teen a few months before my 18th birthday and driven to a homeless shelter and given $60 cash. I ended my K–12th grade experience hurting, angry and hopeless.

CLERESSA BROWN

Cleressa Brown is starting the second year of her career in education working in the same middle school she attended. Her former teachers are now her colleagues. She is already being promoted from an instructional assistant where she supported certified teachers, to a management position and will be the site coordinator for the program, Community in Schools. She feels this job, though challenging, is well-suited for her. She knows what some of these students are dealing with—just a few short years before, their story was hers.

In this new position, she will be helping low-income families connect with social service agencies. As the site coordinator, she will work collaboratively with school staff to learn the academic and nonacademic needs of students. If a student needs extra academic help, Cleressa will find tutors in the business community. If a struggling family needs clothing or has medical needs, it is her job to identify resources and make those connections.

Cleressa is a self-starter, an organizer, and has always been a leader, always climbing to be on that top rung. Her love for learning began during her elementary school years. She realized that when she performed well, the adults at school gave her positive attention. During her middle and high school years, she took advantage of after-school programs and clubs. Her interpersonal skills were such that she got along well with her peers and was elected president of

> *I would tell my 5-year-old self that I now know you shouldn't have seen some of the things you saw. Even though you were happy, you were neglected in other ways. But through it all, you knew you were loved by your mom, your teachers and mentors! You were brave enough to make a way out of no way. You are the reason I am where I am today.*
>
> —Cleressa Brown

the Associated Student Body (ASB) in middle school. In high school, she was a leader in the Black Student Union and the ASB.

When the federal government threatened to cut funding for after-school programming, Cleressa was asked by the coordinator of the programs at her middle school to speak with one of Washington State's senators. The after-school coordinator, Cleressa, and another student flew to Washington, D.C., and met with Sen. Patty Murray. An eloquent and thoughtful speaker even at that age, Cleressa shared how after-school programs helped to provide meaningful balance in her life. The funding for after-school programs around the country was spared.

During the interview, she became emotional when asked what she would say today to her five-year-old self. Cleressa is the first person in her family to graduate from high school and the first to earn a bachelor's degree from a university.

If I could talk to my five-year-old self, I would tell her she was something else. I understand now what a brave little girl she was in all her innocence. Now I know why she loved school so much—she loved the structure it provided. She was so smart and picked up things quickly. And this made her teachers smile and give her positive attention. My five-year-old self associated learning and working hard at school with love. For her, a love for learning had depth and dimension. Learning played an integral part in her emotional and mental survival.

When I reviewed the list of ACEs for this interview, I was shocked by the multiple adverse childhood experiences that happened around me as a little child. Since everyone in my immediate family was dealing with the same dysfunctions, these ACEs were my normal. If there was a family member leading a different life, I didn't know them. When my mom got evicted from an apartment, we went to stay with aunts, uncles, and cousins. When they got evicted, they moved in with us. No toilet paper—I'd look for a paper napkin or used Kleenex before using the bathroom. When a family member drank too much and got angry, you stayed out of the way by playing with your cousins. We were resourceful and supportive of each other in dysfunctional ways.

When my older sibling was born, my mother was just a girl, a beautiful sixteen-year-old girl. She had a lot of family support raising her baby but looking back on it with adult eyes, my sibling had a lot of inconsistent parenting in a family that was not stable. By the time I was born, eight years later, my mother was older and I was always with her. Though our lives may have been chaotic at times, she was a very loving parent. I think because I was with her more, my life turned out differently than my sibling who struggled more.

It wasn't until I started elementary school that I was exposed to a different world. There was structure and every day was the same. I loved school and I learned quickly that when I worked hard, teachers liked me. Actually, I read their approval as love. I thought my teachers loved me and I did all I could to please them. But fifth grade would change my future life. My fifth-grade teacher was a Black woman who dressed and acted like the actors on *The Cosby Show*. Until fifth grade, I had had no contact with Black professionals except for the Cosbys and surely they were not real because they were on TV. My fifth-grade teacher was the first college-educated Black person I'd ever met. I remember thinking, I bet she buys her beautiful clothes at J. C. Penney's.

Some of my classmates thought she was mean. But at ten years old, I felt she wanted something better for me. She was firm and consistent. I remember the first time I got my hair permed and it was straight as a bone. I couldn't help but play with my hair while she was teaching us. Suddenly, she stops teaching, and says something to the effect, "This is not the time to play with your hair; you need to be paying attention to the lesson I am teaching." She didn't direct her eyes in my direction or call my name—she spoke to the class in general and I remember thinking, "In this room full of kids, she sees ME. I am important to her!" Somehow at ten years old, I got the message that my hair was not as important as my learning. Looking back on it, her expectations were high for all of us. She wasn't necessarily the huggy-feely type—she was about business. I got the message that school was business and I needed to always take learning seriously. I learned that it wasn't what was on my head that mattered, but what was in my head mattered most.

By middle school, I began to come to terms that my home life was not the norm. My sixth-grade teacher was a funny, kind of wacky White woman. She made learning fun. But she was also available. I could go to her room during lunchtimes or after school and talk about my home or school life. I could tell her anything and she would listen without judgment. Looking back on it now, here was a White woman who had never experienced what was my reality but that didn't matter. She loved Reesie for Reesie. She truly cared about me and I loved her.

Although I was still adept at cultivating relationships with the adults at school and loving the positive attention good grades and appropriate behavior earned me, by middle school, I realize it was also helping my self-confidence to flourish. By this time, a lot of teachers knew my circumstances and they were members of my village.

I also took advantage of after-school activities. Looking back on it now, I realize that I had found a way to extend time in a structured, more predictable environment with adults who boosted my self-esteem. I also became very close to the woman who was the coordinator of the after-school programs. She is a Filipino woman who worked for Seattle's Parks and Recreation and would mentor me. Toward the end of my eighth-grade year, the Federal government was debating whether or not to cut funds for after-school programs. She selected me and worked with me to complete the application process for a possible meeting with one of our state senators. In working with her, I shared how after-school programs were like a God-send to me because of some things happening at home. I was selected, along with another student, to fly to Washington, D.C. The three of us met with Sen. Patty Murray and I shared with her my dependence on after-school programs. Federal funding remained intact. But when I returned to Seattle, I learned that my apartment had caught fire. My family was safe but we had nothing, everything was lost. My only clothing was what I took to D.C. It was trauma compounding an already traumatic home life.

My middle school teachers, counselors, and principal took up a collection and gave my mom gift cards. Because of their generosity, my mother and I stayed in a motel for two weeks. We were able to eat and buy new clothes. My teachers did things they were not paid to do or were supposed to do. If there were volleyball games I needed to get to, they drove me. And when I left and went to high school, my mentor, the after-school program director at my former middle school, was there for me when I became homeless and my mother couldn't care for me. The two months, I stayed in her home, enabled me to stay in the same high school and gave me time to try and figure out my next steps. Before I graduated from middle school, it was my after-school mentor who contacted a counselor at the high school and told him to find me and look out for me. It wasn't one of my teachers or guidance counselors, it was someone who worked for Seattle Parks and Recreation.

(Continued)

(Continued)

Although he was not the counselor for the freshmen class, the counselor found me. He had a Zen-like quality to him and soon, I would be telling him things that I had been holding in for a long time. I could cry in front of him, be angry or happy—it didn't matter to him. He was there, always in the present, and never judgmental. He taught me life lessons, and would check me when I said something that didn't make sense. He had a way of telling me that my thinking could be wrong and ask me to think of another way to handle things. He could look at me and tell me, "Cleressa, you are tripping!" Those words would bring me back to earth and what had felt overwhelming before our talk was now reduced to something trivial. Manageable and surmountable.

High school years are the most important ones for a student. In just four years, two of which you are still young and immature, you have to be prepared to step out into the world, ready for the next steps in your young adult life. He was my guardian angel. I remember he asked me why wasn't I applying to Harvard or Yale? When I laughed, he didn't. He told me I was Harvard material. I never did apply.

Still, my high school years were probably the most unstable ones in terms of my home life. I was homeless for much of it and on my own. After staying with my mentor for two months, I moved in with my godfather and his wife for a month and a half. They lived twenty-seven miles away from the high school I attended. I would wake up every morning at 4 a.m. to take a commuter bus to get to my school. My school days were long because I stayed after school to participate in extracurricular activities. Like I have already stated, I had lots of support from the adults at high school. Eventually, I would move back to Seattle and stay with people who knew my mother's family before I was even born. My uncle is not my biological uncle. Still he and his family are the people who saved me. When I overslept and missed the school bus, I could call my uncle and he would pick me up and get me to school. I lived with him and at times, with his father, whom I called grandfather, for the rest of my high school years.

Then another mentor came into my life, another strong, confident Black woman. She had contacted the school asking if there was a student she could help. She was willing to buy school supplies or whatever was in her means to support a hard-working student. My go-to Zen-like guardian angel told her about me. She had never wanted to meet any of the students she had previously helped until she heard that I'd told my Zen-like counselor, I didn't need anything. He just looked at me and said, "Cleressa, you need something." Because he told her about me and my thinking that I needed nothing, she wanted to meet me. And another role model came into my life, a college-educated woman who had the financial means to help a struggling student. For this student who needed nothing, she bought me a laptop computer, clothes, and paid for other things I didn't know I needed like fees just to submit an application to attend college.

I loved math and was very good at it. All through my middle school years, I'd managed to be placed in advanced math classes. I skipped Algebra I and was placed in Algebra II my freshman year in high school. I wasn't even in the seat good when the freshman counselor comes to my class and asks me to step out into the hallway. When I got there, she told me she was changing my schedule and taking me out of Algebra II and putting me into another math class. When I asked her what class and she told me, I realized it was an even lower class than Algebra I. I told her no, I was staying in Algebra II. I hadn't failed a math class and told her I was where I was supposed to be. I told the Algebra II teacher and he was puzzled also but he met with her and advocated on my behalf. Another math teacher also appreciated my math abilities. He was from Nigeria and spoke with a heavy accent which frustrated some students but not me. He called me Madame

President and still calls me that. He admired my work ethic and I admired how much he loved math. He would joke in class and tell the other students they needed to be like me, work hard like me. He made himself available when I needed extra help and he didn't do that for a lot of people.

Looking to take advantage of every opportunity, I went to Guatemala and Europe with two different programs. I sold coffee, asked teachers for donations to raise travel money. When I needed extra money to get a passport, the staff at the agency found extra scholarship money for me.

I didn't apply to Harvard, instead, I chose to go to one of the Black Harvards, a historically Black university and was accepted into Hampton University, in Virginia with an academic scholarship. I was also financially aided by two major Black sororities, Alpha Kappa Alpha and Delta Sigma Theta.

There's no telling where I would be had it not been for the many, many adults during my K to12th-grade years.

If I could offer teachers advice, I would tell them that just because a kid comes from a low-income or dysfunctional family, doesn't mean they are unhappy. Just because they aren't growing up like you grew up, doesn't mean it is wrong. It's just different. Just keep searching for the right hook to open up their world. There are so many Cleressas who won't speak up like I did and their silence may be interpreted as not having motivation or not valuing education. Please don't accept their silence. But "see" them and believe in them to the point, they will start to believe in themselves. Many flowers fold themselves up at night and open again in the light of day. Please know that you are that light.

It doesn't take much and it's not always about warm fuzzies. It's about loving with firmness and consistency. Correcting with care. Making learning exciting and relatable. Never giving up on a child. Understanding that you are their normal. Give them five minutes after school or thirty seconds as they walk into the classroom. Eat with them in the cafeteria sometimes. Accept your role in their lives for nine months as an honor. They see you. You need to see them.

CONOR BLACK

One of Conor Black's driving ambitions is a desire to give the world something enduring, something simple that he can build with his own hands. Until recently, Conor worked in New Mexico installing solar electric systems. As he says, "My wages were low and the roof-top temperatures high." It was an occupation that left his Harvard classmates shaking their heads in wonder.

Conor grew up at the edge of an affluent suburban community where subdivisions blended into other subdivisions, streets lined with luxury home after luxury home, all surrounded by perfect lawn after perfect lawn. Realtors market these subdivisions, with names like Northern Heights, Summit Park, Novelty Hill, as the "street of dreams." Conor grew up in an old house, on a three-acre pond that for most of his childhood was undeveloped. It was named Petersen's Pond. When the area became developed, in the early 1990s, developers changed the name of the area to Swan Lake. The public school district for these communities on the plateau is ranked the third-best district in the state for academic achievement.

> *It's because I have the OPTION, I can say no to things if they don't align with my principles. I am riding on the shoulders of those who set me up . . . the long list of people that made me a well-to-do bright kid at a good public school who went to a good college that I mostly didn't pay for!*
>
> —Conor Black

Although he grew up with wealth and at the periphery of extreme wealth, he has never aspired to be wealthy. Instead he wanted to be powerful like Lakota-Sioux Chief Sitting Bull, Nez Perce Chief Joseph, or Malcolm X. In his own words, he wanted to be "strong, dogged, resilient, wise, and speak truth to power." These were the role models that helped to shape him into the man he is today. These were men who lived in tumultuous times, who were willing to confront adversity, take risks, to say and do things for the sake of their people. Conor's exposure to his heroes was encouraged by his father, who he believes wanted to cultivate the same sort of resilience in him. His father wanted him to be curious about the lives of others. His sixth-grade teacher would deepen both resiliency and curiosity for him and at a time when he most needed it.

Conor's home life was tumultuous, unbalanced, and tense. It was during his sixth-grade year that he began to feel ill at ease, a feeling that he wrestled with for many years. The woods that were his back yard, his public school classrooms, and athletic fields were his most comfortable spaces to be in.

Today, Conor is starting his own electrical contracting business in the small community where he, his beautiful wife, and their tow-headed, sharp and hilarious three-year-old daughter live.

My parents' separation happened around the time I turned eleven years old. There was a violent incident the summer before I started sixth grade that led to restraining orders being filed and my Dad gaining custody of my older sister and me. Wealth, a big beautiful home surrounded by woods, vacations skiing or traveling to other countries offered little comfort to what I was experiencing most often. I remember feeling on edge, waiting for chaos, emotionally manipulated, and alone. Looking back, I can see that there was extensive honing of my fight-or-flight response at this age. My choice was often flight, and we lived next to a wooded pond where I felt most at home. Regrettably, it was also during this time that the pond and surrounding area were being rapidly developed as a result of the early 90s tech boom. The family unit had crumbled. And the woods were turning into relentlessly green lawns. I didn't see a whole lot to trust in adults.

Thankfully, my father was always giving me books to read about one culture or another. He was an imaginative kid who was always outdoors in Los Alamos, New Mexico, where artifacts of Native American people are all around—if you look. I think he had that sort of mind-expanding childhood brought on by investigating the outside world and thinking about the ways that previous people lived on the Earth. Just as it became for me—I think it was also an escape for him. It was his way of coping with a tumultuous home life. Perhaps my Dad was thinking son, this will help you cope and build resiliency too!

And then I met my sixth-grade teacher, Mrs. Romero. She was an extraordinary teacher when I needed one. To this day I am thankful she was part of my life at that time of conflict, confusion and vulnerability. She was a no-nonsense woman who at the same time let us know by her actions that she cared for us in more ways than just meeting academic standards. When there were days that were particularly tough, she would take time for me and have thoughtful insight. She was, in my estimation, a ceaselessly compassionate woman, who cared about the young people we were, and she was always talking about the "adults" we would one day become. She taught us how to work as a team and treat each other with love and respect. We were a family. But arguably more functional than the typical family unit that I know and certainly more functional than my own at the time.

Mrs. Romero taught us how to write through reading! We didn't just read a book together, we dissected sentences and talked about the author's word choice. We read genres and her class library was multicultural and multiethnic. When we covered fairy tales, in her collection, there were fairy tales from Europe, Africa, and Asia.

I figuratively met Chief Joseph, Malcolm X, and Chief Sitting Bull when we covered biographies and autobiographies. Because of my father, I was already reading a lot about indigenous cultures but not processing them the way we did in class. Although each student was reading a different biography, we all responded to the same thought-provoking questions and shared our insights and learnings with each other. The culmination of the unit was Romero's Wax Museum and writing a soliloquy where according her directions, we had to get into the heads of the people we were reading about. I chose Chief Sitting Bull.

To prepare for Romero's Wax Museum, we had to imitate the style of clothing our famous person wore. For me, this meant making leather buckskin leggings, a loin cloth (that I wore over khaki pants) and an ornamental breastplate of bamboo, bone, and beads. We set up our stations outside the cafeteria and as classes went to lunch, they were treated to our wax museum. We performed the soliloquys for our classmates. And then, because Mrs. Romero liked to challenge us, we took the wax museum to our neighboring junior high school.

Mrs. Romero told us she had selected some students to do their soliloquies. When she called my name, I was petrified. I did not want to talk about plentiful buffalo and the rapacious white man in front of junior high kids. I told her that I didn't want to present. Evidently, she didn't insist and I thought I was off the hook. So, I was shocked when I heard her announce to the audience, "And next we will hear from Sitting Bull!"

About ten years ago, my dad and I watched the video he made of me and I found myself teary-eyed. My delivery was spot on. To this day, I have difficulty speaking to people about deeper things but on that day, I was able to stand in front of an audience and be my authentic self through Sitting Bull's experiences. The words I had written were parallel to my own feelings of despair and hope, tenacity, and resiliency. The wild applause that came at the end were proof, I think, that these "big" kids got the message too.

Mrs. Romero knew that I was ready. She helped me push through fear, and the life lesson I began to learn and understand through my readings and writings is that adversity is nothing but a challenge to overcome. I can say to this day, I've been able to consistently shirk the easy path my whiteness and economic privilege afforded me in favor of what I deem a more principled one because I am strong in body and spirit. It's because of those tumultuous times in my home, thinking about how other people live and see the world, and my sixth-grade year that helped me to begin to see myself as a resilient and principle-driven person.

(Continued)

(Continued)

My sixth-grade year was a turning point for me. At a stage of vulnerability, when there was tumult at home, and the woods around my home were turning into million-dollar homes and vast lawns, I had a stable and loving environment that was cultivated by a good person that I could trust, who helped us students build on our inner strength, and was one of the most caring human beings I've known.

MARIA GONZALES

Maria Gonzales is an entrepreneur. She owns a dog grooming business. Maria loved animals and at a tender young age, she remembers learning what a zoologist was and decided that she wanted to learn as much as she could about animals. She wanted to be a zoologist. She wanted to take pictures of animals and write books about them like the one she'd read. Although she never became a zoologist, she never lost sight of her desire. She loves working with dogs and the independence being self-employed offers her. She's her own boss.

For most of her PreK to 12th-grade experience, her socioemotional or academic needs were not met. She remembers being a good student in math, science, and art and her teachers in those classes encouraged her and gave her positive feedback. But this was not enough; she would skip the classes that were problematic for her, any class that involved a lot of reading and writing.

She may have been misdiagnosed and placed into an ESL program. Maria spoke backward, using nouns and verbs in the wrong places. Her teachers could not understand what she was trying to say. Her placement in an ESL program may have had more to do with her last name. Although she spoke Spanish, it was not her first language. Her mother is White and her father is Puerto Rican. She spoke and understood both languages. When her mother divorced her father, Maria spoke only English at home. Her family could understand her but her teachers could not. Maria now knows she is dyslexic but she may also have dyspraxia. Dyspraxia is most associated with fine and gross motor difficulties but it can also affect speech, memory, organization, and time management.

Maria is the middle child of three girls. All of them are now young women leading productive lives. Her oldest sibling works for a nonprofit program helping youth from troubled homes learn how to be more independent. Her younger sister manages a store in one of the largest coffee chains on the planet.

The people in their church family who know the story of their lives, nicknamed them the three graces. In Greek mythology, the three graces exude charm and beauty and are favored with power from God. In their own way, these sisters protected each other and in many ways empowered each other to become the women they are today.

I don't remember a lot of good things about my PreK to 12th-grade experience. I remember reading a book or looking at a picture book when I was very young. It may have even been a book my teacher read to the class. It was about a zoologist and when I heard the word and looked at the pictures of the animals, I decided that that is what I wanted to be when I grew up. I wanted to take pictures of animals and write stories about them. I wanted to work with animals.

If I could sum up my childhood years in one word, it would be moving. We moved all the time. First from the east coast to the west. There was never any settling in—we moved all over in the city where we lived. We moved away from my biological father to live with a stepfather. I didn't get along with him. When my mother divorced her second husband, our lives were a series of rotations from moving in with her new boyfriends, to homelessness due to evictions, to cheap motels when we had money. And the cycle would start over—boyfriends, homeless, cheap motels. My mom did her best to stay employed but that was never consistent either. I do remember she did her best to buy us things and treat us to movies even if it meant not paying rent.

Her moods were unpredictable. My mom could be loving one minute and out of control the next. During those times, we were verbally abused and on occasion even physically abused. My stepfather would smack us on the back of our heads and call us names. Once my mother threw a brush at me and hit me so hard, I bled. They had to take me to the emergency room and I remember her telling the doctor it was an accident. For some reason, I believed it was accidental. Then just a few years ago, she told me it wasn't an accident and she laughed as she told me this, oblivious to how hurtful her comments and laughter were. Even when I told her it hurt me, she didn't get it. I love my mom but I don't understand her.

I now know that my mother's mother was an emotionally and physically abusive person. My grandmother was an alcoholic and neglected my mom. So emotional and physical pain is a generational curse in my family.

I was sexually abused at an early age. I was either in first or second grade when my teacher was explaining the difference between good touches and bad touches. I realized that what was happening to me was bad touching. I told my older sister who told my mom. I remember my mom not believing us but the abuse stopped. I guess that was a good thing that happened during my PreK to 12th-grade years. I remember being in foster care. I am not sure if I was already in foster care or if I was placed there because of the sexual abuse. I was really so young. My sisters and I would be placed in foster care again when I was eleven or twelve years old. That I remember.

We moved so many times, I think I went to at least eight different elementary schools and for sure, three middle schools. I had a few friends in each setting, but I was so insecure, socializing was not easy for me. The constant moving made bonding with students hard and impossible with the adults. I was teased by other kids and I remember my older sister always telling me I had to grow some balls and look out for myself. I took her words to heart, as the keys to my survival. I was already struggling in school academically and as I got older, I began to get in trouble for talking when I wasn't supposed to, not paying attention, being disrespectful to adults, and fighting anyone who teased me or looked at me wrong. I once broke a boy's nose. I was always being suspended. At one point, we lived in a middle-class suburb and I didn't last very long in that uptight environment. I hated my teachers and they didn't like me either. I ended up being suspended and reassigned to an alternative school. I was done with school. I remember thinking I am not even in it and I don't want it! School had no meaning. I knew I would not graduate from twelfth grade.

(Continued)

(Continued)

By twelve or thirteen, I was stealing cigarettes from a local drug store. My older sister was smoking weed and asked if I wanted to join her. At first, I said no, afraid I would get addicted. I had a fear of dying so I researched the effects of marijuana and decided it wouldn't kill me and I couldn't get addicted. I told her I wanted to try it. I remember we were with our mom on and off. She worked nights and we would have friends over. We would drink alcohol and smoke. Sometimes my mom yelled at us for having people over and other times, she would smoke and drink with us. We turned my little sister on. She was still in elementary school.

I was sexually active at an early age.

At sixteen, I was living more or less on my own. My mom kicked me out of a house we were sharing with a male friend of hers and his girlfriend. The police were called to their home many times because of their fights. Their landlord evicted them and my mother in her distorted thinking, blamed me because I didn't get along with either of them. I remember feeling uncomfortable about the way he looked at me. Worried that he might do something to my little sister, I would take her with me when I stayed at the home of some friends. I would get us both ready for school.

I used a party-line to meet men. I was looking for someone to take care of me. I became involved with a man who was thirty only I didn't know it. I had lied about my age and told him I was eighteen. He had lied about his age and told me he was much younger. Still, it was a relatively stable time for me and I was able to go to a community college and get a GED. My older sister was living in the YWCA and interning in a special program they'd helped to arrange for her. She helped me to find money to pay for vocational training. I looked over all of the options and when I saw grooming school, I was so excited. Grooming dogs appealed to that early vision of working with animals. I also signed up to volunteer at the local zoo. Both gave me a sense of satisfaction and the adults around me encouraged me.

By the time I was nineteen, I had a job bathing dogs in a grooming salon and had my own apartment. But I got involved with a boyfriend who was very jealous. He was emotionally and physically abusive. I added snorting cocaine to smoking and drinking. I remember the day I decided to end this relationship. I had watched an episode of the *Maury Povich Show* on domestic violence. It was the first time I realized the relationship I was in had a name and it was not a good one—domestic violence. When I told my boyfriend I was breaking up with him, he beat me so badly, I ended up in the emergency room. The social worker helped me to contact the police and I pressed charges. The courts granted me a restraining order and he was out of my life forever. The manager of the apartment changed the locks on my door and my neighbors rallied to support me.

I was able to buy my business with the aid of a loan from a nonprofit agency. I am currently living with a man who loves me and treats me accordingly. We've been together for ten years and have a beautiful, happy and self-assured three-year-old. My business is going well and I love what I do. The relationship I have with my sisters grows stronger as we grow older. We have a bond that cannot be broken. Putting everything all together grounds me and makes me feel whole.

THE SALOMON MARTINEZ FAMILY

About two years ago my husband and I decided to become foster parents. We had mulled over the idea of going to an adoption agency, but after having worked for years with children in the system, I decided that I wanted those same children by fostering. Fast forward to now. I am the proud parent to two amazing boys. When Javier and David were introduced to me, I was given some of their back story. They were a part of a case that involved a parent murdering their sibling in front of them and both boys had been in care for many years. At the time of removal, Javier was four and David was nine months old. Since their first placement, they had gone through a number of foster homes; we would be their fifth placement.

Javier was diagnosed with both ADHD and PTSD. He was on Vyvanse and Adderall while David was set to be evaluated and diagnosed the same. Both arrived with gigantic case files about five inches thick, full of referrals and e-mails tracking disruptive behaviors.

It was a bit overwhelming to read through the cursing, fighting, spitting, and destruction each of them caused in various setting since entering into foster care. When they came to live with us we had six to eight service providers coming into our home weekly and both boys were signed up to have neurological, CT scans, and psychological tests to further investigate what the prior home had identified as dangerous and unmanageable behaviors bordering on an oppositional defiance disorder diagnosis.

So that is where we started, and now eight months later we have two boys who, with the support of teachers and ourselves, are right on track. Javier is in a special education program that is ready to begin mainstreaming him, and his brother is settling in without any behavioral concerns into his elementary school class. Javier is also now no longer on any medications and has been working through his trauma, having built secure attachments with us and his academic supports.

As a parent I was able to work with the teachers to really dig into the trauma piece of their past. The behaviors, although distracting and definitely disruptive, began to vanish once we focused collectively on providing both boys with emotional support and consistency. Oddly enough, it wasn't about being overly nice or attentive either. Neither of the boys took well to being treated kindly or with "kid gloves," in fact, they generally took advantage of that and without exception, left people with the feeling that they had been foolish for going out of their way. The school had a strong behavior management program. The behavior expectations were the same for all of the students, whether they were in general education classes or special education. I physically showed up and kept an open mind. I saw behavior charts, the point systems, and I listened to the language the teacher used and replicated at home. Like their teachers, I focused on their positive behaviors and gave them praise that was specific. They knew that when they came home with good reports, they were entitled to some privileges we had agreed upon. If the report was not good, I was very clear about telling them they were in full control of whether or not they got their due. Using the term their teachers used, natural consequences, was always a part of this unpacking a not-so-great day. If they had a bad day at school, it was because of something they did, not the "bad" teacher or the "mean" parent.

(Continued)

(Continued)

Likewise, if they had a good day it was because of their actions. I learned from observing these highly skilled teachers. The thing I learned rather quickly about my boys was that I had to master being the stone hand in the velvet glove just like their teachers. I could see how they made my sons feel safe and loved in this uncompromising structure. When I made the top of my kitchen cabinets look like an arcade with a point system, they knew exactly what it meant—they could earn or lose points because of the choices they made. Points are earned if they read, draw, or ask for extra math problems. With enough points, they could play video games. They used to strive for more Play Station time; now they enjoy reading and both are reading above their grade levels. It seemed counterintuitive since they had been through so much, but once we were able to create consistency at both home and school (with both of us echoing the same message) the boys' behavior, which had been unaffected by therapists or interventions for the last four years, changed completely.

One way I think that schools could improve working with trauma would be to note that many times trauma is overshadowed by diagnosis and that sometimes when dealing with children who come with a diagnosis, we are tempted to only see the behaviors, assuming that mental health professionals did all the heavy lifting. It sounds simplistic, but all my boys needed was love and it was the one thing no one was giving in a way they could accept it. With trauma, you have to be surgical with how love is administered. If you give it too freely, you may end up with ravenous patients, which I totally understand because they are in need and desperate. However, this is a disservice to them, much like feeding a person starved of food for months on end, too much too soon is damaging and unhelpful. Take time, create structure, be consistent, verify that home mirrors school and make a connection providing love in doses until they are healthy enough emotionally to get full servings. I truly hope that makes sense. There were loads of interventions tossed in there too with point systems and lessons about earning nearly everything, but I tried to distill all that into the core pieces that made everything work. More so than any of the service providers or multiple therapists involved, what made the most impact was the relationship between home and school. In my story, it was teachers who made all the difference and currently the boys are in no additional services and adjusting beautifully.

Additional Reading and Resources

Adams, J. M. (2013). *Schools promoting "trauma-informed" teaching to reach troubled students.* Retrieved from https://edsource.org/2013/schools-focus-on-trauma-informed-to-reach-troubled-students/51619

American Academy of Pediatrics. (2014). *Adverse childhood experiences and the lifelong consequences of trauma.* Retrieved from https://www.aap.org/en-us/Documents/ttb_aces_consequences.pdf

Ansell, S. (2011, July 7). *Achievement gap.* Retrieved from http://www.edweek.org/ew/issues/achievement-gap/index.html

Baker, J., Grant, S., & Morlock, L. (2008). The teacher–student relationship as a developmental context for children with internalizing or externalizing behavior problems. *School Psychology Quarterly, 23*(1), 3–15.

Baron-Cohen, S. (2003). *The essential difference: The truth about the male and female brain.* New York, NY: Basic Books.

Black, C. (1987). *It will never happen to me.* New York, NY: Ballantine Books.

Blad, E. (2017, September 12). *Social-emotional learning: States collaborate to craft standards, policies.* Retrieved from http://blogs.edweek.org/edweek/rulesforengagement/2016/08/social-emotional_learning_states_collaborate_to_craft_standards_policies.html

Bohrnstedt, G., Kitmitto, S., Ogut, B., Sherman, D., & Chan, D. (2015). *School composition and the black–white achievement gap* (NCES 2015-018). Washington, DC: U.S. Department of Education, National Center for Education Statistics. Retrieved from http://nces.ed.gov/pubsearch

Brackett, M., & Rivers, S. (2013). *Transforming students' lives with social-emotional learning.* Retrieved from http://ei.yale.edu/wp-content/uploads/2013/09/Transforming-Students%E2%80%99-Lives-with-Social-and-Emotional-Learning.pdf

Bryant-Davis, T., & Ocampo, C. (2005). Racist-incident-based trauma. *The Counseling Psychologist, 33*(4), 479–500.

Carter, R., Forsyth, J., Mazzula, S., & Williams, B. (2005). Racial discrimination and race-based traumatic stress: An explanatory investigation. In R. T. Carter (Ed.), *Handbook of racial-cultural psychology and counseling: Training and practice* (Vol. 2, pp. 447–476). Hoboken, NJ: Wiley.

Center for Public Education. (2005, August 22). *High-performing, high poverty schools: Research review.* Retrieved from http://www.centerforpubliceducation.org/Main-Menu/Organizing-a-school/High-performing-high-poverty-schools-At-glance-/High-performing-high-poverty-schools-Research-review.html

Chansky, T. (2012, September 6). *How to handle change: It doesn't have to be head first.* Retrieved from https://www.psychologytoday.com/blog/worry-wise/201209/how-handle-change

Cole, S. F., Eisner, A., Gregory, M., & Ristuccia, J. (2013). *Helping traumatized children learn.* Boston: Massachusetts Advocates for Children.

Collaborative for Academic, Social, and Emotional Learning. (2003, March). *Safe and sound: An educational leader's guide to evidence-based social and emotional learning (SEL) programs.* Retrieved from http://www.communityschools.org/assets/1/AssetManager/1A_Safe_&_Sound.pdf

Cummings, C. (2001). *Managing to teach* (3rd ed.). Edmonds, WA: Teaching.

Cummins, J. (1996). *Negotiating identities: Education for empowerment in a diverse society.* Los Angeles: California Association for Bilingual Education.

DeBellis, M. D. (2005). The psychobiology of neglect. *Child Maltreatment, 10*(2), 150–172.

Durso, L. E., & Gates, G. J. (2012). *Serving our youth: Findings from a national survey of service providers working with lesbian, gay, bisexual, and transgender youth who are homeless or at risk of becoming homeless.* Los Angeles, CA: The Williams Institute with True Colors Fund and The Palette Fund.

Dusenbury, L., Weissburg, R., Goren, P., & Domitrovich, C. (2014, January). *State standards to advance social and emotional learning: Findings from CASEL's State Scan of Social and Emotional Learning Standards, Preschool through High School, 2014.* Retrieved from https://www.casel.org/wp-content/uploads/2016/06/casel-brief-on-state-standards-january-2014.pdf

Family Acceptance Project. (2009). Family rejection as a predictor of negative health outcomes in white and Latino lesbian, gay, and bisexual young adults. *Pediatrics, 123*(1), 346–352.

Foster, M., Gower, A. L., Borowsky, I. W., & McMorris, B. J. (2017, May). Associations between adverse childhood experiences, student–teacher relationships, and nonmedical use of prescription medications among adolescents. *Addictive Behaviors, 68,* 30–34.

Graves, K. (2015). Cris Mayo, LBGQT youth and education: Policies and practices [Book review]. *Educational Theory, 65*(1), 79–85.

Hammond, Z. (2015). *Culturally responsive teaching and the brain.* Thousand Oaks, CA: Corwin.

Howard, G. R. (2016). *We can't teach what we don't know: White teachers, multiracial schools* (3rd ed.). New York, NY: Teachers College Press.

Irish, L. (2017). *The impact that adverse childhood experiences and toxic stress have on students.* Retrieved from http://azednews.com/the-impact-adverse-childhood-experiences-and-toxic-stress-have-on-students/

Jackson, R. (2011). *How to plan rigorous instruction: Mastering the principles of great teaching.* Alexandria, VA: ASCD.

Jensen, E. (1998). *Teaching with the brain in mind.* Alexandria, VA: ASCD.

Jensen, E. (2009). *Teaching with poverty in mind: What being poor does to kids' brains and what schools can do about it.* Alexandria, VA: ASCD.

Lamb, A. (2015). *Are "trauma informed" just buzz words or do they actually mean something?* Retrieved from https://www.naccchildlawblog.org/child-welfare-law/what-does-it-mean-to-be-trauma-informed/

McLaughlin, M., & Talbert, J. (1993). *Contexts that matter for teaching and learning.* Stanford, CA: Center for Research on the Context of Secondary School Teaching.

National Education Association. (n.d.). *Strategies for closing the achievement gaps: Steps you can take in your school or district.* Retrieved from http://www.nea.org/home/13550.htm

Pember, M. A. (2015). *Trauma may be woven into DNA of Native Americans.* Retrieved from https://indiancountrymedianetwork.com/news/native-news/trauma-may-be-woven-into-dna-of-native-americans

Public Agenda. (2012, November 12). *Failure is not an option: How principals, teachers, students and parents from Ohio's high-achieving, high-poverty schools explain their success.* Retrieved from https://www.publicagenda.org/pages/failure-is-not-an-option

Quinn, Patricia. (n.d.). *Misdiagnoses of females with ADD (ADHD)*. Retrieved from http://www.addvance.com/help/professionals/female_miss.html

Radesky, J., Kristin, C., Eisenberg, S., Gross, J., Block, G., Zuckerman, B., & Silverstein, M. (2016). Parent perspectives on their mobile technology use. *Journal of Developmental & Behavioral Pediatrics, 37*(9), 694–701.

Shade, B. J., Kelly, C., & Oberg, M. (2005). *Creating culturally responsive classrooms.* Washington, DC: American Psychological Association.

Sotero, M. M. (2006). A conceptual model of historical trauma: Implication for public health practice and research. *Journal of Health Disparities Research and Practice, 1*(1), 93–108.

Southern Education Foundation. (2015, January). *A new majority: Low income students now a majority in the nation's public schools*. Retrieved from file:///C:/Users/val erie/Downloads/New-Majority-Update-2015-4.pdf

Topitzes, J. (2014). *Adverse childhood experiences (ACEs), high school dropout and crime: Extending the study of ACE effects beyond health outcomes and with mediation analyses.* Indianapolis, IN: Wiley. Retrieved from https://sswr.confex.com/sswr/2014/web program/Paper21328.html

U.S. Department of Justice. (2006). *Criminal victimization in the United States—Statistical tables, 2005* (Tables 3, 4, 9, 10). Washington, DC: Bureau of Justice Statistics.

ADDITIONAL RESOURCES

ACEs Too High

ACEs Too High offers a bounty of information about ACEs, including research, a tool to calculate your ACEs score, strategies for supporting students, and self-care tips.

https://acestoohigh.com/

COMPASSIONATE SCHOOLS

The Heart of Learning: Compassion, Resiliency, & Academic Success by Ray Wolpow, Mona M. Johnson, Ron Hertel, & Susan O. Kincaid

This book can be downloaded for free from the Washington state Office of the Superintendent of Public Instruction's Compassionate Schools Initiative's website. The book contains information about the impact of ACEs and trauma as well as strategies that schools can use to foster compassion, resilience, and success.

http://www.k12.wa.us/CompassionateSchools/HeartofLearning.aspx

Culturally Responsive Teaching & the Brain: Promoting Authentic Engagement and Rigor Among Culturally and Linguistically Diverse Students by Zaretta Hammond

An excellent resource to support educators in learning how their respective cultural roots process data and affect the teacher-learner relationship. Shares ten key moves to build students' learner operating systems and approaches for designing and implementing brain-compatible instruction that is culturally responsive.

Trauma and Learning Policy Initiative (TLPI)

TLPI is a partnership between Massachusetts Advocates for Children and Harvard Law School. TLPI offers several free resources for educators as well as ways to advocate for trauma-sensitive education reform.

https://traumasensitiveschools.org/

RESTORATIVE PRACTICES CLASSROOM CIRCLES

Teaching Restorative Practices with Classroom Circles by Amos Clifford

This manual is available at no cost on the Center for Restorative Process's website. It is an excellent resource for teachers and administrators interested in implementing classroom circles and restorative practices.

http://www.centerforrestorativeprocess.com/

EQUITY, INCLUSION, JUSTICE

Racial Equity Tools

Racial Equity Tools offers hundreds of resources (including articles, videos, research, curricula,) to support educators in working for equity and justice in their schools.

https://www.racialequitytools.org

Gay, Lesbian, and Straight Education Network (GLSEN)

GLSEN provides resources for educators on ways to support the academic and socioemotional well-being and success of LGBTQ students.

https://www.glsen.org/

National Association for the Education of Homeless Children and Youth (NAEHCY)

NAEHCY focuses on research, policy, and school-based supports for students experiencing poverty and homelessness.

http://www.naehcy.org/

Teaching Tolerance

Teaching Tolerance is an excellent resource for K–12 educators who are committed to developing their students' critical thinking skills, while building school communities that are free from discrimination based upon race, immigration status, gender, ability, sexual orientation, or religion.

https://www.tolerance.org/

BEHAVIORAL SUPPORTS

Positive Behavioral Interventions & Supports (PBIS)

PBIS is a multitiered system of support that identifies and supports students with behavioral issues. The PBIS framework is not in and of itself trauma sensitive; however, it should be supplemented with socioemotional learning and trauma-informed interventions.

http://www.pbis.org/

PBIS World

PBIS World offers a variety of strategies and interventions that align with the three tiers of the PBIS framework. Many of these interventions can be tailored to the needs of students impacted by ACEs and trauma.

http://www.pbisworld.com/

Art with Heart

Art with Heart uses creative expression to support young people experiencing trauma or adversity. Therapeutic activity books for youth and resources for the adults who serve them transform pain into possibility.

https://www.artwithheart.org/

Bounce Back Project

The Bounce Back Project is a collaborative of physicians, nurses, hospital leaders, and staff who come together for a single purpose to impact the lives of individuals, communities, and organizations by promoting health through happiness. Numerous studies have shown using simple tools, a person's mind can be retrained to focus on the positive, which increases feelings of well-being and decreases feelings of depression. These tools also improve social connections, restful sleep, memory, and stronger immune system function. This is an excellent resource for working with Tier II and III students.

http://www.bouncebackproject.org

Check & Connect

Check & Connect is an evidence-based approach to mentoring students that includes goal-setting, intervention, family partnerships, and progress monitoring.

http://checkandconnect.umn.edu/

EMOTIONAL REGULATION

Mind Yeti

Mind Yeti is a mindfulness app designed to help children feel calm and refocus.

https://www.mindyeti.com/

Yoga Calm

Yoga Calm is an organization that provides training on the use of yoga in schools to support mental, physical, and emotional well-being.

https://www.yogacalm.org/

Dr. Daniel Siegel Presenting a Hand Model of the Brain

In this video, Dr. Dan Siegel uses the hand as a model for the human brain and discusses what happens when we "flip our lid."

https://www.youtube.com/watch?v=gm9CIJ74Oxw

GROWTH MINDSET

Growing a Growth Mindset: Unlocking Character Strengths Through Children's Literature by Kevin Sheehan & Jessica Ryan

This book helps educators to incorporate positive psychology and growth mindset into their instruction through children's literature. The book can be ordered via a link on the website.

http://growingagrowthmindset.weebly.com/

ABUSE

Substance Abuse and Mental Health Services Administration (SAMHSA)

SAMHSA's website offers information about trauma-informed care, substance abuse prevention and treatment, and related research.

https://www.samhsa.gov

Sample Tier I Schoolwide Behavior Expectations for Teachers and Students

How to Use: The first two months of school, staff teach the vocabulary and have students define and demonstrate behaviors. School staff describe their teaching behaviors to students to help them understand teaching and learning is a partnership. Principal should organize assemblies explaining what they will be looking for when observing students in the classroom, moving in the building, or in the cafeteria, for example.

PREAMBLE

At our school, teachers and students are kind, considerate and caring because they are:

Respectful of themselves and others;

Responsible citizens; and,

Reasonable human beings!

RESPECT

- Speak politely to classmates and adults.

- Think positively about yourself. Use phrases like "I can" and "I will."

- Accept and appreciate our differences in all areas: skills, learning styles, culture, physical.

- Listen actively.

- Control yourself from head to toe. Be a calm and quiet presence in the building.

- Share your materials and talents.

RESPONSIBLE

- Take care of your classroom and school. Clean up after yourself in the lunchroom, bathroom, hallways, playground, and in the classroom.

- Honor your obligations. Be prompt coming to school and in from recess. Return library books, homework, school–home communications on time.

- Help. Be an involved participant in group projects and activities. Work cooperatively with others.

- Come to school prepared to learn. Leave toys, gum, candy, and other distractions at home.

- Build a caring school community by being thoughtful of others. Be kind and compassionate.

REASONABLE

- Be patient with peers and adults. Continue the conversation until each person understands the other.
- Practice the steps in problem solving: ignore, move away, talk nicely, warn, and get adult help.
- Accept the consequences of your behavior willingly.
- See the problem from the other person's point of view. Try to understand his or her feelings.
- Know your anger triggers. Choose acceptable ways to manage them.

Sample Format for Restorative Conversation

How to Use: Sometimes for adults, it is helpful to sort through feelings and write them down before scheduling a meeting. For students, writing their thoughts is part of the Ready to Learn Process.

Steps	"I" Statements—Your Point of View
Name the issue.	
Select a specific example that exemplifies what you think should be changed.	
Describe your emotions about the issue.	
Clarify what is at stake.	
Identify your contribution to this problem.	
Indicate your wish to resolve the issue.	
Invite the other person to respond.	

Source: Smothers (2018)

VIDEOS

You Tube Videos—Good Tips With Laughter

Supporting the socioemotional needs of teachers: Principal Gerry Brooks
https://www.youtube.com/watch?v=oMhcSWiF5hs

Teachers supporting the socioemotional needs of their principals: Principal Gerry Brooks

https://www.youtube.com/watch?v=25_nUfhxx6s

Facial Behavioral Management System: Principal Gerry Brooks

https://www.youtube.com/watch?v=JI4y_VeJSmQ

My Daily Classroom Behavior Interventions—High School: How to Survive Your First Year of Teaching: Real Rap with Reynolds

https://www.youtube.com/watch?v=8HIJUfbi9Dw

How to Build Relationships With Students: Real Rap with Reynolds

https://www.youtube.com/watch?v=QCtEx4ai_yk

How to Deal With Bullying: Real Rap with Reynolds

https://www.youtube.com/watch?v=utZ8_sSUb8A

Principal Gerry Brooks impersonation . . . I'm Too Sexy for This Job! https:// https://www.youtube.com/watch?v=x0FpG1t6G_U

TED Talks

How to Practice Emotional Hygiene: Dr. Guy Winch

https://www.youtube.com/watch?v=rni41c9iq54

Mindfulness in Education: Learning From Inside Out Teacher: Amy Burke

https://www.bing.com/videos/search?q=mindfulness+for+educators+tedtalks&view=detail&mid=FF80998382C4B08D55B1FF80998382C4B08D55B1&FORM=VIRE

A Self-Care Revolution: Megan McCormick

https://www.youtube.com/watch?v=sUKKJapwUXc&t=15s

Every Child Needs a Champion Educator: Rita Pierson

https://www.youtube.com/watch?v=SFnMTHhKdkw

Self-care for Teachers Artfully, Mindfully

https://www.youtube.com/watch?v=F2pLNxIOBS0

Transforming the Heart of Teaching: Care for Teachers: Tish Jennings

https://www.youtube.com/watch?v=00TSpqilzz0

A Self-Care Revolution: Megan McCormick

https://www.youtube.com/watch?v=sUKKJapwUXc&t=15s

Glossary of Terms

Adverse Childhood Experience (ACE): a stressful or traumatic childhood event (e.g., abuse, neglect, domestic violence, divorce) that happens before the age of eighteen. These events have been correlated with the development of immediate and long-term cognitive, emotional, and physical health impairments.

Bloom's taxonomy: simple taxonomy (knowledge, comprehension, application, analysis, synthesis, and judgment) that can be used as part of a teacher's management system. Students are taught the needed teacher and student behaviors for each level of learning; helps to reiterate the significance of the teacher–student relationship and cooperation. It also helps students apply growth mindset and resiliency behaviors.

Check & Connect: a mentoring program that includes frequent formal and informal meetings between a student and their mentor. The program includes goal-setting, personalized interventions, problem-solving, family outreach, and progress monitoring.

Check-in/Check-out: a behavioral intervention, typically for Tier II or Tier III students, that utilizes behavioral goals, incentives, and a daily behavior chart to monitor and improve student behavior. The program can be modified to better support ACEs students through the addition of mentoring and socioemotional goals.

class circle: a style of class meeting, or conversation, in which the students and teacher sit in a circle. Typically, classroom circles include agreements for participation, a talking piece, center piece, open-ended questions, and routines for opening and closing the circle.

classroom Cool Down Spot: an area of the classroom designated for emotional self-regulation. Typically includes a comfortable place to sit, a timer, and sensory tools.

community agencies: social service agencies, public health, child protective services, family services, community police, community health and mental health organizations, Big Brothers Sisters, Boys & Girls Club, local sports leagues, public library, among others.

compliant behaviors: students who give the appearance of a healthy well-being because they function within a classroom or school culture. A good rationale for teaching all students socioemotional competencies and using growth mindset and resilience-building strategies. The effects of students living with ACEs is not always observable.

cultural and linguistically psychological assessment: nonverbal problem-solving tests that are considered to be less culturally and linguistically loaded.

School psychologists who administer these assessments must be culturally competent.

culturally responsive teaching: using instructional strategies and creating learning environments affirming students' cultural and ethnic roots. Regardless of the ethnic make-up of their classes, these teachers provide opportunities for students to learn about other ethnic, religious, and family groupings. Teachers also blend a number of cultural learning preferences—for example, rap and rhyme have universal appeal with today's youth as tools for memorization. They integrate art in a variety of content areas as another form of expression. They use different student groupings, cooperative to individual, to support students in developing peer relationships and autonomy.

equity: knowing each school staff member and student by name and need. Both thrive in working and learning environments that develop socioemotional competencies, foster resilient behaviors, and promote growth mindset. Combined, these three approaches support the well-being of adult survivors of adverse childhood experiences and students who are living with ACEs.

exclusionary discipline: suspending or expelling a student from school.

formative evaluation (for teachers): writing measurable objectives for self-care and professional development.

general education staff: certificated instructional staff and classified paraprofessionals or instructional assistants. Certificated instructional staff are classroom teachers, academic coaches like literacy specialists, remedial teachers, ELL teachers, and librarians.

looping: refers to the practice of a master teacher remaining with the same group of students for more than one school year. For example, the teacher who taught Antwone Fisher from fourth to sixth grade.

new normal: term used to describe the differences between the students who attend our schools now from their counterparts in classrooms fifteen or more years ago; this is especially true if the school population has become more ethnically or economically diverse. Some veteran teachers may still be teaching in the same ways they taught students who are no longer in their classrooms. Incoming teachers may not be prepared for the behavior challenges.

Positive Behavioral Interventions & Supports (PBIS): a multitiered framework for behavioral intervention that equips school personnel with evidence-based strategies to support student behavior. Should be coupled with a curriculum that develops socioemotional competencies to provide students opportunities to practice and apply new ways to communicate.

psychotropic medications: prescriptive medications that effect the mind, emotions, or behaviors (e.g., treatments for chronic depression, bipolar disorder, anxiety).

racialized: refers to the moment a student for example, realizes that race makes a difference in how the teachers respond or treat them or their peers.

Ready to Learn (RTL) room: room dedicated to supporting students to successfully reengage in the classroom following an emotional or behavioral escalation. In the RTL Room, the student is assisted, by a member of the student support team, in completing a three-step process (deescalate, repair, and prepare to reengage) prior to being returned to the classroom.

Response To Intervention (RTI): a multitiered approach for identifying and supporting students with academic and/or behavioral needs.

responsiveness: being receptive to and aware of the cultural, emotional, social, and academic needs of students, especially in the instant it is most advantageous; teachable moments making learning more meaningful.

restorative conversation: a conversation that seeks to repair a harm that has been done. The conversation includes those who have been impacted by the incident or issue. The conversation seeks to identify the harm, encourage empathy and perspective-taking, and conclude with a plan or agreement to repair the damaged relationship(s).

restorative practices: a philosophical framework, and an alternative to punitive discipline, that seeks to repair harm while fostering and maintaining healthy relationships. In schools, restorative practices often take place within conversations or circles, in which affected students and staff play an active role in resolving problems.

rounding: formal or informal observations of students and/or school staff. Usually conducted in a group with each person focused on a specific target or having a specific objective. Team debriefs by sharing observations and giving practitioner multifactorial feedback. Term borrowed from clinical psychology and medical fields.

school counselors and school-based social workers: school staff with state and/or national certification in their respective fields. These individuals are able to provide therapeutic services to students and staff. They are also able to communicate with their professional peers working in community physical and mental health agencies.

school psychologists: staff trained in both psychology and education. They team with educators, parents, and other mental health professionals to assist in planning academic and behavior objectives for students. They can assess academic skills, learning aptitudes, personality, and emotional development. They can also provide therapeutic services to children and families.

school-to-prison pipeline: zero-tolerance policies and practices school districts adopted beginning in the 1980s to manage student behaviors had an unintended effect—students were being suspended for relatively minor misbehaviors. Males and students of color are disproportionately impacted by these policies (Elias, 2013). Perhaps a more insidious concern is that according to the most recent data from the U.S. Bureau of Justice, 56 percent of federal inmates, 67 percent of inmates in state prisons, and 69 percent of inmates in local jails did not complete high school (Alliance for Excellent Education, 2013).

self-contained special education: the most restrictive instructional service model usually for students with serious medical disabilities (epilepsy, severe autism, etc.). However, there are students who are placed in restrictive settings for behavior or conduct disorders before they are given adequate interventions and time to change behaviors. The data in most school districts around the country show a disproportionate number of African American and Latino males from low-income families being diagnosed with behavior disorders (VanHook, 2012).

SocioEmotional Learning (SEL) curriculum: curriculum that teaches important socioemotional competencies (e.g., empathy, resiliency) that are necessary for success in school and life. Popular SEL curriculums include Second Step, MindUP, RULER, Zones of Regulation, Art With Heart.

support staff: bus drivers, food service staff, custodians, family support workers, office staff, for example.

toolkit: a term school personnel use to describe the various instructional and interpersonal skills they use to meet the diverse social and academic needs of their students.

trainer-of-trainers: provide designated in-district staff members initial professional development so they can train and mentor district staff. This model supports systemic sustainability.

transformationist learning: instructing in a way that students' beliefs, mindsets, and behaviors are changed because instructional strategies engage them on an intellectual and interpersonal level.

transformationist teaching: using strategies that affirm students' cultural connections, managing classroom with caring control, engaging students in their learning, ensuring personal biases do not impact professional decision-making, and reinforcing growth mindset and resiliency. These instructors change how students feel about themselves as learners.

trauma: an intensely stressful or injurious mental, emotional, or physical event.

trauma-informed: understanding how adverse childhood experiences affects brain functioning, recognizing behaviors are a form of communication, then using interventions and strategies to teach students new ways of communicating and behaving within a school culture.

trauma-informed care: a framework for identifying, understanding, and caring for the impacts of trauma.

turnaround schools: high-poverty, high-performing schools.

2 × 10: a relationship-building strategy in which a teacher spends 2 minutes a day, for 10 consecutive school days, conversing with a student about a topic related to the student's life or interests.

References

Alliance for Excellent Education. (2013). *Crime rates linked to educational attainment.* Retrieved https://all4ed.org/press/crime-rates-linked-to-educational-attainment-new-alliance-report-finds/

American School Counselor Association. (n.d.). *Appropriate activities for school counselors: Inappropriate activities for school counselors.* Retrieved from https://www.school counselor.org/asca/media/asca/home/appropriate-activities-of-school-counsel ors.pdf

Anda, R. F., Dong, M., Brown, D. W., Felitti, V. J., Giles, W. H., Perry, G. S., . . . Dube, S. R. (2009, April 16). The relationship of adverse childhood experiences to a history of premature death of family members. *BMC Public Health, 9,* 106.

Arnett, A. A. (2016, March 23). *Promoting growth mindset means checking biases at the door, experts say.* Retrieved from http://www.educationdive.com/news/promoting-growth-mindset-means-checking-biases-at-the-door-experts-say/416134

ASCD. (2005, March 15). *Characteristics of high poverty, high performing schools.* Retrieved from http://www.ascd.org/publications/researchbrief/v3n06/toc.aspx

Ashe, A. (1992, December 1). *Address before the United Nations.* Retrieved from http://www.arthurashe.org/about-us.html

Aspy, D., & Roebuck, F. (1978). *Kids don't learn from people they don't like.* Amherst, MA: Human Resources Development Press.

Babbel, S. (2014, July 4). *Compassion fatigue: Bodily symptoms of empathy.* Retrieved from https://www.psychologytoday.com/blog/somatic-psychology/201207/compassion-fatigue

Baglivio, M., Epps, N., Swartz, K., Huq, M. S., Sheer, A., & Hardt, N. S. (2014). *The prevalence of adverse childhood experiences (ACE) in the lives of juvenile offenders.* Retrieved from https://www.ncjrs.gov/pdffiles/246951.pdf

Barnett, J. (2008). *Psychological wellness and self-care as an ethical imperative.* Retrieved from http://www.apa.org/careers/psychological-wellness.pdf

Baumeister, R. F., & Leary, M. R. (1995). The need to belong: Desire for interpersonal attachments as a fundamental human motivation. *Psychological Bulletin, 117(3),* 497–529.

Benard, B. (1991a). *Fostering resiliency in kids: Protective factors in the family, school, and community.* Portland, OR: Western Center for Drug-Free Schools and Communities.

Benard, B. (1991b). *From risk to resiliency: What schools can do.* Retrieved from http://www.tanglewood.net/projects/teachertraining/book_of_readings/benard.pdf

Blackwell, L. S., Trzesniewski, K. H., & Dweck, C. S. (2007). Implicit theories of intelligence predict achievement across an adolescent transition: A longitudinal study and an intervention. *Child Development, 78,* 246–263.

Boccanfuso, C., & Kuhfeld, M. (2011). *Multiple responses, promising results: Evidence-based, nonpunitive alternatives to zero tolerance.* Washington, DC: Child Trends.

Bowen, W. (2009). *Complaint free relationships: Transforming your life one relationship at a time.* New York, NY: Doubleday.

Bradley, A. (1996, March 13). *Education week on the web.* Retrieved from http://nuatc.org/articles/pdf/sizemore.pdf

Branch, G., Hanushek, E., & Rivkin, S. (2013). *School leaders matter: Measuring the impact of effective leadership.* Retrieved from http://educationnext.org/school-leaders-matter

Cal Fire. (2015, August 14). *Rocky fire incident information.* Retrieved from http://cdfdata.fire.ca.gov/incidents/incidents_details_info?incident_id=1161

Centers for Disease Control and Prevention. (2010). Adverse childhood experiences reported by adults—five states. *National Library of Medicine, 59*(49), 1609–1613.

Centers for Disease Control and Prevention. (2016a). *About the CDC-Kaiser Study Definitions.* Retrieved from https://www.cdc.gov/violenceprevention/acestudy/about.html

Centers for Disease Control and Prevention. (2016b). *Sexual identity, sex of sexual contacts, and health-risk behaviors among students in grades 9–12: Youth Risk Behavior Surveillance.* Atlanta, GA: U.S. Department of Health and Human Services.

Chapman, D. P., Anda, R. F., Felitti, V. J., Dube, S. R., Edwards, V. J, & Whitfield, C. L. (2004). Adverse childhood experiences and the risk of depressive disorders in adulthood. *Journal of Affective Disorders, 82,* 217–225.

Chernow, R. (2004). *Alexander Hamilton.* New York, NY: Penguin.

Comer, J. (1988). Educating poor minority children. *Scientific American, 259*(5), 42–48.

Darling-Hammond, L. (2004). What happens to a dream deferred: The continuing quest for equal educational opportunity. In J. A. Banks (Ed.), *Handbook of research on multicultural education* (2nd ed., pp. 607–630). San Francisco, CA: Jossey-Bass.

Darling-Hammond, L. (2006). Constructing 21st century teacher education. *Journal of Teacher Education, 57*(3), 300–314.

Dweck, C. (2015, March 2). *Carol Dweck: A summary of the two mindsets and the power of believing you can improve.* Retrieved from https://www.farnamstreetblog.com/2015/03/carol-dweck-mindset

Edelstein, B. (2012). *The need for authentic meaning.* Retrieved from https://www.psychologytoday.com/blog/authentic-engagement/201210/the-need-authentic-meaning

Edmonds, R. (1977). *Search for effective schools: The identification and analysis of city schools that are instructionally effective for poor children.* Retrieved from https://eric.ed.gov/?id=ED142610

Edutopia. (2011, October 6). *Social and emotional learning: A short history.* Retrieved from https://www.edutopia.org/social-emotional-learning-history

Elias, M. (2013). *The School-to-Prison Pipeline.* Retrieved http://www.indiana.edu/~pbisin/docs/School_to_Prison.pdf

Engel, D., et al. (1999, November 17). Scores on standardize tests don't tell the whole story. *The Seattle Times.*

Felitti, V. J., Anda, R. F., Nordenberg, D., Williamson, D. F., Spitz, A. M., Edwards, V., . . . Marks, J. S. (1998). Relationship of childhood abuse and household dysfunction to many of the leading causes of death in adults. *American Journal of Preventive Medicine, 14,* 245–258.

Finkelhor, D., Turner, H., Ormrod, R., Hamby, S., & Kracke, K. (2009, October). *Children's exposure to violence: A comprehensive national survey.* Retrieved from https://www.ncjrs.gov/pdffiles1/ojjdp/227744.pdf

Frankl, V. E. (2008). *Man's search for meaning* (4th ed.). Retrieved from http://novelinks.org/uploads/Novels/MansSearchForMeaning/Concept%20Analysis.pdf

Fredericks, A. (n.d.). *Too many tasks, not enough day.* Retrieved from https://www.teachervision.com/too-many-tasks-not-enough-day

Gardner, H. (1993). *Multiple intelligences: The theory in practice.* New York, NY: Basic Books.

Grayson, J. L., & Alvarez, H. K. (2008, July). School climate factors relating to teacher burnout: A mediator model. *Teaching and Teacher Education, 24*(5), 1349–1363.

Griffin, A., & Kovner, J. (2013, December 28). *Lanza's psychiatric treatment revealed in documents.* Retrieved from http://articles.courant.com/2013-12-28/news/hc-lanza-sandy-hook-report1228-20131227_1_peter-lanza-adam-lanza-nancy-lanza

Gruenert, S. (2008). *School culture, school climate: They are not the same thing.* Retrieved from https://www.naesp.org/sites/default/files/resources/2/Principal/2008/M-Ap56.pdf

Habegger, S. (2008). *The principal's role in successful schools: Creating a positive school culture.* Retrieved from https://www.naesp.org/sites/default/files/resources/1/Principal/2008/S-O_p42.pdf

Hakuta, K., Butler, Y., & Witt, D. (2000). *How long does it take English learners to attain proficiency?* Retrieved from http://cmmr.usc.edu/FullText/Hakuta_HOW_LONG_DOES_IT_TAKE.pdf

Halford, L. (2016, January 30). *Mother Teresa and compassion fatigue.* Retrieved from http://www.eastsidecenterforfamily.com/mother-teresa

Hamilton, A. (1788, July 8). *Representation: Federalist No. 36.* Retrieved from http://press-pubs.uchicago.edu/founders/documents/v1ch13s26.html

Haynes, J. (n.d.). *How long does it take students to learn English?* Retrieved from http://teaching.monster.com/benefits/articles/8517-how-long-does-it-take-students-to-learn-english

Howard, G. (2016). *We can't teach what we don't know: White teachers, multiracial schools* (3rd ed.). New York, NY: Teachers College Press.

IMPACT. (2010). Mental health disorders, psychological distress, and suicidality in a diverse sample of lesbian, gay, bisexual, and transgender youths. *American Journal of Public Health, 100*(12), 2426–2632.

Izumi, L. (2002, September). *They have overcome: High-poverty, high-performing schools in California.* Retrieved from https://eric.ed.gov/?id=ED469963

Jensen, E. (1998). *Teaching with the brain in mind.* Alexandria, VA: ASCD.

Jensen, E. (2009). *Teaching with poverty in mind: What being poor does to kids' brains and what schools can do with it.* Alexandria, VA: ASCD.

Jerald, C. D. (2001). *Dispelling the myth revisited: Preliminary findings from a nationwide analysis of "high-flying" schools.* Retrieved from https://eric.ed.gov/?id=ED462485

Kagi, R., Jinkins,L., and Frockt, D. (2011–12). SHB 1965 Concerning Adverse Childhood Experiences. Retrieved from http://apps2.leg.wa.gov/billsummary?BillNumber=1965&Year=2011&BillNumber=1965&Year=2011

Kannapel, P., Clements, S., Taylor, D., & Hibpshman, T. (2005, February). *Characteristics of high-performing, high-poverty schools.* Retrieved from http://www.ascd.org/publications/researchbrief/v3n06/toc.aspx

Larkin, H., Felitti, V. J., & Anda, R. F. (2011). Social work and adverse childhood experiences (ACEs) research: Implications for practice and health policy. *Social Work in Public Health, 29*(1), 1–16.

Leithwood, K. (1994). Leadership for school restructuring. *Educational Administration Quarterly, 30,* 498–518.

Leithwood, K. (2010, July 7). *Characteristics of school districts that are exceptionally effective in closing the achievement gap.* Retrieved from http://ecadmin.wdfiles.com/local—files/at-risk-children-families/Characteristics%20of%20Schools%20-%20Closing%20Gap.pdf

Leithwood, K., Louis, K. S., Anderson, S., & Wahlstrom, K. (2004). *How leadership influences student learning.* Retrieved from http://www.wallacefoundation.org/knowledge-center/Documents/How-Leadership-Influences-Student-Learning.pdf

Maslow, A. H., Frager, R., Fadiman, J., McReynolds, C., & Cox, R. (Eds.). (1987). *Motivation and personality* (3rd ed.). New York, NY: Pearson.

McKinley, J. (n.d.). *Leveling the playing field and raising African American students' achievement in 29 urban schools.* Retrieved from http://education.jhu.edu/PD/newhorizons/strategies/topics/Differentiated%20Instruction/playing-field/index.html

MedicineNet.com. (2016). *The classic and modern versions of the Hippocratic Oath.* Retrieved from http://www.medicinenet.com/script/main/art.asp?articlekey=20909

MedicineNet.com (2017). *Neuroplasticity.* Retrieved from http://www.medicinenet.com/script/main/art.asp?articlekey=40362

Mezirow, J. (1997, June). *Transformative learning: Theory to practice.* Retrieved from http://onlinelibrary.wiley.com/doi/10.1002/ace.7401/abstract

Michael, R. (2016, August 10). *What self-care is and what it isn't.* Retrieved from https://psychcentral.com/blog/archives/2016/08/10/what-self-care-is-and-what-it-isnt-2

National Child Traumatic Stress Network. (2008, Oct.). *Child trauma toolkit for educators.* Retrieved from http://www.nctsn.org/sites/default/files/assets/pdfs/Child_Trauma_Toolkit_Final.pdf

National Education Association. (2011). *C.A.R.E.: Strategies for closing the achievement gaps.* Retrieved from www.nea.org/assets/docs/CAREguide2011.pdf

National Policy Board for Educational Administration. (2015). *Professional standards for educational leaders 2015.* Reston, VA: Author. Retrieved from http://www.wallacefoundation.org/knowledge-center/Documents/Professional-Standards-for-Educational-Leaders-2015.pdf

Neason, A. (2017, July 23). *Half of teachers leave the job after five years. Here's what to do about it.* Retrieved from http://www.huffingtonpost.com/2014/07/23/teacher-turnover-rate_n_5614972.html

Norcross, J. C., & Barnett, J. E. (2008). *Self-care as ethical imperative.* Retrieved from https://www.nationalregister.org/pub/the-national-register-report-pub/the-register-report-spring-2008/self-care-as-ethical-imperative/2008

Nyhan, C. (2016, June 12). *Compassion fatigue for educators* [Video]. Retrieved from https://prezi.com/d1ag6s4wuz67/compassion-fatigue-for-educators

Olah, K. (2017, Sept.). *Is it still the "Three R's"?* Retrieved from https://en.wikibooks.org/wiki/Foundations_of_Education_and_Instructional_Assessment/Curriculum/Three_R%27s

Overman, S. (n.d.). *Fighting the stress of teaching to the test.* Retrieved from http://www.nea.org/tools/fighting-stress-teaching-to-Test.html

Palmer, P. (1997). *The courage to teach: Exploring the inner landscape of a teacher's life.* Retrieved from http://www.couragerenewal.org/PDFs/Parker-Palmer_The-Heart-of-a-Teacher.pdf

Parrett, W., & Budge, K. (2011, November 9). *Turning high-poverty schools into high-performing schools: A synthesis of research on what works in high-performing/high-poverty schools.* Retrieved from https://csi.boisestate.edu/wp-content/uploads/2011/08/2011-Educational-Strategies-Conference-1.pdf

Philips, O. (2015, March 30). *Revolving door of teachers costs schools billions every year.* Retrieved from http://www.npr.org/sections/ed/2015/03/30/395322012/the-hidden-costs-of-teacher-turnover

Pierson, R. (2013, May3). *Every child needs a champion* [Video]. Retrieved from https://www.youtube.com/watch?v=SFnMTHhKdkw

Popkin, S., Rich, H., Hendey, L., Hayes, C., & Parilla, J. (2012, April 4). *Public housing transformation and crime: Making the case for possible relocation.* Retrieved from http://www.urban.org/research/publication/public-housing-transformation-and-crime-making-case-responsible-relocation

Richmond, E. (2013, March 29). *Two takes on the "well-being" of teachers.* Retrieved from http://www.ewa.org/educated-reporter/two-takes-well-being-teachers

Richmond, E. (2014, June 26). *US teachers love their job but don't feel valued*. Retrieved from http://www.huffingtonpost.com/emily-richmond/report-us-teachers-love-t_b_5534127.html

Rimm-Kaufman, S., & Sandilos, L. (n.d.). *Improving students' relationships with teachers to provide essential supports for learning*. Retrieved from https://www.apa.org/education/k12/relationships.aspx

Roberson, R. (2013). *Helping students find relevancy*. Retrieved from http://www.apa.org/ed/precollege/ptn/2013/09/students-relevance

Ruiz, L. D. (2016). *The role of school climate in mitigating the effects of neighborhood socio-economic status and violence on academic achievement* [Doctoral dissertation]. Retrieved from Via Sapientiae, DePaul University Libraries, http://via.library.depaul.edu/csh_etd/194

Sacks, V., Murphey, D., & Moore, K. (2014). *Adverse childhood experiences: National and state level prevalence*. Retrieved from https://www.childtrends.org/wp-content/uploads/2014/07/Brief-adverse-childhood-experiences_FINAL.pdf

Shade, B., Kelly, C., & Oberg, M. (2005). *Creating culturally responsive classrooms* (7th ed.). Washington, DC: American Psychological Association.

Shannon, S. and Blysma, P. (2007). Nine characteristics of high performing schools. *State of Washington Office of Superintendent of Public Instruction*. Retrieved from http://www.k12.wa.us/research/pubdocs/NineCharacteristics.pdf

Shonk, S. M., & Cicchetti, D. (2001). Maltreatment, competency deficits, and risk for academic and behavioral maladjustment. *Developmental Psychology, 37*(1), 3–17.

Sizemore, B., Brossard, C., & Harrigan, B. (1983). *An abasing anomaly: The high achieving predominately Black elementary school*. Retrieved from http://files.eric.ed.gov/fulltext/ED236274.pdf

Sternberg, R. J., Wagner, R. K., Williams, W. M., Horvath, J. A., et al. (1995). Testing common sense. *American Psychologist, 50*, 912–927.

Strauss, V. (2018, February 20). How mass school shootings affect the education of students who survive [Web log]. *Washington Post*. Retrieved from https://www.washingtonpost.com/news/answer-sheet/wp/2018/02/20/how-mass-school-shootings-affect-the-education-of-students-who-survive/?utm_term= .49a85dd50bdf

Stronge, J. (2007). *The qualities of effective teachers*. Retrieved from http://www.ascd.org/publications/books/105156/chapters/Section-II@-Teacher-Responsibilities-and-Teacher-Behaviors.aspx

Substance Abuse and Mental Health Services Administration. (2014). *Trauma-informed care in behavioral health services: Tip 57*. Retrieved from https://store.samhsa.gov/shin/content//SMA14-4816/SMA14-4816.pdf

Thapa, A., Cohen, J., Higgins-D'Alessandro, A., & Guffey, S. (2012). *School climate research summary: August 2012* (School Climate Brief, No. 3). New York, NY: National School Climate Center. Retrieved from https://www.schoolclimate.org/publications/scholarship

TheyDiffer.com. (2015, July 10). *Difference between compassion fatigue and burnout*. Retrieved from https://theydiffer.com/difference-between-compassion-fatigue-and-burnout

University of Houston. (2011, May 25). *Job stress in teachers linked to student achievement*. Retrieved from https://www.sciencedaily.com/releases/2011/05/110525181422.htm

U.S. Department of Education. (2017, January 30). *Teacher Shortage Areas, 2015–16*. Retrieved from https://catalog.data.gov/dataset/teacher-shortage-areas-2015-16

U.S. Department of Education, National Center for Education Statistics, Schools and Staffing Survey. (n.d.). *Public School Data File, 2007–08*. Retrieved from https://nces.ed.gov/surveys/SASS/tables/sass0708_2013027_s1n_04.asp

VanHook, C. R. (2012). *Racial disparity in the diagnosis of conduct disorder* [Undergraduate Research Awards, Paper 12]. Retrieved from http://scholarworks.gsu.edu/univ_lib_ura/12

Walker, W. R., & American Psychological Association. (2003, June 8). *Remembering the good times, putting the bad times in perspective—How our memory helps make life pleasant.* Retrieved from http://www.apa.org/news/press/releases/2003/06/happy-memory.aspx

Werner, E., & Smith, R. (1992). *Overcoming the odds: High-risk children from birth to adulthood.* Ithaca, NY: Cornell University Press.

Wolpow, R., Johnson, M. M., Hertel, R., & Kincaid, S. (2009). *The heart of learning and teaching: Compassion, resiliency, and academic success.* Olympia, WA: Office of Superintendent of Public Instruction (OSPI) Compassionate.

Wyre, S. (2013). *The importance of relevancy in improving student engagement and learning.* Retrieved from https://www.facultyfocus.com/articles/faculty-development/the-importance-of-relevancy-in-improving-student-engagement-and-learning

Zakrzewski, V. (2012). *Four ways teachers can show they care.* Retrieved from http://greatergood.berkeley.edu/article/item/caring_teacher_student_relationship

NOTE: Page references in *italics* refer to figures.

CORWIN

A SAGE Publishing Company

CORWIN HAS ONE MISSION: to enhance education through intentional professional learning.

We build long-term relationships with our authors, educators, clients, and associations who partner with us to develop and continuously improve the best evidence-based practices that establish and support lifelong learning.